Autumn Passage to the Himalaya

Treks, Travels and History

I Hold the Heights

I have not lost the magic of long days;
I live them, dream them still.
Still I am master of the starry ways,
And freeman of the hills.
Shattered my glass, ere half the sands had run—
I hold the heights, I hold the heights I won.

Mine still the hope that hailed me from each height,
Mine the unresting flame.
With dreams I charmed each doing to delight;
I charm my rest the same.
Severed my skin, ere half the strands were spun—
I keep the dreams, I keep the dreams I won.

What if I live no more those kingly days?
Their night sleeps with me still.
I dream my feet upon the starry ways;
My heart rests in the hill.
I may not grudge the little left undone;
I hold the heights, I keep the dreams I won.

Geoffrey Winthrop Young

(Geoffrey Winthrop Young (25 October 1876 – 8 September 1958) was a British climber, poet,educator, and author of several notable books on mountaineering. He lost a leg in First World War, 1914, but continued climbing for decades after that.)

Autumn Passage to the Himalaya

Treks, Travels and History

Harish Kapadia

Sketches by
Geeta Kapadia

Aryan Books International
New Delhi

AUTUMN PASSAGE TO THE HIMALAYA
Treks, Travels and History

ISBN: 978-81-7305-678-9

First Published 2023

Published by
Aryan Books International
Pooja Apartments, 4B, Ansari Road, New Delhi-110002 (India)
Tel.: 23287589, 23255799; Fax: 91-11-23270385
E-mail: aryanbooks@gmail.com
www.aryanbooks.com

Printed in India

To my soldier – son

Lt Nawang Kapadia

He loved the Himalaya and gave his life defending them

'It is better to die in valour than be a coward'

What's so good in your life if you are not willing to chance it. Take all the precautions once you have started, take all the precautions that you possibly can but don't be put off because it is dangerous or supposed to be dangerous or looks dangerous.

(*Dr Tom Longstaff on his accident on Gurla Mandhata*)

Foreword

I've often heard people complain that nowadays, in the Twenty-First Century, there are no longer any unknown places on the map, no new frontiers to explore, and no explorers to go where nobody else has gone before. While there may be some truth in this lament, it ignores the fact that exploration can occur in almost any corner of the world, even in a city like Mumbai, so long as the person who goes there is intent on discovering something new. And in the Himalaya, with its well-trodden paths and high passes, there are still those places that hint at wildness and more than enough stories that haven't been heard or told. One of the few people who can still legitimately call himself an explorer is Harish Kapadia. He has gone to remote and lonely places in the mountains that may often seem untouched by the hand of man, but even when he is following in the footsteps of others, he is on a quest for experiences and encounters that nobody else can claim.

Harish's many books and articles are testimony to his insatiable desire to seek out new routes and new approaches in the Himalaya. As a mountaineer, he has stood on numerous summits and ventured up challenging slopes. More than once, he has cheated fate and has the broken bones to prove it. The Royal Geographical Society awarded him its Patron's Medal, which is the ultimate recognition for an explorer, an honour he shares with Eric Shipton, Edmund Hilary and Pandit Nain Singh Rawat, among a host of other names that are etched upon the Himalaya. He has received many other honours including the Tenzing Norgay Award and a Piolets d'Or, but he has never been one to rest on his laurels and continues to search out new destinations in the Himalaya.

This book, *Autumn Passage to the Himalaya,* takes its title from his treks, travels and studies of the Himalayan ranges. Harish retraces his treks and climbs in Himachal Pradesh, explores many different regions from Sikkim and Kashmir to Uttarakhand and Bhutan, as well as a few trans-Himalayan forays in the Karakoram and Tibet. As much as he is an explorer, Harish is also a raconteur – anyone who has attended his lectures will confirm this. His stories are full of adventure, a knowledge of history and mountain lore, along with an acute awareness of geography. Whenever he tells a tale it is always laced with humour and an endearing sense of mischief, though he can be dead serious too.

This collection of stories will take you in search of circular rainbows, hidden valleys and treacherous "death trails," as well as famous routes pioneered by early explorers like Francis Younghusband. It will also revisit what has been called the Golden Age of mountain travel and exploration, between the two World Wars. Unlike the tale of the Italian prisoners of war in this collection, Harish Kapadia has always been free to roam his beloved Himalaya, though at the same time, because of his curiosity and a persistent desire to see what lies beyond the next ridge, these mountains have held him captive.

Stephen Alter
Landour, 28 May, 2022

Preface

Decades ago, during my school days, our Principal and educationist, MT Vyas inculcated a habit of keeping a daily diary, notes of activities of that day. That led me to maintain a diary of all my Himalayan treks, starting from 1964. These notes helped in writing articles about the trekking experiences and events of each trip. Daulat Desai, a brilliant history teacher, prompted me to research the history of every region I went to and the valleys that I trekked in. Many of these articles were published in *The Himalayan Journal* and other publications. With the notes on my treks in the Western Ghats, I published my first book *Trek the Sahyadris* in 1977, a guide to trekking in local hills. Its sixth edition is in print today.

In the early nineties, ML Gidwani of the Indus Books approached me to publish selected articles in the form of a book. Even though these had been published in a mountaineering journal, he was confident that general readers would be interested in such a collection. Thus, the first book *High Himalaya Unknown Valleys* was published in 1993 and ran into four editions. Soon two other books of the same genre: *Meeting the Mountains* and *Into Untravelled Himalaya* followed in next decade, each running into multiple editions. Later with Soli Mehta, I published a book *Exploring the Hidden Himalaya* about unknown Himalayan mountain peaks. This was followed by books on the Siachen glacier, Spiti, all major regions of the Himalaya, an anthology of articles, a book about Himalayan maps, and Himalayan trekking guidebooks, both from Indian as well as foreign publishers. Thus, I was able to make available a vast collection of knowledge about the Himalaya in general and my adventure activities as well.

In the recent years, I supplemented my work by launching my own website, www.harishkapadia.com. It helped me bring into the public domain almost all my treks, climbs and explorations and I further added many events and references that are not present in the above series of books. Sketch maps, full reports on expeditions, book reviews, the awards received, small articles on few friends and events, webcasts and films of my treks and expeditions have also been made available on the website. Thanks to my son Sonam Kapadia who cajoled me to host the material digitally and brilliantly executed the ideas.

In the last decade, I have continued to regularly visit the mountains, which has led to this book *Autumn Passage to the Himalaya.* The book contains many memories, articles on exploration, treks, studies, historical events, the changing Himalayan scene, tribute to adventure personalities and travels to remote areas which are unique. Hopefully these should prove useful and interesting.

Indus Books closed down, but luckily, equally enthusiastic, Vikas Arya of Aryan Books International took over. I am grateful to both these publishers who have specialized in the titles on the Himalaya. I am grateful to several mountaineers and authors who have contributed to the Foreword of my various books. I feel highly privileged that Stephen Alter, a celebrated and award-winning author who writes about the Himalaya and also on nature, fiction and a variety of subjects, has written the Foreword to this book. My Himalayan exploits, which are the real source of my writing, would not be possible without the companionship of so many friends, from teenagers to peers of my age. Over the years many have helped to edit my books, apart from professionals appointed by the publishers. I am grateful to Nandini Purandare, Muslim Contractor and, for the current collection, Smruthi Ranganathan for the support. I am thankful to all of them.

My wife Geeta Kapadia, herself a renowned Himalayan artist, the backbone of all my Himalayan endeavours, has been 'mapping' my Himalayan work by contributing excellent sketches.

Zerksis Boga, my trekking companion of many decades gave me an advise as he departed to greener pasture abroad: "Don't give up going to mountains or being in touch with the mountain spirit if you wish to have a healthy autumn and winter of life." I continue my love affair with the Himalaya in many ways – reading, writing, podcasts, webcasts, helping adventurers with any queries, and, of course, visiting the mountains as often as I can.

And Deering's woods are fresh and fair,
And with joy that is almost pain
My heart goes back to wander there,
And among the dreams of the days that were
I find my lost youth again.

(From the poem "My Lost Youth",
by Henry Wadsworth Longfellow, 1807–1882)

Harish Kapadia

Contents

	Foreword	*vii*
	Preface	*ix*
	Books by the Author	*xv*
	List of Illustrations	*xvii*

SIKKIM

1.	Memories: Training, Sherpas and Friends from 1964	1
2.	Chasing Circular Rainbows or the Brocken Spectre: Trekking on the Sandakphu Ridge	12
3.	An Autumn Trek to Tholung Monastery: Trekking in the Dzongu Valley of North Sikkim	22
4.	The Plateau: Mountains of the Sikkim–China Border	26

KASHMIR – KARAKORAM

5.	Old Trails, New Companions: Treks in Kashmir	36
6.	Two Walks in the Kishtwar: The Kablas Lakes and Bhut Nala	48
7.	Younghusband: 'Damned Rum Name' – The Life and Times of Sir Frances Younghusband	60
8.	On the 'Death Trail': A Journey across the Shyok and Nubra Valleys	72

HIMACHAL PRADESH

9.	Prisoners of the Himalaya: 'YOL – Your Own Locations'	82
10.	Ramblings in Chhota Bangahal: Kullu Valley	93

11. Mobile with a Mobile in the Himalaya: A Ringing Revolution 99
12. A Peak, a Pass and a Monastery: Hanle – Hangrang and Gyundi 105
13. A Road Much Travelled: Treks on Trails by Early Explorers 116

UTTARAKHAND

14. The Valley of Flowers: A Trek to the Bhiundhar Valley, Garhwal 125
15. The Valley of Friends: My Companions from the Saryu Valley, Kumaun 132
16. An Autumn Walk to Kedar Kantha 142
17. We Are the Pilgrims: Mountain Ranges and Temples of Garhwal 147
18. In the Valleys of Eastern Kumaun: Byans, Johar and Danpur 155
19. Obra Gad – the Hidden Valley: Western Garhwal 167
20. The Age of Exploration: Dhauli Valley, Niti Pass and Bara Hoti 172

TIBET AND BHUTAN

21. A Hundred Years after Younghusband: Travels in Tibet 185
22. Across Bhutan in Eighteen Days: A Journey across the Dragon Kingdom 201
23. Himalayan Disaster – Nature's Fury or Man-made Calamity?: A Look at Himalayan Floods in Recent Memory 212

Select Bibliography 219
Index 225

Books by the Author

1. *Trek the Sahyadris*
2. *High Himalaya Unknown Valleys*
3. *Meeting the Mountains*
4. *Into the Untravelled Himalaya*
5. *Spiti – Adventures in the Trans-himalaya*
6. *Exploring the Hidden Himalaya*
7. *Battle of Roses – Siachen Glacier*
8. *Across Peaks and Passes – Kumaun*
9. *Across Peaks and Passes – Garhwal*
10. *Across Peaks and Passes – Himachal Pradesh*
11. *Across Peaks and Passes – Ladakh and East Karakoram*
12. *Across Peaks and Passes – Darjeeling and Sikkim*
13. *Himalaya – More than Mountains*
14. *A Passage to Himalaya*
15. *Trekking in the Indian Himalaya* (Outlook Publishers, New Delhi)
16. *Trekking and Climbing in the Indian Himalaya* (by Globetrotter Publishing, London)
17. *Legendary Maps from the Himalayan Club*, General Editor Harish Kapadia.

List of Illustrations

MAPS

		Page No.
Chapter 4:	The Plateau, North Sikkim	32
Chapter 5:	Kashmir treks	41
Chapter 6:	A. Kablas lake, Kishtwar	50
	B. Eastern Kishtwar	55
Chapter 8:	Eastern Karakoram	75
Chapter 12:	A. Hangrang Pass, Kinnaur	109
	B. Karcha-Gyundi valleys	113
Chapter 16:	Har ki Doon area – Kedar Kantha	145
Chapter 19:	Obra Gad valley	169
Chapter 20:	Dhauli Valley – Niti Pass	178
Chapter 21:	A. Central Tibet	189
	B. Western Tibet	196

SKETCHES

A. Kolahoi peak, Kashmir 47

B. Monument created by the Italian Prisoners of War 92

C. Temple bells at Chiltha Devi, Kumaun 184

COLOUR PLATES

I. Jannu peak (left) and Kangchenjunga – view from trek to Sandakhpu.

II. Gurudongmar lake and peak, North Sikkim.

III. Rare view of Pandim peak, North Sikkim.
IV. Historic Niti pass and Ganesh Ganga. Central Garhwal.
V. Routes to Bara Hoti, east of Niti pass. Central Garhwal.
VI. View from Panar Bugiyal, en route to Rudranath. Vishnu Ghar Dhar peaks seen.
VII. Tarsar lake with campsite.
VIII. Zajimarg valley (Mukund R.).
IX. Sundersar lake (Grp Capt Nitin).
X. Marsar lake (Mukund R.).
XI. Gashibrar – highest peak of Kolahoi.
XII. Peaks of Kishtwar from Kablas Lake – Shankh Padri (Amrita Dhar).
XIII. Regimental arcs erected at entrance to the Siachen glacier.
XIV. Mule caravan approaching the Galwan valley.
XV. On Karakoram Pass.
XVI. On the Teram Shehr plateau. Peaks behind: L to R. Padmanabh, Laxmi and Teram Kangri group.
XVII. On the East Rimo glacier. Peak Rimo on right.
XVIII. Saltoro Kangri I (left) and Saltoro Kangri II, on the Siachen glacier.
XIX. Potala Palace at Lhasa.
XX. Kumbum monastery at Gyantse.
XXI. Khojarnath monastery (lord of animals) near Purang.
XXII. Grave of Zorawar Singh at Tola, near Purang.
XXIII. Tirthapuri, Western Tibet, origin of the Satluj river.
XXIV. Tholing Math, established by Shankracharyya at western Tibet.
XV. Tsaprang hills, Western Tibet.
XVI. On top of Guge Fort, Tsaprang, Western Tibet.

B/W PLATES

1. Kangchenjunga massif and Zemu peak in foreground, from Mangan.
2. Simvu twin peaks from Mangan.
3. Siniolchu from Mangan.
4. Tholung monastery (Kartik Bhagat).
5. Tholung monastery with faded, ancient paintings at bottom.
6. Pauhunri peaks, the highest peaks on 'The Plateau' in North Sikkim.
7. Dongkhya Ri, 6190 m.

8. Khangchenjau with Yulehkang seen from Lachen.
9. Chomo Yummo above Gigong, North Sikkim.
10. Kolahoi north face above Dodsar lake (Mukund R.).
11. Kolahoi group, Kashmir.
13. A Shepherd girl helping a trekker to cross bridge.
12. A Gujjar lady, Kashmir.
14. Madhav Rigo peak above Machail, Bhut nala, Kishtwar (Amrita Dhar).
15. Gharol peak in Bhut nala.
16. Agyasol and Spear peaks, Bhut nala (Amrita Dhar).
17. Arjuna peak from about 5000 meters across the valley (Ranjit Jakli).
18. Road carved out from rock-wall fron Gulabgarh to Killar.
19. Spear peak, Bhut nala (Ranjit Jakli).
20. Phabrang peak viewed from Killar in the Pangi valley.
21. Mules crosing the Shyok river.
22. Sultan Chushku stream.
23. On historic Karakoram Pass.
24. Yurgolak ancient fort, the Shyok valley.
25. Chhongtash camp, the Shyok valley.
26. Peaks of Aksai Chin plateau from the Depsang plains.
27. Two 'Polu Stone Shelters', near D. B. O. Karakoram. In foreground, memorial stones to Ph. C. Visser 1935, (left) and Kaivan Mistry 2002.
28. On 'Col Italia'. High peaks of Rimo III (right) and Rimo IV seen.
29. Teram Sher plateau. Peak Rimo I at the centre behind.
31. Memorial to Ferdinand Stoliczka at Leh cemetery.
30. Historic Jesuist church at Leh.
32. Camp on Teram Shehr plateau, Peak Padmanabh behind.
33. Kiangs – wild donkeys at Hanle.
34. Black-necked cranes at Pangong lake.
35. Hanle monastery, southeast Ladakh.
36. Monument created by the Itailan prisoners at YOL Cannt.
37. Chamba Kailash peak from 'The Jot', Chamba, Himachal Pradesh.
38. Prayers being recited by a Lama over mobile.
39. Author discussing mobile phones (S. Venables).

40. Kinnaur Kailash peak, from Hangrang pass.
41. Traditional dancers at Shailkhar, Kinnaur.
42. Hansbeshan peak from Kedar Kantha.
43. Swargarohini I, II and III (R to L) from Kedar Kantha walk.
44. Rangrik Rang from Kedar Kantha walk.
45. View from the Hangrang pass, Kinnuar. Leo Pargial peak (left) and Rio Purgial peak.
46. View from Valley of Flowers. Rataban Peak in centre and Bhuidhar pass to its right.
48. A young Garhwali girl working with grains.
47. Nanda Singh Chauhan, guide with Frank Smythe during his two visits to the Valley of Flowers.
49. The Valley of Flowers.
50. Harish Kapadia left, with Harsinh Junior and Harsinh Senior.
51. Ladies in a Kumauni carved house in the Saryu valley.
52. Camp at Devkyari. Dhodu peak behind, Obra gad.
53. Ranglana, Obra gad.
54. Villagers dancing at Devkyari to celebrate Obra Devta.
55. Priest dancing with knieves in his mouth.
56. Niti village.
57. Rarely seen Geldhung peak, Niti pass area.
58. Trekker on way to Dayara bugiyal. Peak Jaonli seen behind.
59. View from Chandra Shila, Tungnath (Monesh Devjani).
60. Januhut from Deoria tal (Monesh Devjani).
61. Hardeol peak from Bansi Narayan.
62. Bethartoli Himal main (left) – and South from Bansi Narayan.
63. Nanda Devi from Bansi Narayan.
64. View from Bansi Narayan, Garhwal. Peaks Left to right: Dunagiri, Changabang and Kalanka.
65. Trisul peak from Panar bugyal, Garhwal.
66. Peaks on The Plateau.
67. Hathi Parvat (R) and Ghori Parvat (L) from Bansi Narayan.
68. Kora chorten at Trashiyangtse, Eastern Bhutan.
69. Takstang monastery (Tiger's Nest) near Paro.
70. Punakha dzong, western Bhutan.

71. Trongsa dzong, Central Bhutan.
72. Chomolahri peak (left) and the range, in Bhutan.
73. Jokhang temple, the spiritual centre for Buddhist at Lhasa.
74. Norbulinka, residence of the Dalai Lama at Lhasa.
75. Northern view of Everest peak from Pang La (Kunj Trivedi).
76. Pilgrims with prayer wheels at Jokhang temple, Lhasa.
77. Paryer wheels at Tirthapuri, Tibet.
78. Gyantse fort, Tibet.
79. Karo la pass and glacier, en route to Lhasa.
80. Kailsh peak and Rakastal lake, Tibet.
81. Kailash peak, southern face, Tibet.

1

Memories

Training, Sherpas and Friends from 1964

TRAVEL TO DARJEELING

It seems like ages ago. Yes, I went to Darjeeling for my Basic Course in Mountaineering in 1964! It was course no. 43, if my memory serves me right. If you know the history of the Himalayan Mountaineering Institute (HMI), this was its first decade. The courses were for 35 days – and for me it was plus almost eight days for travel to and from Bombay (now Mumbai). We spent the first five and the last three days at Darjeeling; took ten days to walk to Base Camp, trained for ten days at Base Camp and took eight days to walk back. It was training at its best. These long marches and the stay at the Base allowed us to interact with the great Sherpas who accompanied us, including Tensing. We could enjoy the mountains and immerse ourselves in understanding the area very well. A very sensible thing.

During and before the sixties, travel to Darjeeling was long and tedious. HMI was authorised to offer a special railway concession to students and that allowed me to travel 'first class' at half rate.[1] Bombay to Calcutta (now Kolkata) by *1Dn Calcutta Mail* via Nagpur was a memorable experience with its views, rhythm and the dining car, which has now been discontinued. I changed to the *Darjeeling Mail* at Calcutta. Early next morning, the train

1. All British officers always travelled First Class. As F M Bailey put it, "I had never travelled Second Class in India, not even speculated what it was like. First-class travel was not merely the officer's prerogative, it was his duty to the British Raj." Baily, F M, *No Passport to Tibet*, The Travel Book Club, London, 1957, p. 271.

halted at Sahib Ganj, which was on the banks of the Ganga. In those days, the railway bridge on the river had yet to be constructed. All the passengers and their luggage had to be transported to a train waiting on the other side. The porters arrived and all the luggage was carried to and loaded onto the waiting ferry – many local cars too were being ferried. Thanks to my upper-class ticket, I sat on the upper deck restaurant and enjoyed breakfast while the ferry made its way across the Ganga over the next two hours.

The scene repeated itself at Manihari Ghat, on the north bank opposite. As we embarked on the train, we realised that it was almost a replica of the train by which we had arrived, only it was now 'meter gauge'. It was late in the afternoon, and we were on the move again. It was astonishing to think that all the British officers, administrators and the early Everest expeditions travelling to Darjeeling, had to go through this procedure. After a long sea voyage to Bombay, it was probably a test of endurance.

From Siliguri you had to catch a narrow-gauge train to Darjeeling. Comprising about 15 bogies pulled and pushed by three engines, this was indeed a remarkable experience. After chugging along for two hours through the plains, the train was divided into three sections of five bogies and one engine each. Two great engineering marvels were designed to help the engines haul the train up. First, a climb up a very steep slope with each train going up the slope. Then they would reverse to be able to climb up higher. This way all the bogies were hauled up. Later, at Batasia Loop, the train would make the climb in rounds, one section going over the other. This still exists today.[2]

At the Darjeeling railway station two Sherpas displaying large badges of HMI were awaiting the arrival of the new students. A very grand gesture, I felt. We walked to Jawaher Parvat, about 3 km away. Soon, we were settled at the Student's Hostel.[3]

Of the 30 students in my course, we were just two civilians – Dilip Bhide and I from Bombay. There were 28 young army lieutenants or captains

2. *Darjeeling Hill Railway*. Many references are available on the web.
3. The memories came back as I visited the area again – HMI and a trek to Dzongri in 2020, almost fifty-five years after doing the course. Many things had changed of course. For starters, we flew from Mumbai to Bagdogra (near Siliguri) in two hours and were in Darjeeling in just two more.

as other students. But we were immediately welcomed by these young officers – as we were almost of the same age. I was teamed with (then) Lt Prem Chand of the Gorkhas (not of Kangchenjunga fame, but from the 11 Gorkhas). We became instant friends and shared many things, and remained friends until he died in 2011. There were differences in our physical fitness and abilities, but we civilians were not too far behind. I was glad I had come well prepared with many historic facts about the area, as I realised that some of the Sherpas, including the great Tensing, were keen to know more about the history of their area.

THE COMPANY OF SHERPAS

To my regret, three of the best amongst Sherpas, Nawang Gombu, Lhatoo Dorjee and Ang Kami, were joining the 'pre-Everest expedition to Rathong peak'. Indian teams had attempted Everest twice before and 1965 was considered almost the last chance for them to achieve the ascent. So, instead of the usual Advance Course, which was generally held on same dates as the Basic Course, HMI dedicated this period to the selection of future Indian Everesters. In a way we were lucky, as we were interacting with the future legends and were witnessing the senior-most mountaineers of the country in action. Our instructors were Tensing, Miken Gyalzen, Sirdar Khamsang Wangdi (or simply Ongdi K.), Ang Temba, and Da Namgyal – each in his own way a great man and worth a separate story.

All these Sherpas had been to Everest on various expeditions – that was their bread and butter, and fame. But they had done other climbs too. Apart from Tensing, two of the most senior sherpas were with us. Gyalzen Mikchen, the senior instructor of the course, had climbed with the Japanese and is credited with the first ascent of Pyramid peak in 1949 as well as the first ascent of the difficult Manaslu peak in 1954. Da Namgyal was part of the Sherpa group that carried heavy loads to South Col in 1953. The next day, with Lord John Hunt, he carried loads to Camp VII on the southeast ridge, the final camp, that helped Hillary and Tensing make the historic first ascent of Everest two days later.

Tensing Norgay is, of course, renowned and there are several books on him. The first Prime Minister of India, Nehru, told him to "Produce a thousand Tensings for India". To that end the HMI was established with

Tensing as Director of Field Training, a post he held until he retired. Upon his death, he was cremated on the grounds above the HMI – his statue stands there today. His soul certainly rests at HMI.

On the same grounds above HMI, was a lovely nineteenth century memorial built in memory of Diri Dolma, wife of Forest Ranger Kanta. It was demolished to make way for a grotesque building to house a museum – an irreparable loss. So much for those who care about history!

Other Sherpas were not so lucky as Tensing. Many years later, while visiting Darjeeling, I saw the great Gyalzen and Da Namgyal selling woollens to tourists in the streets of Darjeeling to make ends meet. They had families to stay with and were doing this to supplement their daily expenses.

They were the senior-most Sherpas and, after decades of service at HMI, were the first to retire. Though celebrities in their own right, as per government classification, they were not entitled to pension. I was shocked and disturbed to see them reduced to such a pitiable condition. The Japanese and the British, with whom they had much success, immediately offered help. But they thought it was best to fight for their rights in an attempt to bring awareness of the situation for the benefit of both themselves and their community, and decided to demand an official pension instead of living off voluntary support and assistance. The government, as in all such cases, was adamant and the rules were not changed.

I was with erudite Sherpa Dorjee Lhatoo, the then Deputy Director of Field Training at HMI. We took a picture of Lhatoo in the bazaar, posing between these two great men selling woollens. The photo was captioned: 'Two sweater sellers of Darjeeling and one future sweater seller of Darjeeling'! It was circulated widely, especially in foreign journals and magazines, causing much pressure on authorities. It had the desired impact on Indian bureaucracy and rightful pension for the staff of HMI was introduced.

A MEMORABLE EXPERIENCE

Our course began the next day. Principal Col. Jaiswal, delivered a welcome lecture. "You will have a great experience. The mountains you will see and the great personalities you will trek with, will be a delight. The base camp at Chaurikiang will be your home for almost two weeks". Some of us chuckled at this Sikkimese name. "You can laugh now, but I assure you this name you will remember all your life".

We spent five days in Darjeeling. The first thing was getting used to stuff: PT (physical training) army style, a run to the bazar, lectures on various subjects, a movie on the Institute and training, various activities such as the issuing of equipment, lectures on medical aspects, safety and getting to know our Sherpa instructors. There was a cricket test match going on and, as I had a radio, I was in great demand. I was caught listening to it during one lecture. Luckily the speaker, a doctor, was also a cricket fan and was happy to get to know the score! After the day's events, we would go off to the Bazar, food at the Glenary's, ice-cream and milk shakes at Keventers and books at the Oxford Book Shop. All these establishments are still there. Five days flew by in an instant.

In December/January each year, rock climbing training courses were conducted in the hills near Bombay. As they were free from routine courses during that time, Sherpa instructors from Darjeeling would come to Bombay to teach. I had done a course there and hence, knew some of the Sherpas. All were seniors but very easy to get on with. So, sometimes I took some liberties and joked around with them – our disciplined army friends would enjoy that.

After five hectic days, the time came to start from Darjeeling. The pre-Everest team had already left. With heavy luggage on our backs, we started on our 10-day trek to the base camp, down from Darjeeling to Singla Bazar, on the banks of the Teesta river, from where we enter Sikkim. Early the next day, a cold October morning, we were asked to jump into the river for a bath. I was aghast and caught hold of one of the instructors known to me and begged to be excused. "I am from Mumbai, we never take a bath in such cold water. If I am forced to do so, I will be sick for rest of the course." Then I added in jest "I am the only son of my father so why send me home sick!" They all laughed, and I was excused, but I am sure I was marked as a weakling.

We soon settled down to the routine of trekking and arrived at Yoksum where a day was spent acclimatising. That evening pots, one for each of us, of the famous Sikkimese 'tomba' were brought. The drink is made of fermented barley in a bamboo container, on which hot water is poured. You sip this mildly alcoholic drink slowly, adding more hot water as you go along. It was a gift from the Sikkim government to popularise their national drink! How successful was their ploy: to date, I ask for tomba as soon as I am in those parts, and I am sure my army friends, as they advanced the ranks, have made their entire battalion drink it!

The climb started from Yoksum. We went up a steep terrain to Sachen, Bakkhim and Tsoka to Phedang. This last climb in particular, was very steep and many of us found it challenging. But our army friends rose to the occasion, encouraging us and even sharing some of our load. I was later told that people have died out of exhaustion or have had a heart attack on that section.

The next major camp was at Dzongri. No place in the Himalaya could be better I thought – rhododendrons, grassy meadows with yak herders, Kangchenjunga and other peaks rising all around. We spent an extra day here to acclimatise before we walked the last section to Chaurikiang. As we pitched our tents, I said to myself that the principal was right, this is a place I will never forget in my life. The camp, situated in a bowl, was next to a glacier and many giant peaks of the Sikkim Himalaya surrounded the vista. This is where we settled for 10 days of training.

I remember Tensing, visiting our tents every morning – anyone who was not up would get a shout. There were no excuses, even if you were ill. He would almost pull down the tent and ask you to re-pitch it as an exercise to get fit. We were divided into smaller groups, each called a 'rope', of six each, with one Sherpa instructor in charge, for better training. I was in the rope led by Sherpa Sirdar Wangdi, someone almost as senior as Tensing. Every day we would line up for a short lecture by Tensing and then go off with our rope instructor. Rock climbing, ice and snow work, rappelling, crampon climbing, use of ropes and rescue work – we were taught all these mountain activities. Due to these expert instructors, the small group size and sufficient time, we had the best of the training.

REMEMBERING THE SIRDAR

My rope instructor, Sirdar Wangdi, was a very different class of Sherpa. Educated and well trained abroad, he knew his ropes well and was a good teacher. He was 'Sirdar' (leader of a Sherpa team) of several expeditions in

Nepal, and he received this honourable title.[4] He was also on the international women's expedition, led by Madam Cloude Kogan in 1959. The team had three Sherpanis, daughters of Tensing: Pem Pem and Nima and his niece Doma from Darjeeling, thus establishing his future connection with HMI. In that expedition, Kogan, Claudine van der Straten-Ponthozone and Wangdi were trapped in an avalanche. Kogan and Claudine died, buried in the snow, but after struggling for almost three hours on his own, Wangdi came out of the debris and survived.[5]

His crowning glory was as Sirdar of the 1962 French expedition to Jannu (Kumbhakarna) with Lionell Terray. He was one of the summiteers on one of the most challenging mountains. On the summit, "Wangdi got a big Indian flag out of his bag, then a Nepalese flag and finally the colours of HMI." wrote Terray.[6]

We remained in contact for many years after the course. He was well ahead of his times. There were no trekking agencies in the 1960s and he thought of starting a 'Sherpa Guide School'. Not all Sherpas in Darjeeling were earning regularly, but only when, if lucky, they went on some expeditions in a year. Wangdi managed to arrange a group of six Sherpas, experts but less employed. He agreed to give them a monthly payment plus extra when climbing. This group settled at Manali, far away in the western Himalaya. As Wangdi had married a girl from Kathmandu, he could manage funds and much of the equipment. Soon, his agency became known and some groups started using them.

---

4. Sirdar Wangdi, born in 1932, first broke in on the Himalayan mountaineering scene with Raymond Lambert on Cho Oyu in 1954. Since then Wangdi has mostly been associated with French mountaineers: Makalu with Franco in 1955, Trisul in 1956 with Franco again and Jannu in 1959, yet again with Franco. He was awarded the Himalayan Club Tiger Badge and he became an Instructor at the Himalayan Mountaineering Institute. Wangdi was a quiet, gentle soul, he looked rather frail, but was terribly wiry and tenacious in purpose. He was more intellectual than other Sherpas and his independent spirit burnt fiercely inside him. (Mehta, Soli, in *The Himalayan Journal* Vol 13 1973–74, p. 226.
5. Kohli, Capt M S, *Sherpas,* UBS Publishers and Distributors New Delhi, 2003, p. 47.
6. Franco, Jean, & Lionell Terray, *At Grips with Jannu,* Victor Gollancz Limited, London, 1967, p. 191.

Unfortunately, this sparked a lot of jealousy from the local babus. The mountaineering institute at Manali did not appreciate his presence as it was thought that he was encroaching upon their territory. In 1967, I sent a large group of students from the University of Mumbai to train under Wangdi. His Sherpas took them to a glacier far away for training. At the same time, supported by Wangdi's company, an Indo-British team was climbing Mukarbeh, a challenging peak. They got caught in a storm and called for rescue. Wangdi went to the institute for help, and to arrange a helicopter but was denied any help even in this emergency. Finally, he recalled one of his Sherpas and a student, Zerksis Boga from the training camp and they went ahead with the rescue. Unfortunately, three climbers, Geoff Hill, Suresh Kumar, and Sherpa Pemba were found dead, suffocated in their tents.[7] This incident was picked by local administrators and politicians to ruin Wangdi.

Business suffered because of the many inquiries and notices directed at him, so did his health, and he took to heavy drinking. On one of my later visits, I walked with him to the Mission Hospital in town. Walking small distances had become a challenge and he had to rest often. The doctor's verdict was that he had TB, and if he would not stop drinking and smoking, he would not survive. It was soon thereafter that he passed away.

CAMPFIRE

Soon, our days of training were over and we started on the return trek. In three days, we were at the meadows of Yoksum. The same night, the Pre-Everest team also reached there, in high spirits as they had climbed Rathong, a first ascent. To add to the pleasure, Tensing had arranged permission to invite his friend, the famous Swiss climber Raymond Lambert and his wife to join us. Ordinarily, foreigners were not permitted to visit Sikkim, but Tensing was no ordinary person.

Prem Chand, my tent partner, was an army intelligence officer: "Harish, I see a large box of whisky in Mr Lambert's luggage. We should try and manage to get some bottles." Being army officers, he and others could not ask, so the task fell on me, a civilian. I chatted with Lambert as I knew something about

---

7. Ashburner, John, 'Mukarbeh 1968', *The Himalayan Journal*, Vol 28, 1968, p. 21. Details of accident and death on the peaks in 1967 on page 22. Full details in *The Alpine Journal*, 1967, p. 315.

his Everest record. Slowly, I broached the subject, "Sir, we are all tired, may I request you to share a little whisky with us?"

Lambert laughed and said, "Ok if you give me a damn good campfire, I will consider it". That was no problem – we had students from every part of the country. Prem Chand organised wood and lamb, which was skinned and hung above the roaring fire to roast as we performed songs, skits and stories from different regions. After about half an hour, Lambert signalled to me offering a couple of bottles of whisky! Tomba added more, the party took off. The senior team presented a Punjabi Bhangra, we had an Assamese dance, someone sang a serious Bengali song and even managed a classical south Indian piece! I presented a Gujarati garba where you go round and round in a large circle, taking special, delicate steps, in tune with a song. Since I cannot sing and neither could the strong army officers take small, delicate steps, it was probably the funniest garba ever!

Soon, Tensing got up and with a group of Sherpas began the traditional Sherpa dance – rhythm and grace personified. It was a unique experience to see these senior Sherpas dance, and one thought they could dance only on summits! Ang Kami Sherpa, who became the youngest person to summit Everest next year (1965), took out a colourful scarf and performed a solo dance with Sherpanis singing songs. These were performances to treasure. As the fire turned to embers and the party was suitably drunk, Dorjee Lhatoo, joined in with a guitar and started singing as only he could. We all gathered around him. The forest, cold Sikkim air, embers, moon and the singing were a cocktail to sip on for hours.

It was time to return to Darjeeling. In a couple of days, we were again at Singla Bazar. The last climb to Darjeeling was planned as a night walk. Porters carrying lanterns, some of us with torches and the heavy breathing of all of us in silence of the night was truly something to experience.[8]

Next evening, the selection of team for the 1965 Everest was announced to great joy for many and some disappointment for others. Capt. Mohan Kohli, was elected leader of the team, and there were celebrations that we juniors also joined in. The fun, frolic and midnight drunken brawls are difficult to describe!

---

8. After my 2020 trek on the route to and back from Dzongri, I asked Dorjee Lhatoo about how many times he has done this trek. "More than 100 times", he replied casually and without any hesitation.

GRADUATION AND GRADES

As for every Basic Course, a graduation ceremony was held. This time Mr S S Khera and Mr H C Sarin, both presidents of the Indian Mountaineering Foundation, were chief guests and awarded us the 'Ice-axe badge' as memento for completing the course. Thirty-five days had flown by, we never knew how quickly the course was over, but to this day, I have remained friends with most of the Sherpas and army officers.[9]

After a month, the graduation certificate from HMI arrived by post. I had received a 'B' grade, as expected. In fact, other than two students, the entire batch had received a B. Those days, grading was strict but honourable and we were allowed to undertake an Advance Course of training with this grade. Next year, I went on to the newly established Nehru Institute of Mountaineering to successfully complete my advance training, the first advance course of the Institute.

I had my sweet revenge after about 40 years, in 2005. Having done much climbing and exploration, I was invited to be the Chief Guest at the Graduation Ceremony at HMI. After pinning ice-axe badges on students, I gave a short speech that went something like this: "You are at an important stage of your mountain training. Do not worry about grades, just learn from the experience. Freedom of the hills is something you must enjoy. I am the most long lasting 'B' grader from HMI, but you can imagine the standard of training, that I still could do so much. On our course only two students were A grade, and I do not know what happened to them! What you do after the course, like 'After Everest', is important. You will remember this training, various places, various names and cherish the new friends you have made, and it will be in your memory – always."

---

9. In 1970, six years later, Geeta, then my fiancé went to HMI to undertake the Basic Course. She was treated royally as the Sherpas knew her relationship with me, and she received an 'A' grade as the systems and syllabus had been revised.

I. Jannu peak (left) and Kangchenjunga – view from trek to Sandakhpu.

II. Gurudongmar lake and peak, North Sikkim.

III. Rare view of Pandim peak, North Sikkim.

IV. Historic Niti pass and Ganesh Ganga. Central Garhwal.

V. Routes to Bara Hoti, east of Niti pass. Central Garhwal.

VI. View from Panar Bugiyal, en route to Rudranath. Vishnu Ghar Dhar peaks seen.

VII. Tarsar lake with campsite.

VIII. Zajimarg valley (Mukund R.).

IX. Sundersar lake (Grp Capt Nitin).

X. Marsar lake (Mukund R.).

XI. Gashibrar – highest peak of Kolahoi.

XII. Peaks of Kishtwar from Kablas Lake – Shankh Padri (Amrita Dhar).

XIII. Regimental arcs erected at entrance to the Siachen glacier.

XIV. Mule caravan approaching the Galwan valley.

XV. On Karakoram Pass.

XVI. On the Teram Shehr plateau. Peaks behind: L to R. Padmanabh, Laxmi and Teram Kangri group.

XVII. On the East Rimo glacier. Peak Rimo on right.

XVIII. Saltoro Kangri I (left) and Saltoro Kangri II, on the Siachen glacier.

XIX. Potala Palace at Lhasa.

XX. Kumbum monastery at Gyantse.

XXI. Khojarnath monastery (lord of animals) near Purang.

XXII. Grave of Zorawar Singh at Tola, near Purang.

XXIII. Tirthapuri, Western Tibet, origin of the Satluj river.

XXIV. Tholing Math, established by Shankracharyya at western Tibet.

XV. Tsaprang hills, Western Tibet.

XVI. On top of Guge Fort, Tsaprang, Western Tibet.

Soon it was time and the Darjeeling experience was over for this time. That last Darjeeling evening ended in the warm balcony of Nawang Gombu's house. As the time passed, more and more drinks flowed. Gombudaju was in his elements. "You must take one more, Harish" he kept insisting. When I was reluctant I was threatened, "If you don't take more, you no friend Harish".

How can I refuse for I count these warm hospitable Sherpas as some of the finest friends I have. It was a different matter that two very drunk friends staggered home that night !

– Harish Kapadia

WANDERLUST

When I was a little lad -
Sometimes I feel it still -
A yearning strange I always had,
To see beyond a hill.
What would I find?
It seemed, I must reach the other side.
And so, for many, many years,
I travelled far and wide.

Seeking things beyond the hills,
Seeking something new,
But always on the other side,
More hills came into view.
So I travelled on and on
And like the rolling stone,
No moss I gathered on my back
Nor much else did I own.

In my own home now I sit
And pass my idle time,
By thinking of the things I've seen
And putting them in rhyme.
But sometimes I grow restless,
My heart with longing fills,
And once again I get the urge
To see beyond the hills.

– Ernest Jack Sharpe

2

Chasing Circular Rainbows or the Brocken Spectre

Trekking on the Sandakphu Ridge

"Have you trekked to Sandakphu, uncle?" Yangdu asked me. "It is one of the best treks in the world". She was calling me 'uncle', which in India, is a title you receive as you age. Yangdu has a long experience of trekking, particularly around Darjeeling, where she was born and has lived for half her life.

"Sandakphu is a window to one of the finest views of the snowy mountains, from the mighty Everest in Nepal to the revered Kangchenjunga in Sikkim and the legendary Chomolhari in Bhutan. From here Everest is 144 km as the crow flies", she added with an infectious enthusiasm.

"This trek takes you along the famous Singalila Ridge. Singalila is a prominent spur of high ground that lies at the southern end of a long crest that runs down from Kangchenjunga itself. It forms the border between Sikkim and Nepal. The trek along this ridge takes you through small settlements and is renowned for being one of the most scenically rewarding in the entire Himalaya. Apart from these giants, there are views of a host of other peaks in the eastern Himalaya, all seen at one stretch – quite a sight even from about 3500 m, which is the maximum altitude you get to on this trek." And as final advice she added, "Go in autumn, you will get the clearest views". So, there I was, en route to Darjeeling in November 2000, to feast on the best views as promised by Yangdu – and she was on the mark.

There are two major advantages of trekking around Darjeeling. First, is the great flight from Delhi to Bagdogra (make sure that you have a left-hand side window seat). We viewed the entire Himalayan range starting from Bandarpunch, Nanda Devi, Everest and the complete range of Nepal's high mountains. When you see the Kangchenjunga massif you know that you are nearing Bagdogra. Second, is the journey from Bagdogra. Going up, the *Himalayan Hills Railway* can be a long and laborious process and as a result, most people now travel to Darjeeling by road and take the little toy train ride from Darjeeling back to Ghoom. This Hill Railway has been declared a 'World Heritage Railway'. This is what we did along with a visit to the memorial at the Batasia loop to the heroes of the Indian army's Gorkha soldiers. We visited the Himalayan Mountaineering Institute and spent time with old friends. Like all other visitors, a trip to view the sunrise from Tiger Hill early in the morning was mandatory. I will no longer vouch for the peace and sanctity of the surroundings as a large crowd had gathered there, and we were told that such crowds are there almost every day now. As the sun rose over the horizon, on one hand the peak of Everest lit in an exquisite change of colours but on the other, the people next to us burst out beating drums, shouting and dancing. There was such a big commotion that one felt as if the sun had done something wrong. People have different ideas of enjoyment and shattering the silence in such surroundings was theirs.

I was to trek to Sandakphu in the company of some wonderful friends. Ajit and Usha Mehta are Gujaratis like me from western India, who migrated to Chicago, USA, many decades ago. They, like several other friends of mine, adopted USA as their country.

It was on 1st of November that we were ready to start on our trek and drove about 30 km to a village called Manebhanjang. As I started walking, a young lady from our group, Sejal, started walking with me. She was a student from USA who appeared quite strong and fit. I casually asked her, "So Sejal, have you been trekking before?" In an American accent she replied, "No, but I have been doing plenty of walking around, plenty of training, long distance jogging and have been for short walks around places in the US". Then, after a pause, she looked at me and asked, "How about you, have you been to the Himalaya before?" I just smiled. I wished I was coming for the first time. For that infectious enthusiasm of the 'first time', that first view of the snow and that first smell of pines is something I miss now after so many years in the Himalaya. As Martin Conway had put it:

Later we may know more, we understand more, we may even come to love more; but the first vision of a young man's love is surpassed by no further splendour, and the glory of a mountain view never comes again.

The trail started with a rather steep climb as one reaches the Singalila ridge. Luckily, the first part was a climb for a short distance, about 3 km, and around noon we stopped at a small hamlet called Chitrey, where we had lunch. As lunch was being prepared in a small dhaba, some of the local boys about 200 ft above us were playing loud music and making so much noise that it reminded us of the Tiger Hill incident. As we had to sit here for a while, Nilesh Kothari from our group climbed up to them and waved. The boys did not pay any attention. So he waved out a Rs 50 note and shouted, "How about stopping this noise?" He was an American and this was his capitalist method of conquering the natives. The boys did not listen and, in fact, they turned the speaker towards us, increased the volume and started dancing. Finally, it was the tall figure of Dr Mark Jalakas who climbed up and gave them a piece of his mind. That did the trick. The authoritarian approach certainly succeeded over the capitalist one.

We were to climb more than 1100 m to reach the top of the Singalila ridge at Tonglu. By 4 o'clock, with such a steep trek to overcome, we were dehydrated and fatigued. But, as the sun went down, everything looked lovely in the autumn light. As we turned a corner on this long winding road, Mark Jalakas who was slightly ahead of me and feeling little tired, suddenly stopped: "Harish, look at the Brocken Spectre".

Mark always knows more about things and as I looked around, I saw a lovely circular rainbow riding on the clouds in the valley below. What was incredible was that our shadows were falling right into the centre of that rainbow. It felt as if we were riding on a cloud, at least our shadows were. (Such a phenomenon was first noticed in the German mountain range of the same name, Brocken).[1] It was an amazing sight and Sejal, who was with

1. Brocken, also called Blocksberg, highest point 1142 m (3747 feet) of the Harz Mountains, lying 13 km (8 miles) west-southwest of Wernigerode, Germany. A huge, granite-strewn dome, the peak commands magnificent views in all directions, and a mountain railway, 19 km (12 miles) long, reaches the summit. When the sun is low, shadows cast from the peak become magnified, and seemingly gigantic silhouettes are cast on the upper

me, went crazy taking photographs. The clouds were rushing towards us, and it felt as if we were riding towards heaven in the centre of a rainbow. All Sejal could say repeatedly was, "It's awesome, it's awesome".

I had seen such a phenomenon before in the local hills near Mumbai, in the Sahyadris (Western Ghats). A historical fort of the great Maratha warrior Shivaji, named Harishchandra Gad, has steep, high walls facing the west. In late May, as the build-up to monsoon clouds swirl up from the valley to the fort and the morning sun rises from the east, it casts long shadows on these clouds making one feel as if one is walking on them. During the days of the Raj, a British officer once stood at the edge on a horse. His shadow 'riding' on the clouds was seen by the simple villagers and a folk-tale was born – about British officers who could even ride on clouds, and hence no one dared to challenge them!

All tiredness left behind, we reached Tonglu with the memory of this brilliant spectre. Tonglu has a small trekker's hut and if you are lucky, you may be treated to a spectacular sunset over the Kangchenjunga range as you stand on the balcony. We were lucky and looking at this brilliant spectacle again revived many memories. On the second day we had to proceed to Tumling, which is at around 2860 m. We were walking on a very broad but rough jeepable trail on the famous Singalila ridge about which I had heard a lot, and on which people have travelled for centuries. To the left of the ridge, towards the west, lies Nepali territory and to the east, or right, is India. Thank God both are friendly countries and no armies face each other here. In fact, trails regularly zig zag into Nepal and back to India. We entered the Singalila National Park after paying a minor fee and descended 6 km to Garibas. From Garibas, the motorable road continued along the ridge, but there is a lovely foot track that crosses west into Nepal to reach the small village of Jaunbari. We were not an unusual sight for people in the village, they had seen many trekkers. There were small eating joints, and people nonchalantly spoke to us while busy with their work.

---

surfaces of low-lying clouds or fog below the mountain. This effect is known as the Brocken bow, or Brocken spectre, and is given a mystical significance in the mountain's folklore. Long after the introduction of Christianity, traditional rites continued to be enacted there annually on Walpurgis Night, or Witches' Sabbath (April 30). The peak is represented in a famous scene in J W von Goethe's drama *Faust*.

The trail climbed up back to the Singalila ridge rather steeply and once again we followed the ridge till we reached Kala Pokhri, literally meaning 'Black Lake'. In fact, as we reached there late in the evening, the lake certainly looked very black.

On the third day we were to proceed via Bikhey Bhanjang to Sandakphu. It was a steep ascent of almost 5 km till we reached Sandakphu, a place that almost defies description. Right on top of the ridge we were on an international boundary with a police post and several excellently situated bungalows.

It was quite cold that evening, but who cared – right in front of us was the majestic Kangchenjunga and all its surrounding peaks with lovely deodar and pine forests. Peace was all around, and the backdrop was magnificent. Towards the west Everest appeared as a very small dot, almost peeping out from behind Makalu. But then there were many who were more excited about looking at Everest than Kangchenjunga. I think being tallest in the world has its advantages and attractions. The next day we woke up early to see the golden sunrise. It was as has been mentioned by an early explorer.

> From Sandakphu, the wild elemental grandeur of the snows begins to assert itself, till the climax is reached at sunrise, when it soaks the snow-laden peaks in crimson and mauve, orange and gold, Kangchenjunga and Everest are seen in all their glory against the background of an azure sky speckled with lazily floating, fleecy clouds. The whole snowy range of Bhutan, Sikkim and Nepal, about 320 km in length, a wonderful square mass of mountains looking like a wall of snow, is visible, but the gigantic height and breadth of towering Kangchenjunga, with its attendant peaks, Kabru, Jannu and Pandim dominates the scene; Everest (8848 m), now looking rather graceful and majestic, 160 km away, soars above, peeping shyly from the northern horizon with Lhotse on the left.

After breakfast we started on the trail on the ridge towards Molley. As we walked along, we could view the beautiful valleys of both India and Nepal. From Sandakphu, the same broad trail continued and now all the steep climbs were behind us. As we passed through beautiful open areas with Kangchenjunga on our right and Everest on the left, we crossed a few Nepali villagers who were carrying fresh peas from Nepal and descending into Sikkim to sell them to villagers there. You could easily buy some from them, which is what we did. Eating fresh peas and walking with such a grand view is certainly a different experience. For about 4 km the trail was flat, until finally we reached a long steady climb to Sabagram (totally about 5 km further away). To break the long walk to Phalut, a slight detour has been made and after a short descent you reach a trekker's hut at Molley, about 2 km off the road. Molley[2] was once a camping ground for shepherds. From here, a long ridge led down into the Ramam valley, making this a convenient camping spot for shepherds travelling from Nepal to Sikkim. Molley is at 3600 m with alpine vegetation, and an undulating ripple of dwarf rhododendron bushes and shrubs of poisonous aconite.

Going on from Molley the next day, the trail at first climbed back to join the main trail then, after descending a bit, we came to a 3 km steep ascent to Phalut, which is an important viewpoint on the trail. A bungalow has been built little below the highest point.

Phalut forms the junction of Nepal, Sikkim and West Bengal and is one of the most beautiful places to visit. The hills are all bare and from here Kangchenjunga is only 48 km as the crow flies. Unfortunately, as it was cloudy that day, we did not get much of a view. Our discussions cantered around from being serious, sublime, to simple laughter. There were many stories from America and many concerns about India. Our NRI friends were very much in touch with everything Indian and in love with the country of their origin. We had heated discussions regarding different aspects of politics, which livened up the evening. We were trekking with mules, which were carrying our heavier loads. That afternoon we had reached early and had sat down for a chat in the bungalow when Mark Jalakas suddenly rose, and very politely murmured, "I will go out and check the horses". I looked at him and said, "Mark, the horses would not have arrived as yet". He looked at me in amazement: "Haven't you heard the term before?" And everybody smiled. He had used a polite American expression, to announce that he was going out for a nature's call.

The route ahead of Phalut to Gorkhey was certainly not for anyone with weak knees – it descends 1200 m in 15 km. But this descent took us through the most wonderful forest. The trail was well trodden. Bamboos and firs ultimately replaced deodars and pines in a day's wonderful walk.

2. Explanations of place names are given at the end of the article.

The lower hills were covered with moss-laden trees, different varieties of rhododendrons, silver firs, pines, spruce, chestnuts, oaks, giant magnolias and hemlocks.

Tired but satisfied, we reached the small village of Gorkhey at 2390 m. Gorkhey is on the border with the northern part of western Sikkim, though foreigners are not allowed to cross into Sikkim via this point. We were on the Ramam river. This is a small river but an important one as it is the boundary of West Bengal and Sikkim to the north. We continued descending both that and next day; our destination was Siri Khola.

For those who love plants and people, this route is paradise. With a forest of different varieties of indigenous trees, Samanden, a beautiful village, was worth taking a halt at to meet the simple folks there. The villagers are basically from a Sherpa clan that migrated here from Nepal many years ago. The main source of income for the villagers is potato farming, fields of which we saw around the lower villages of Rimbick and Ramam. But there is also a legend that attracts many curious visitors and Lepcha pilgrims to this quiet village. It is said that many years ago the legendary Himalayan 'Yeti' fought with a Lepcha hunter for supremacy of the hunting grounds here. Eventually, since both sides were of equal strength, they came to a joint solution and made a treaty. So, in the quiet woods, a huge stone was erected as a symbol of friendship between the Lepcha hunter and the Yeti!

As we trekked ahead, we walked out of the forests. There were small villages we constantly passed through. Early in the morning, a little after we started on the trail, Usha and Gina sat down to play a match of carom with the local villagers. While walking from that point we logged on with a forest party. The forest officer was a mine of information and narrated various legends, stories and happenings in the area. When walking between villages one can pick up so much from the locals or officials posted there that it makes your trek really interesting and worthwhile.[3]

---

3. A recent legend we heard was 'Hamjaya', about a taxi driver who drove to Sandakphu. The road to Sandakphu is steep and rough. Many times, thick fog and rain makes driving rather dangerous, hence most taxi drivers are reluctant to drive there. Once day, a pretty lady came to the stand and asked in Hindi 'Kaun Jaya' ('Who will go to Sandakphu'). Only one taxi driver replied 'Hamjaya' ('I will go'). When he did not return for a few days, it was

The trekker's hut at Siri Khola was built overlooking the river. It was well placed with small hotels clustered around, and gave us welcome relief. We cooled off that day and in the evening everyone had a most relaxing time. The last day's walk was to Rimbick village. It was a flat walk again on a broad trail. That day we almost had a competition as to who would reach the camp last.

Each one walked leisurely, chatting with villagers, sitting at small wayside shops, drinking tea at the roadside dhabas and, of course, food and a glass of beer also went well with trekking. The trail was well decorated with flowers, for the local festival of Dusherra had recently been celebrated. Yellow flowers were hanging from all windows. The villagers let these hang till they dry up and then plant the seeds – an age-old eco-friendly tradition. At the end of the road was the small village of Rimbick.

Rimbick (2286 m) is a small, important town and is mostly quiet but gets busy on the main market day, which is Tuesday. It is lovely to watch simple people from different villages coming to buy and sell their local products. Rimbick, which is a Lepcha word meaning 'Ling-gip' – a place where there is a swing.

Suddenly, we were amongst modern facilities. A hot shower, a good clean room and change of clothes made us feel a contentment that only civilisation can give. We talked of having completed a lovely trek, of hardships faced and loosened our tired limbs.

We got a different perspective soon. There was a sudden commotion in the bazaar and as we looked around, we saw runners arrive. A Himalayan run was being held in the area and what we had trekked in about 8 days, these enthusiasts were running in that many number of hours! But then to each his own, as they say. We saw some runners staggering in very tired. They collapsed on the ground and could be heard murmuring, "Never again, never again". However, I am sure they were running again the next day and returned next year. It is the spirit that counts and looking at these runners we were amazed at what the human body can do.

---

feared that both had perished on the road. As the mourning was underway the taxi driver appeared smiling with the lady as his wife. They had married and spent their honeymoon at Sandakphu. The taxi driver is still known as 'Mr Hamjaya' after the reply he had given.

All that remained for us now was the 130 km long, 7-hour drive to Kalimpong, our last destination. Kalimpong, once an important trade centre between India, Bhutan and Tibet, is a small cosy town that retains the old British charm. There are many educational institutions, particularly Dr Graham's Home, which is legendary. With its pleasant climate and famous for its orchid nurseries and handicrafts, this lovely laid-back town was surely the best place to wind up the trip and relax before going home.

Everybody was now in great form and a sense of satisfaction enveloped us. The dinner table was lively and memories of the trek were pushing us on. Unfortunately, like all good things it had to end and the next morning we parted company. My friends took a bus and a flight on their way back to Delhi and I took a taxi back to Darjeeling to meet my Sherpa friends. Each one of us was going back to our Brocken Spectre in a different way.

Explanations of some names on the Sandakphu trail.

Bikhe Bhanjang	Bikhe is a special medicinal plant which is available in this valley.
Garibas	Gairi – lower place, bas – place to stay. Thus, a place to stay at lower location.
Jounbari	Joun, Nepali for barley. Bari – village. A village where barley grows.
Mane Bhanjang	Mane – old mane stone, stupa which is erected here. Bhanjang – valley. A valley where Mane is erected.
Molley	'gobar', excrement of cows which is applied to floors in village houses. Many cowherds used to stay here. So, it was named 'a place where gobar is available'.
Phalut	was originally called 'Phale Lung'. Phale – stone, Lung – steep place. A steep, stony place. Another explanation given is that Phalu means head of a cock. There is a rock here of a similar shape.
Samadeen	This is a small village hidden between two valleys. Simply put, it can be called a 'lost village'. But a legend is sometimes quoted for this name. There was a dispute between Lepcha and Topcha communities. During a fight both groups were trapped in this valley and heavy rain followed. One group was above

the ridge and the other on the river. As a stalemate grew, wiser counsel prevailed and both communities decided to settle here together. The agreement reached is called 'samadeen' in the local language.

Sandakphu

There are different explanations available. But the most likely is told in a legend from almost a century ago. A local Nepali guide named Santa Bahadur who roamed the ridge here, was buried in heavy snow and perished. Pur in Nepali means 'buried in snow or someone who died accidentally'. Thus, the place came to be called 'Santapur' – the place where Santa died. Over the years, Sikkimese pronunciation made it 'Sandakphu'.

Mine are the torrents and the timeless hills,
The rock-face and the heather and the rain,
The summits where the life-wind thrums and thrills,
And, answering, the glad heart sings again :
The good grey rock that loves a grasping hand,
The stress of body, and the soul's rebirth
On the tall peak where gods and men may stand
Breathless above the kingdoms of the earth :

Epilogue from *The Mountaineer's Week-End Book*
by Showell Styles, (p. 404)

3

An Autumn Trek to Tholung Monastery

Trekking in the Dzongu Valley of North Sikkim

Lepchas, the original inhabitants of the valleys in North Sikkim, are known by different names: Rong (tribe name), Rongkup (children of Rong), Mutanchi Rong (beloved people of God), and their land was called Mayal Lang (hidden Land or the land blessed by God). These nature worshippers continue to possess a vast knowledge of their natural surroundings – the forests and the flora and fauna – as well as of traditional medicine that they have accumulated over many generations. They have also built several monasteries.

Their population, once estimated to be about 50,000, has dwindled considerably and only a few are alive today. They live in Dzongu, a valley west of Mangan in North Sikkim, which has been declared a restricted area, but permits to visit it are easily obtained.

Four of us arrived at Mangan (via Gangtok) in early October 2015. The view from the homestay opened onto Siniolchu and surrounding peaks. In the crisp autumn air, the snowy ridges looked resplendent. This made one appreciate why Douglas Freshfield in his book *Round Kangchenjunga* called it the most beautiful peak in the world. Though he did not enter Dzongu, he was at its foot on the Zemu glacier which lies to the immediate north of the Dzongu valley. From Mangan, we proceeded on rough roads to the Teesta river at Sangkalang (19 km) and reached Passingdang, the first large village in the valley. Similar rough roads lead in various directions to beautifully situated villages in the valley. Lingthem (10 km) and Tingvong (eight km from Sibim) are a couple of larger noteworthy villages.

We drove on to Lingzya (10 km) which is marked by a huge waterfall. The village was lined with white prayer flags and mani walls. Our drive ended at Be (six km) and we settled at a comfortable homestay. Our hosts produced wonderful meals from different vegetables available in the forest nearby and revealed indigenous knowledge about how many of these vegetables could combat lifestyle-related diseases like high blood pressure and diabetes.

We started our trek to Tholung monastery from here. Sporting a thin beard on his chin, our guide, Mingtu, looked like a traditional Lepcha. He was very familiar with the terrain as he had explored different areas along with Anindya Mukherjee of Kolkata. Mukherjee has written about his trek looking for 'Bon Manchi', a local name for the elusive Yeti, which Lepchas believe lives here.[1] The valley to the east of Lingzya leads to the foot of Guicha la (pass) in the south. In the north is Zemu gap leading to Zemu glacier. The former is visited by many while the latter is rarely visited, let alone crossed. At the head of the valley, on the border with Nepal, stands Talung peak.

After a leisurely trek followed by a camp at Dijim next day, we reached Tholung monastery, which was deserted as the lamas had moved to lower altitudes. A major earthquake in 2011, with Tholung as its epicentre, had partly destroyed the monastery. A new monastery is being built next to the existing one. There were several old wall paintings and a stupa studded with jewels, also said to contain bones of earlier kings. Despite the damage, it still carried an air of serenity.

The monastery, said to have been established in 1789, is considered the most sacred in Sikkim. Following a Gorkha invasion of Sikkim during the reign of Chhogyal Tensing Namgyal, all precious collections, write-ups, religious objects from large monasteries like Dubde and Sanga Choling were brought here to upper Dzongu. After a few years, a monastery was built at Tholung and all the items were stored here under the charge of the family known as Tholung Nangpa. They were in charge till 1940, when

---

1. Mukherjee, Anindya, 'The Land of Mythical Paradise', *The Himalayan Journal* Vol 67 2011, p. 30; 'Zemu Gap from South', *The Himalayan Journal* Vol 68 2013, p. 37; 'Quest for the Bon Manchi: The Wildman of Sikkim', *The Himalayan Journal* Vol 70 2015, p. 1; 'The Curious Case of De Nga' on exploring High altitude lakes in Dzongu, https://adventuremania-india.blogspot.com/2017/04/the-curious-case-of-de-nga.html, 29 April 2017.

the Ecclesiastical Department of the Government of Sikkim took over, though the Nangpa family continues to be the chief patron of this gompa. These treasures are aired and displayed to the faithful once in three years. A monastery, the one destroyed by the earthquake, was built in 1980, and now another new structure is under construction.

UPPER VALLEY TO KISHONG LAKE
(by Dr Kartik Bhagat)

With a group of selected porters, we left for the upper valley on a short trek. This was an uphill route for the faithful leading to various holy sites. At first, we crossed the Rimbi river through rocky and slushy terrain with fallen trees across the path at various places along the route. The route gradually climbed up to a cave known as Thugong (locked box of treasure). We continued along the valley to Ritzim Ferong and finally to Themrong, at the junction of Zumthul chu meeting with Rimbi chu which we were following.

On the second day, we progressed uphill through small nalas. At Thinsung, we saw the Kishong waterfall with a small meditation platform for Guru Rimpoche. From Lapyok, the trail climbed steeply through shrubs with mulberries and blue berries. We walked through thick fog, light rain and cold wind so camping at Tholukpe was a relief.

The next morning, we had some views of the upper valley with Lama Angden seen rising above Kishong lake. As we were exhausted from the previous day, instead of proceeding to Kishong lake, a mere three hours away, we decided to return. Though the porters were in good spirits, we could see plenty of snow ahead of us. We stuck to our decision and completed our descent in two days to join the rest of the party.

On the way back, we halted briefly at Passingdang to meet a young Lepcha scholar. He had studied in different parts of India but chose to settle in his ancestors' valley. After trekking to most parts of the valley and studying its traditions and mythology, he published a book with historic photos. As long as young, motivated people live in Dzongu, the area is safe for posterity. As we sipped tea, he enthralled us with his amazing collection of folklore. What better way to end a trek to a beautiful valley?

Gone are the days when in the evenings, children used to flock around the elders, to listen to the stories, sitting around the fireplace in their small, warm, and cosy kitchens. The elders also got an occasion to share their day to day sweet and sour moments with the young ones. In this age of technology where the younger generation remains attracted to various modern gadgets and social networking sites, this beautiful evening 'past time' is fast disappearing.

KT Lepcha[2]

Most times, the worst situations can become a compass to best of situations.

– Anonymous

My Divine Forms

Among the light I am the radiant sun
Among the stars I am the moon
Among the lakes I am the ocean
Among the mountains I am Kailash
Among the immovable I am the Himalaya

Lord Krishna, *The Bhagavad-Gita*

2. Lepcha, Sonam Wangchuk, *The Myths of Mutanchi*, Privately published, 2015, 142 (contact author: sonamWC.lep@gmail.com).

4

The Plateau

Mountains of the Sikkim–China Border

This was my fifth visit to the mountains of Sikkim. In 1964, as a young student I took a training course at the Himalayan Mountaineering Institute. The mountains of west Sikkim – Kabru, Rathong, Pandim and a host of others – attracted my youthful eyes and I returned in 1976. No sooner had Sikkim became a state of India than two of us, Zerksis Boga and I, obtained permits and, for more than a month, roamed the valleys of northwest Sikkim, covering Zemu glacier, Lhonak valley Muguthang, Lugnak la, Sebu la and returning via Lachung valley.[1] Even after that trip, I returned to Darjeeling and the Sikkim valleys quite a few times, visiting the Singalila ridge, lakes of lower Sikkim and surroundings of Gangtok and Kalimpong. If you stretch the area to the south, I made several visits to Darjeeling and hills nearby over the years. In Sikkim, the approach to different valleys is so varied that it gives a feeling of trekking in different Himalayan zones.

In no other country on earth can one find such a variety of micro-climates within such a short distance as Sikkim, declared the eminent English botanist and explorer Joseph Hooker in his *Himalayan Journals* (1854), which documented his work collecting and classifying thousands of plants in the Himalaya in the mid-19th century.[2]

---

1. Kapadia, Harish, *High Himalaya Unknown Valleys,* Indus Publishing Company, New Delhi, 2001, 156. Also *The Himalayan Journal,* Vol 35 1979, p. 181.
2. Mayer, Kurt, and Pamela Deuel Meyer, *In the Shadow of the Himalayas: Tibet, Bhutan, Nepal, Sikkim – A Photographic Record by John Claude White 1883–1908,* Reprint, Mapin Publishing, Ahmadabad, 2005, p. 50.

But one prize had escaped me – the northern-most valley of Sikkim near the China (Tibet) border. Known as 'the Plateau', this area has some of the highest (after the Kangchenjunga group) and most beautiful peaks. Though visited by several early explorers, after the 1962 India–China war, it became highly restricted, especially as in later decades Chinese tried to assert themselves in these valleys. To its east lies the Chumbi valley which drains the Amo chu. It was through here that much trade with Tibet was carried out. The Younghusband Mission to Tibet passed through this valley in 1903–1904. The early Everest expeditions either passed through the Chumbi or across the high passes of Naku la or Karpo la on the west of the Plateau. These early climbers, with spirit and stamina, climbed a few of the high peaks on their way back, even after months spent on Everest.

It was a few political officers, posted to the Darbar of the Chogyal in Sikkim by the British, who travelled to remote parts and recorded their journeys. Claude White at the end of the nineteenth and beginning of the twentieth century, was a well-travelled man. F M Bailey and F Williamson explored the area between the two world wars. Experienced botanical explorers and naturalists F Kingdon-Ward, F Ludlow and George Sherriff added much to the knowledge of northern Sikkim. Amongst the climbers Dr A M Kellas stands out. He made six expeditions to Sikkim between 1907 and 1920 and many first ascents. He was especially active on the Plateau, and in 1910 alone, he climbed 10 peaks above 6000 m, all first ascents. He had a special attraction to the highest peak on the Plateau, Pauhunri (7125 m).

In August and October 1909, Dr Kellas attempted Pauhunri in two separate attempts, reaching within 100 m of the summit. Not one to be defeated, he returned in May – June 1910 and Pauhunri yielded to his efforts and he summited after a five-day struggle from 13 to 17 June. All these efforts were on the northeast face, approached from the Chumbi. His route was repeated by C W F Noyce (24 Sept 1945) and French climber R Walter (24 Sept 1949). After three decades, an Indian army team (Col V Y Bhave) made an ascent from the Plateau and northwest face (20 Sept 1983), a climb that was repeated by a team of paramilitary forces (Sonam Wangyal) on 1 November 1989.

The three of us, Atul Rawal, Vijay Kothari and I arrived in May 2012 to trek in the north Sikkim area and the Plateau. We were all above 65 years in age and were supported by our three dependable Kumauni porters. At first, we had to acclimatise to the altitude to reach the Plateau, as the average height is almost 19,000 ft. However, with such strong winds, it is not possible to stay long enough to acclimatise. So, we entered the Lachung valley first.

LACHUNG, DOMBANG AND BORUM LA

Half a day of travel on a rough road from Gangtok brought us to Lachung which was at grips with tourists, or what they call 'Package Travellers'. A group is offered a 'package' starting from Kolkata, with travel overnight by train to Siliguri and a drive to Gangtok. The following day a long drive takes them to Lachung. On the third day, this horde drives up to what is known as 'Zero Point' (at the foot of Donkhya la), rambles for half an hour on snow, returns to Lachung, and remarkably, goes on to Gangtok same evening. On the fourth day they drive to the railway station and return by night train to Kolkata. In between they see a monastery or two and do some shopping! We were amazed at their stamina, lack of curiosity and time, to see anything more.

Lachung was a small village, now with a few hotels and many guest houses. It was well spread out and with a strong army presence as several routes from here lead to the border between Chumbi valley and China. There was no trace or memory of the Scottish missionary Miss Doig, who had spent decades here and was well known to the early expeditions.

After about five kilometres, a road bifurcates east to the Dombang valley. This is a long valley, almost parallel to the main Lachung valley. On one side are the steep slopes to the border with Gora la (5248 m), once an easy pass to the east. The ridge between the Dombang and Lachung valley, 'the Dombang ridge', comprises several peaks, not higher than about 5800 m but attractive. The Dombang valley was thoroughly explored by Trevor Braham in 1949 with M Hruska, a Czech climber. They elected to go in November, facing the cold but hopefully enjoying clear weather, a rarity in Sikkim. With them was the famous Sherpa Ang Tharkay. Tharkay's reputation was founded, I think, not just on his natural qualities as a mountaineer, but also on his ability as a manager. "The confidence and trust which he inspired gave one the comforting assurance that if a solution to any problem existed, he would find it."[3] After reaching the foot of Gora la, they followed a smaller

3. Braham, T H, *Himalayan Odyssey*, George, Allen and Unwin, London, 1974, pp. 54–55.

tract to the northwest over the Karpo la (5383 m). They then followed the Khangkyong glacier and found a way to the Plateau via Donkhya la. 'The Plateau was almost two miles deep, it was surrounded by a row of five peaks, two over 23,000 feet and the remainder over 22,000 feet...'[4]. This was a fine exploration of an alternate approach to the Plateau. We were soon to see these peaks and the 19,000-feet pass reached by him from the north.

Our association with the journey of Trevor Braham continued. We spent two delightful days at the forest rest house at Yumthang, after passing the rhododendron sanctuary. This vast open ground is surrounded by sharp, rocky mountains to the west and the Dombang range to the east. If developed, this ground can challenge any climbing centre in the world.

The trek to Borum la (4883 m) starts about three kilometres ahead of Yumthang. A board had been put up at the junction with Lako chu, encouraging tourists to walk '1.5 km to Hot Springs'. We went up a well-made path which soon disappeared and, for at least 15 kilometres till where the valley ended, there were no hot springs. After a camp, the trail entered a narrow valley and led to the small lake almost near Borum la, fed by the Borum glacier. In 1949, Braham could not cross the lake and we faced with the same situation.[5] We were advised by the army not to cross Borum la as the trail on the west, towards the Lachen valley, was destroyed by the earthquake in 2011. The earthquake was about 10 km below the surface and the areas near the epicentre, full of ancient monasteries of Tholung, were left relatively untouched. But it was far away areas like this Lachung-Lachen ridge that bore the full force of destruction. Anyway, reaching the pass was all that we desired, and our acclimatised party now returned to Lachung and from there by road to Lachen for the second part of our trek.

THE PLATEAU

The Giagong Valley is a desolate, windswept spot lying in the centre of a gorge between Chomoiomo (*Chomo Yummo*) 23,000 feet on the west, and Kangchenjhau, 24,000 feet, on the east, and is a veritable funnel up which the wind is always howling. I managed, however, to find a fairly sheltered spot for my camp and stayed a few days. One day I climbed a hill to the west called Tunlo, and from the top I had a magnificent view to the north Sikhim up to the rounded hills forming the

4. Braham, ibid., p. 56.
5. Braham, ibid., p. 60.

watershed and the true boundary. Looked at from this elevation, the scene is a most desolate one truly typical of, and only to be found in, Tibet: with the exception of the valley immediately below me, nothing was under 18,000 feet, without shrub, much less a tree, to be seen, and the wonder was how the large flocks of sheep scattered about, numbering perhaps 10,000 or 12,000, found enough grazing to keep them alive.[6]

We were heading to the Giagong valley, described by White. In fact, we were to make a sort of base camp at Giagong to visit the Plateau twice. But first we spent two days at Lachen, which I had visited in 1976. It had changed completely of course, and all my enquiries following up on old memories bore no fruit. The old monastery, now fully renovated, stood next to a modern hotel. There was no sign of family of the famous guide, Kondup lama, who had accompanied me. He was as legendary as Tensing Norgay Sherpa, having undertaken several journeys to Everest via Tibet with him. No one remembered the Scottish Mission at Lachen. The old forest bungalow where I had spent wonderful days, was surrounded by hutments, and had now turned ugly, and into a non-functional radio broadcasting station. It was here that I had seen the logbook in which most early Everest team members had signed; some signatures were missing for the 'return' entry – of those who had perished on the mountains. There was no sign of this logbook at any forest establishment till Gangtok. The system of 'Phipun' (village headman) was prevalent but now it was an elected post within the village.

The mountain scenery was to change rapidly in the next two days. Driving to Thango, we had our first views of the twin Lama Angden peaks (5868 m), first climbed by A J M. Smyth and Wing Commander Ford in September 1942. Soon the southern view of the peaks on the Plateau emerged, looking like a huge block of snow-clad peaks of Gurudongmar and Kangchenjau. Both these peaks have a long history.

On his return from Everest in 1936, Eric Shipton and E G H. Kempson separated from the main party to enter the Plateau from Kongra la (5133 m). On 1 July, in a long, day push, two of them made the first ascent of Gurudongmar (6715 m), by reaching a col from the shores of the lake to climb the steep west ridge. The second ascent was made only in 1991 when

6. Mayer, Kurt, and Pamela Deuel Meyer, op. cit., p. 63.

a para-military force team (G T Bhutia) climbed it on 3 October, along with nearby Sanglaphu (6224 m). Kangchenjau (6889 m) was Dr Kellas' territory. In August 1912 he reached a col from Sebu la and reached the upper rocks. He turned to the north ridge from here to reach the summit plateau and the top. The other creditable attempt was made by Trevor Braham in 1949. The mountain also killed five Indian in an avalanche in 2005.[7]

We spent the first night at the Giagong camp of the Indian army. In fact, winds were so strong that it would be a major effort to set up small mountaineering tents. Next morning, we walked towards Tunlo, a small hill in the west, which was mentioned by White. There were some yak herders camped there and the view of the vast plateau was rewarding. In the distance we could see remains of a *sangar* (rock wall), which we passed the next day, built by Tibetans to protect themselves against invaders.[8]

Kangchenjau rose fearfully in the east with huge blocks of ice hanging on its face. On the west was Chomo Yummo (6829 m). Both these and their surrounding peaks were to be seen all along till we turned east on the Plateau. Chomo Yummo broadly straddles the ridge between the Giagong valley and the Tibet border. The attempt by T H Tilly with Ang Tharkay in 1945 from Donkung, and the northeast approach, failed. Then came Dr. Kellas again! In 1910 he climbed the northwest ridge to make the first ascent. In 1986, this peak was to suffer an assault by 39 summiteers of an army team (Maj Gen P L Kukrety). They fixed ropes till the top and all climbed up – a far cry from the ascents by Dr Kellas.

To our west was Chummankang (6212 m), earlier known as Laschi. Leaving their luggage with the legendary Karma Paul, Bill Tilman and his Sherpas climbed this rather gentle peak. It was the rainy season so route

7. While attempting the summit, the party was hurled down by an avalanche and got entangled in the ropes they were tied to. In all, five climbers died on the spot and two survived with serious injuries. Those who died were Dr Paras Moni Das, Inder Kumar, Ms. Nari Dhami (these two had summitted Everest), Dawa Sherpa and Dawa Wangchuk, instructors from mountaineering school at Gangtok. Dr P M Das was a high-ranking police officer and a well-known climber. Dr P. M. Das's obituary can be read in *The Himalayan Journal*, Vol 62 2006, p. 270.

8. 'About a mile north of this camping ground (Giagong) are the remains of the wall built by the Tibetans as an obstruction to the British Mission to Tibet in 1903–04.' (Brown, Percy *Tours in Sikhim*, W Newman and co, Ltd, Calcutta, 1944, p. 128).

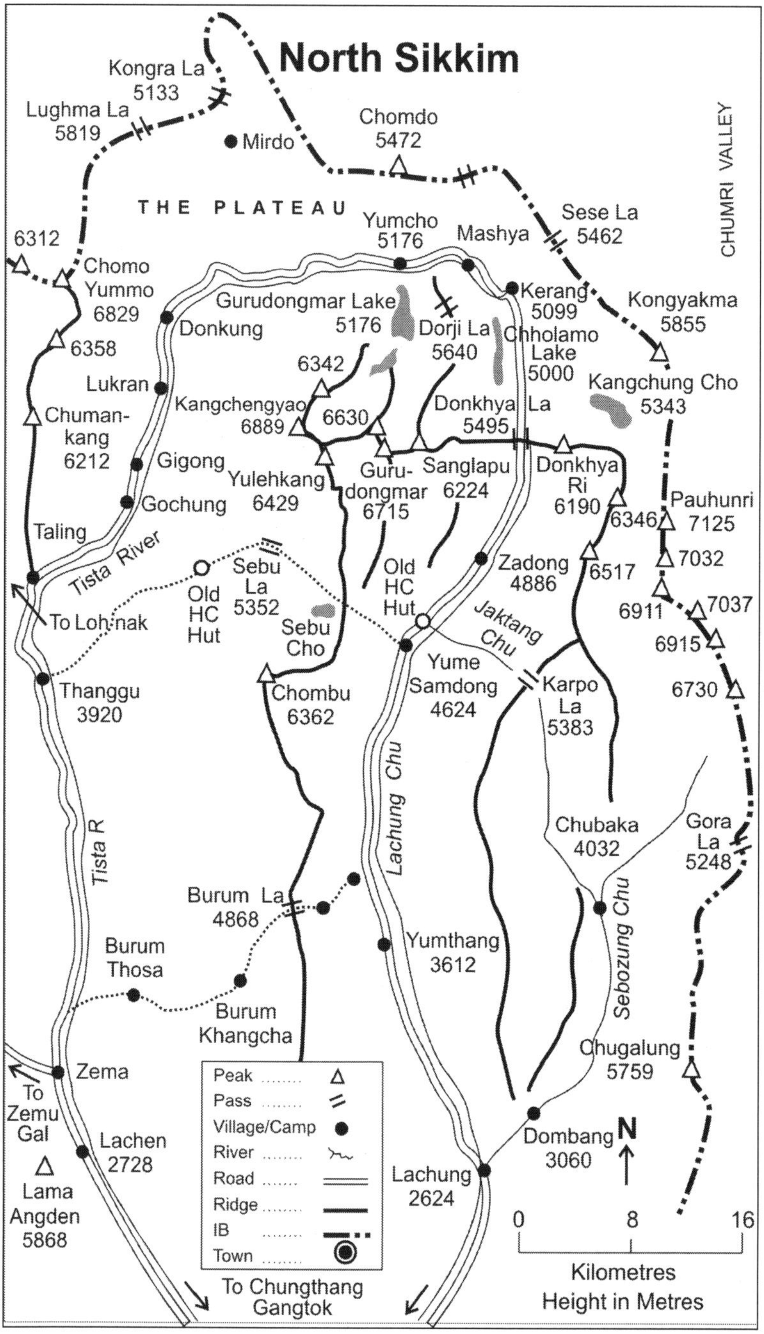

The Plateau, North Sikkim.

finding was complicated, and they hardly had any views. But Tilman turned that to virtue and wrote:

> The great disadvantage of the monsoon period of seeing neither where one is going nor the surrounding scenery is compensated for in small degree by the surprises and shocks occasionally administered by a momentary lifting of the clouds, and by the fun of guessing where one is. A journey in this season can also be recommended to those who enjoy discomfort.[9]

We were soon heading for the Plateau. Little ahead at Donkung, a bifurcation led to Mirdo, which is known as the 'Finger area' because the border juts out on the Tibetan plateau like a finger. This was the route of early expeditions to Tibet, going across Kongra la (5133 m). But then this area became 'sensitive' due to the Chinese designs. We were fortunate to get permission to spend some wonderful time on the Plateau, which is strictly regulated after the India–China War of 1962.

The Plateau was vast and wild, more than anything we had imagined. As we passed Yumcho plains (with a small lake), the wind, which explorers had called 'a veritable curse', was starting to build up. Travellers were glad to lie down in some hollow or crouch behind stones so as to be out of it even for a few minutes! The Gurudongmar lake (5176 m) with its deep blue water and the white peaks of Gurudongmar and Kangchenjau as backdrop, was sublime. There were tourists making their fleeting visit and praying at the temple built by the army – this was the grand finale of their 'package'! Our next objective was the high Dorji la (5640 m). The view to a vast number of peaks opened up from here and can be best described by quoting White.

> There is something exhilarating in these high altitudes, the tremendous expanse of snow around gives a feeling of freedom not experienced at lower elevations, while there is always a fascination in arriving at a summit of a mountain, (*or a pass*) particularly when the unknown is on the other side. (*Italics mine*)[10]

As we turned towards south, looking towards Kerang, the mountain landscape that we had come looking for opened out in front of us. It is

---

9. Tilman, H W, 'Laschi and the Zemu Gap', *The Himalayan Journal*, Vol 11 1939, p. 148.
10. Mayer, Kurt, and Pamela Deuel Meyer, op. cit., p. 70.

one of the most remarkable landscapes in the world, and alone worth the journey to see it:

> Cholamu lake is in front, beneath the feet of the spectator, beyond is a desert with rounded hills. Farther away, range after range of mountains, some of them covered with snow, extend to a distance the eye cannot appreciate. The total change of colour and form from the valleys of Sikhim, the utter barrenness, the intense clearness of the atmosphere, produce such an effect as if one were gazing upon another world in which the order of this is no longer preserved; where a tropical desert is seen amongst snow-capped peaks, beneath the unnaturally clear atmosphere of the arctic regions.[11]

The Donkhya la (5495 m) was in front of us, flanked by peak Donkhya Ri (6190 m) and Sanglapu (6224 m). The southeast was dominated by Pauhunri (7125 m) and its five satellite peaks were leading to the south on the ridge dividing the Plateau and the Chumbi valley. The peaks were: 7032 m, 6911 m, 7032 m, 6915 m and, 6730 m, all unclimbed and unattempted. This would be one of the highest walls separating two valleys.

Cho Lhamo (or Tso Lhamo) had many attractions. Birds from Siberia and Russia come here during the summer. There is much wildlife and vegetation. It is reported that geologically the Plateau is important. "Messers G B Gourlay and J B Auden spent October and early November 1934 on a visit to north-eastern Sikkim. At a height of about 17,300 ft, they found a series of highly fossiliferous shale and limestone, the preliminary examination of which suggests that these beds are Triassic in age. This find is important in that these Tso Lhamo beds fill the gap between Lower Permian Lachi beds first found in 1933 by L R Wagner when on the Everest Expedition, and the Jurassic system which has long been known to cover so much of Tibet."[12]

The Tibetan frontier ran to our north for a long distance, a high ridge with passes of Kongyakma (5605 m), Sesse la, (5462 m), Chulung la (5447 m) and ending at the 'Finger area' and pass of Kongra la (5133 m). The famous Kampa Dzong, where Dr Kellas was buried, was about 35 km from here.

---

11. Blanford, W T, 'Journey through Sikkim', *Journal of the Asiatic Society of Bengal*, 1871, p. 407.
12. Mason, Kenneth, 'North-East Sikkim', *The Himalayan Journal*, Vol 7, 1937, pp. 139-41.

Thus, Kampa Dzong was closely related to the mountains of Sikkim.

Just before reaching Kampa Dzong, Dr Kellas died of heart failure. He had been ailing since the march through the Chumbi valley. He had strained his heart during the previous year on Kamet and Narsing (19,128 ft) and in the early spring of 1921 in camps over 20,000 feet on Kabru. The country between Phari and Kampa Dzong, mostly above 16,000 feet was now too severe for him. He was buried on 6 June (*1921*) on the slopes of the hills south of Kampa Dzong facing the mountains of Sikkim, which he alone had climbed.[13]

If there was a high, windy, and desolate frontier anywhere, it was here. One could see a hint of Tibetan borderland of Chumbi valley. to quote White again: "It was a magnificent afternoon and the view over Tibet was glorious. The power of sun's rays at this height in the very clear atmosphere was extraordinary, and I have never before or since felt it in the same way"[14] We were on the shores of the Cho Lhamo lake and though it had much snow on it but the location and surroundings were so beautiful that we forgot the strong wind and remained there in silence for some time.

The final word should belong to John D. Hooker, who, having seen most parts of the Himalaya pays the ultimate compliment to the Plateau and Cho Lhamo:

I doubt whether the world contains any scene with more sublime associations than this calm sheet of water, 17,000 feet above sea, with the shadow of mountains, 22,000 to 24,000 feet high, sleeping on its bosom.[15]

13. Mason, Kenneth, *Abode of Snow,* E P Dutton & Co, New York, 1955, p. 157.
14. Mayer, Kurt, and Pamela Deuel Meyer, op. cit., p. 70.
15. Brown, Percy, op. cit., p. 129.

5

Old Trails, New Companions

Treks in Kashmir

Holdsworth, a senior teacher at Doon School holds a record for smoking a pipe on the summit of Kamet, a 7,756 m peak! After retirement he continued trekking to different parts of the Himalaya. His article, 'Moderate Mountains for Middle-aged Mountaineers' gave a classic coverage of the ranges suitable for persons with whom age was catching up.

There comes a time for dwellers in the Indian subcontinent, when they have climbed their own particular Everests and are no longer young enough, or perhaps wealthy enough, to take part in a large-scale expedition to one of the few remaining 8,000-metre peaks, but when the urge to spend their holiday in the high places is still insistent. For such as these there are still literally hundreds of mountains between 18,000 and 22,000 feet which are accessible without grandiose arrangements for stores, porters or equipment. I have long since reached this age and perhaps a few memories of such moderate mountains will be of interest to some readers of the *Himalayan Journal* who are approaching this stage in their life.[1]

"A mountaineer never retires. In a sense he never hangs his boots to call it a day. As he grows in years he continues with trekking and loving the hills ..." wrote Chris Bonington. So, ignoring age as a factor, I planned a trek in Kashmir. But after a two-year hiatus at home due to Covid restrictions, I realised that it was a difficult choice. Where to go? What are the tests, mandatory to be able to fly out? How much difficulty can we face after so

1. Holdsworth, R L, 'Moderate Mountains for Middle-aged Mountaineers', *The Himalayan Journal* Vol 25 1964, p. 85.

many months of being confined to a flat in Mumbai without much exercise, and who would be my companions?

"I am no longer that young, Harish Uncle. I am now fifteen!" Shreya (Ranganathan), who had trekked with me for the last 5 years announced. This was a declaration of independence – of being a youth not just 'young'– as all growing children do, as early as they can! I had to respond to her exuberance. "I am also not that old, only five times your age plus one,76!" We formed the age bracket for the team and the rest fitted within this wide range!

As what was termed the 'second wave of Covid' ended in India and the third wave was still expected, we chose to take advantage of the in-between period. Protocols and rules of engagement were to be complied with, a new for a trekking holiday. RT-PCR tests for travel both ways, airlines regulations such wearing a mask, face-shield and if you have a middle seat, then a protective suit. The more careful wore hand gloves and double masks! A feeling of being in a spacecraft – not an aircraft.

Youth packed for the trek with the usual paraphernalia but the old had additional tasks – medical check-up, blood tests, blood pressure, cardiogram and dental checkup... perhaps, if I continue going to hills long enough, the list may include dentures! Having walked in the Himalayan valleys for more than 5 decades I was ready to match steps with the youth, imbibe their enthusiasm and maybe teach them a thing of two. Rajan Dalal, nearly my age, was fitter and wiser than me!

We spent two days at Pahelgam. Rajan played at the beautiful Golf Course, some walked along the Lidder river, and some concentrated on partaking of Kasmiri Wazwan food and trout in the bazar. Pandemic-induced changes were here with us too, as young Sharmila (Ranganathan) who was not on vacation, continued to attend classes online, in proper school uniform, from a hotel room!

OLD TRAILS

For more than a century now, the trail to Lidderwat (camp on Lidder river) has been in use. Any Britisher worth his salt would not have gone back home without a visit to Kashmir. Kashmir, in addition to the Shikara ride, houseboats and natural beauty, was also a favourite trekking destination. Amongst many other places, treks from the Pahelgam area were the most popular as they can be short or long as desired. This led to the mushrooming of many trekking agencies in Kashmir. It is said that in the past so many groups camped there, that there was no camping place available at Lidderwat. Till Nepal fully opened its door to trekkers, most of the valleys here were popular. Sonamarg, in the adjoining Sind river valley, developed as a major climbing centre with a guidebook *Sonamarg Climbing and Trekking Guide*, first published in 1944 by Wilfrid Noyce, H Tilly and Whittle. A revised and updated version was published by John Jackson in 1976. The fame of the beauty of Kashmir was well known across the world since early times. The famous book, *The Tourist Guide to Kashmir, Ladakh and Skardu* by Major Arthur Neve, was written in 1910 and, after his death, Dr Ernst Neve published the revised fifteenth edition in 1933.

Nepal opened its doors to trekkers and climbers in 1949, which almost coincided with Indian freedom and the Kashmir war of 1947–48. Soon, there were fewer trekkers and, eventually, adventure activities stopped when full-blown terrorism hit the valley in 1989. From then on, it was always touch and go – an incident and suddenly the state would be closed. It is only in 2019 that the situation improved but again, the pandemic forced a closure. Now, in 2021, it was new start again for the old trails.

THE LIDDER VALLEY

This was my third visit to the Lidder valley, each time with a different group and different circumstances. After an accident on the high mountain of Nanda Devi Sanctuary, and a hip operation in 1974, I was advised to stay on crutches for two years. It was too long a period not to visit the Himalaya. So, in 1975, four of us visited the Lidder valley. Those days travel to Srinagar was challenging. We arrived at Pathankot railway station after two days of travel by the *Frontier Mail* from Bombay and rushed for a plate of cutlets and omelet at the railway restaurant managed by Naorojis of Dharamsala. These two dishes are major gift of the British to Indian cuisine and hundreds of plates are now gorged on Indian trains daily. From the railway station, buses by N D Radhakishan, agency for railways, would drive you to Srinagar with a night halt en route. After a change of buses at Srinagar, one would arrive at Pahelgam for the start of the trek.

I rode a horse all along, like the early British travellers here. A long day brought us to Lidderwat and after two days on the meadow, we went to the Kolahoi Base camp. It was a different type of adventure. My horseman, Abdulla, was an great storyteller and in the evening, he would offer special namaz for my recovery. As we returned to Lidderwat, we were trapped in the forest rest house for three days as it poured heavily. The chowkidar went down to his village to get more supplies, leaving the rest house in our charge. We had a unique mix of stranded trekkers in the rest house. Two French air hostesses gave us gentle company and when their turn came, sang a soft song. Two Belgians, not understanding a word of English, caused hilarious confusion. They picked up one word from a full English statement and would repeat it with gusto. When told, "Your rucksack is getting wet in rain" one of them picked up the word and kept saying, "Rucksack, I have, I have" till he was actually shown that his rucksack had almost filled up with water!

My companions from Himachal Pradesh sang lusty songs. And that evening an American reporter joined us. He was from *Washington Post*, responsible for unearthing the Watergate Scandal and was in India to interview the then prime minister, Mrs. Indira Gandhi. He had been given an appointment for after a week so here he was, in Kashmir for a trek with a liaison officer, and now trapped with us. He was at a loss when we said that he would have to sing a song, just as we all had. After some deep thought, he went out of the room and returned, thumping his shoes as he marched and sang that American anthem, 'When the Saints Go Marching In.'

I went camping again at Lidderwat in 2012, with group of friends and their children whom I had known for so long. We climbed slowly up towards Tarsar lake, but had to camp early as there was heavy snow on the ground. Ravi and Paula Mariwala led the children who were playing in the snow as around them, gaddis slowly crossed the snowfield with their flock. But we missed the chance to see the clean blue waters of the lake; the pass ahead was snowbound and we had to return the same way, so we missed visiting any other lakes as well. So here I was again after nine years, hoping to complete the trail.

2021 TREK

We started from Aru, the traditional starting point for this trek. A flat track led along the valley for 12 km to Lidderwat. I was a little apprehensive about my ability to walk the distance because of the long absence from hills due to the lockdowns. However, I reached the camp safely – later than the others but with verve. With the wisdom of age, I had planned to stay here for next few days while the others proceeded to the base camp of Kolahoi and Dodsar, a high-altitude lake. They left the next day. Vikas Manhans from Jammu, who also stayed back, and I became 'green card holders' of the vast beautiful green ground. It was interesting to watch many local trekkers visiting and enjoying the trail in their backyard. On the second day we saw a yellow flag walking towards us, hoisted on the rucksack of a lady. She turned out to be from Mumbai, my city, and was arranging treks for various groups. In the modern way, she had no office but operated only through Instagram and Twitter. The yellow flag, with her name, announced her treks to attract customers. When we met her, she was keen to take selfies and pictures, with her standing on a rock holding the yellow flag high.

The same evening a large group of a curious mix of elderly and young arrived and settled nearby. Young students sat in a tent and were lectured by their leader. Later, they all climbed up to a ridge and we could see the teacher giving them 'gyan'. I wondered at this and if they were from a local school. Kashmir has a tradition of outdoor schooling in their summer courses. Tyndale Biscoe School, founded in 1880 is one of the oldest schools in Jammu and Kashmir. The school was started by Christian missionaries and was named after Canon Cecil Tyndale-Biscoe (1863–1949), a well-known name in the field of education. Eventually, five other mission schools were set up, one each in different parts of the capital city and one in Anantnag, which still function as the backbone of education in Kashmir.

Mallinson Girls' School was founded in 1912 by Miss Violet B Fitze as the Girls' Mission High School. Its name was later changed to Mallinson Girls' School in honour of Miss Mallinson, a missionary who served in the school from 1922 to 1961. Many such schools take students out in the field for trekking, and education is imparted on treks.

I could not hold back my curiosity and visited their camp in the evening to talk to the teacher, who introduced himself simply as 'Gotu'. But behold! they were also from the suburbs of Mumbai and were a group of family and friends. Mr Gotu was well travelled, and this was his way of passing on his experiences to the youth in his family. He narrated experiences in the tent and for practicals, took them to the ridge.

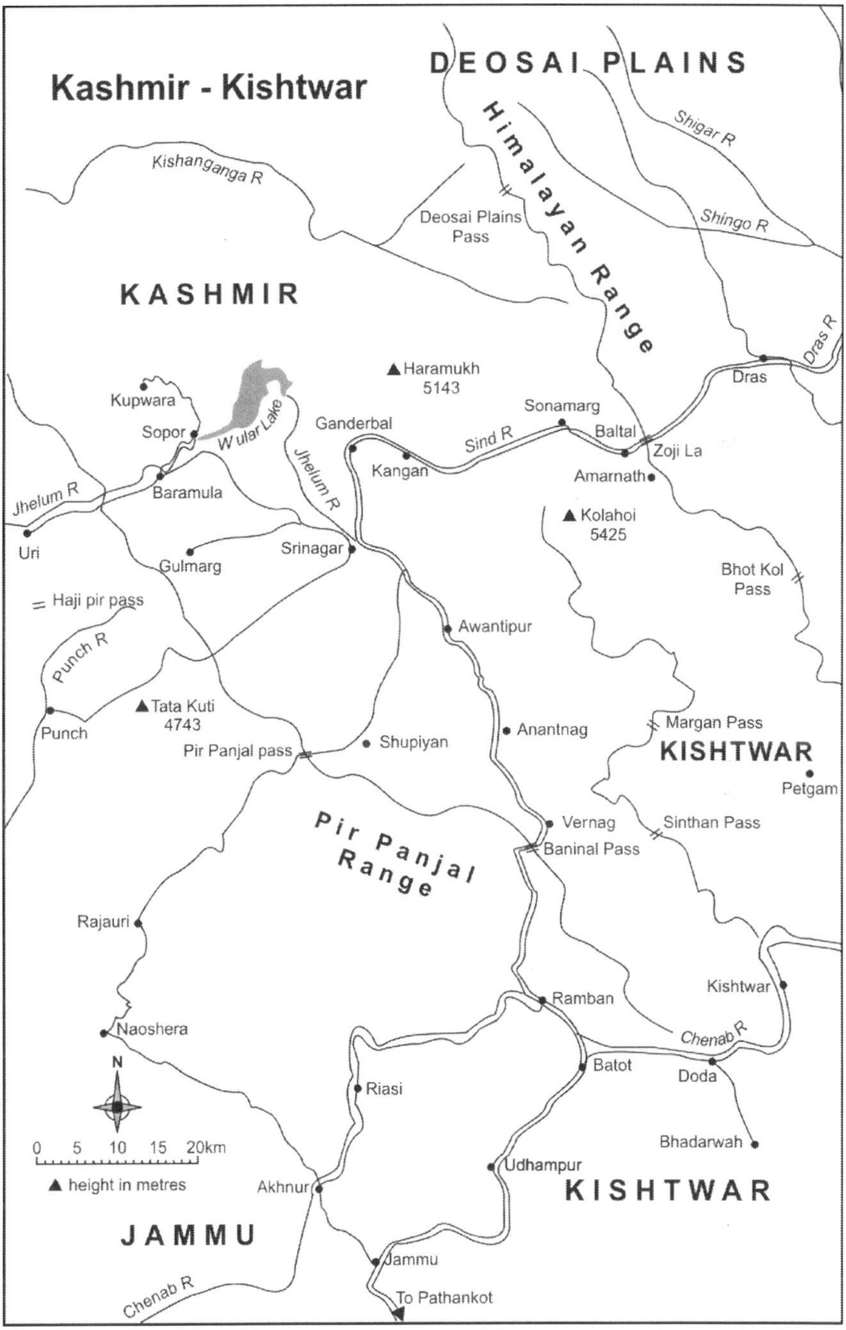

Kashmir treks.

KOLAHOI

We were camped in the shadow of Kolahoi,[2] the highest peak of the Kashmir valley and were to admire its view all along the trek. This legendary peak can be admired from many angles on this trek. But it's steep walls will succumb to modern day rock climbers only when they are allowed to climb here in peace.

Amongst the early explorers in Kashmir were the Neve brothers: Dr Ernest Neve, a fine climber and a medical doctor, and Major Arthur Neve, who was more of an explorer and had joined with leading names such as Dr Tom Longstaff to visit the Karakoram range and the Siachen glacier. Ernest was a regular visitor to the Lidder valley, particularly to the Kolahoi peak.

Ernest Neve was a leading mountaineer and a founding member of the Himalayan Club. https://en.wikipedia.org/wiki/Ernest_Frederic_Neve - cite_note-:0-1 He made the first ascents of Kolahoi (5,425 m) in 1912 and Mount Tatticooti (4,765 m) in 1901. Along with his brother Arthur, Ernest also climbed various other Kashmiri peaks such as Sunset Peak, Rajdain, and Sachkach.

Arthur Neve was a priest, a medical doctor and a mountaineer. When he was able to take time off from the hospital, Arthur found great enjoyment in discovering the outlying parts of Kashmir for either travel, medical work for people who could not reach his hospital, or evangelical work. His first tour in 1882 to the outskirts of Kashmir sparked this passion, as it allowed him to see other tribes, villages, people, and terrains. This first tour also led him to believe that there was more medical need and work to be done throughout these parts of Kashmir, and this vision drove him to begin the long process of building the Kashmir Mission Hospital.

While on these excursions, Neve travelled to places like the Hindus valley, the Saltoro valley, and Tagur. He became a reputable mountaineer, and some of his notable climbs include a climb to Nun and Kun at 7,077 m, as well as in the Nubra valley in Zanskar and Ladakh:

Kashmir is, for mountaineers, associated with the names of Karakoram, Nanga Parbat and the Nun Kun group. These are all big mountains and possibly beyond

---

2. Leeson, Farnces, 'The Kolahoi Group, An Historical Sketch' *The Himalayan Journal* Vol 16 1951, p. 112.

the reach of the middle-aged. But perhaps some people do not realize that above the Kashmir Valley proper the Great Himalaya comes down to heights of no more than 18,000 feet. In the east, easily accessible from Pahalgam and the Liddar Valley there is the fine peak of Kolahoi, 17,800 feet looking remarkably like a minor Matterhorn. It has, I believe, been climbed two or three times, first, in the first decade of the century by Doctor E Neve. New routes might be invented.

So wrote Holdsworth. And now we were camping at foot of it.

Kolahoi, at 5,425 m, the highest of the peak in the vale of Kashmir, is an interesting climb, varying in difficulty according to the amount of snow. Its highest and central peak is Gashibrar (The Goddess of Light). The two other main peaks are Buttress peak (4,420 m), a mile to the south of Gashibrar, and Bur Dalau (5,110 m feet), a mile and a half to the south-east. Dr Ernest Neve and Kenneth Mason made the first ascent of the latter on 21 June 1911, by the eastern arete.

The first ascent of Gashibrar was made by Kenneth Mason and Dr Ernst Neve on 28 June 1912. They followed the Armiun Narr, crossed the Har Nag pass, and reached the icefield south of Kolahoi to the summit. G R Cooke and Lt B W Battye climbed the peak on the 9 July 1926. In 1938, John Hunt (later Lord Hunt) with Rowland Brotherhood made an ascent by a different route.[3] Kolahoi proved difficult for later parties and it defied many attempts. In September 2018, a group of nine trekkers from Kashmir went on an expedition to the Kolahoi peak. Unfortunately, the group was caught in rock fall near Burdalaw region on the glacier during their descent and lost two of its members: Adil Shah, founder of Alpine Adventures group and Naveed Jeelani, who was a junior administrative officer from Srinagar. Their bodies were later retrieved from the glacier after two days due to bad weather.

With some reading and walking and such interesting visitors, our days at Lidderwat passed quickly and soon it was time for the party to return with their experiences of the trek to Kolahoi base camp.

---

3. Hunt, John, 'Kolahoi by the South Face', *The Himalayan Journal*, Vol 8 1936, p. 106. Also, Wormald, Peter, 'Another Route on Kolahoi, *The Himalayan Journal* Vol 16 1951, p. 112.

LIDDERWAT, SATLANJAN, KOLAHOI BASE CAMP AND DODSAR (*by Shekhar Jaywant*)

After settling Harish and Vikas at Lidderwat with sufficient rations and a person to look after them, the rest of us set course for the Kolahoi Base Camp (BC) with a night halt at Satlanjan.

The route gradually climbed along a valley, with the fast-flowing Lidder for company. Though the walk was long, there were conifers and shaded grassy areas to rest along the way. Nitin (Kanitkar) was, as usual, scampering all over the slopes on either side with his camera ready to capture any birds or animals. There were camps of Gujjars along the way with cows and some buffaloes grazing in the meadows with the lovely mountains as a backdrop. Stopping and taking in the beauty also gave us an opportunity to catch our breath and replenish our energy with the dry fruits and snacks carried by Mukund and Urvashi. Gradually, the trees turned sparse and the ground started becoming rocky. We reached Satlanjan (place with seven streams) at lunch time and decided to camp close to the river at a site chosen by Shreya. The horses came up shortly and the hot Maggie noodles served were welcome. The afternoon and evening were spent resting and after an early dinner it was into the sleeping bags. The temperature was dropping as the sun went down – we had gained about 1000 ft during the day.

The next day, after an early breakfast, we were off to the Kolahoi BC. Rain was expected later in the day and we were hoping to reach the campsite before that. The walk this time was shorter, about 5 km, but the area was rocky, with no shade. The views continued to fascinate. Sure enough, it soon started clouding up, which was a relief, but then the wind picked up and there were indications that it would rain. We tried to pick up pace to beat the rain and were lucky to find shelter in a bakarwal's (shepherd) hut, with a hot cup of kahwa and a kangdi to keep warm, while the others found shelter under a rock overhang.

The next day started with a river crossing on our way to Dodsar lake towards Kolahoi peak. Though a rope was put across the fast-flowing river, it wasn't much use as it was held very loosely and most of us took a dip in the river. Mukund ended up with a wet camera which remained non-functional for the rest of the trip. The climb thereafter was steep and very tiring, but at the end of it we were rewarded with an awesome view of the bluish green

Dodsar lake, some portions of which were frozen, with the glacier and Kolahoi peak in the background. It was very windy and there was a slight drizzle, so we were unable to spend too much time at the top. After eating our packed lunch, we set course to return by a different route as our guide Arafat had planned. He had already gone ahead to recce it and luckily was spotted on a ridge at some distance. The route had a more gradual descent, but was more treacherous with slippery scree slopes and traverses over sections of snow. The guides had the difficult task of ferrying each of us across. En route, we saw Huksar lake. We got back into the valley between Satlanjan and the base camp. This was the most tiring day of the entire trek. We had climbed about 1300 ft on a steep slope and descended the same height over treacherous terrain.

The next two days were spent on the return trip to Lidderwat over familiar ground but an easier walk, descending along the valley.

ONWARDS TO THE LAKES

(*Harish Kapadia continues*)

A satisfied team gathered again, and our trek to the upper valley started. We chose to go up slowly with a camp at Homwas and Sekiwas. The trail was very easy, but the trekkers wanted a challenge, so halfway through, Sonal Jain left with Vikas to visit a small lake higher on the ridge and to join us at the camp. We could see the Yemhar Pass (Pass of Yem, 'god of death') a direct trail to Sonamarg. On the northern side of the pass a steep rocky staircase was built but several mules had fallen to their deaths.

Next morning, we were woken up by much noisy bleating of goats as they fussed over the salt that they were given as a morning ritual. The trail climbed up to Tarsar lake steadily without posing any difficulties. The *Gazetteer* narrates a legend of a fakir staying in a cave at Kolahoi glacier. He accepted a challenge and successfully swam across Tarsar lake (Tar: swim, Sar: lake) but later drowned in Marsar lake (Mar: dead). Our day at this lake was peaceful despite the many visitors around. An afternoon hailstorm, a rainbow and calm waters in morning left us with a sense of beauty and peace. A pass of the same name across a ridge in the north led us to Zajimarg valley. This vast valley had just a few shepherds' huts, and a river that flowed quietly through it, and thus the valley's nickname – silent valley – was most appropriate. A huge square rock called 'Handoobeta' marks almost the centre of the valley. A rich trader and owner of a flock of sheep visited us. With him we discussed the future of meat production as a traditional occupation and whether the next generation would agree to roam the hills with the flock. No one has an answer to that question, of course. On the northern wall of the valley, a beautiful shapely peak Deo Masjid (4440 m) stood. The curious conjunction of words: Deo, meaning god in Hindu terminology and masjid, the Muslim prayer house, represents the traditional culture of the valley.

From the higher camping ground in the Zazimarg valley, a major portion of the team separated and gradually climbed further to Sundersar (beautiful lake). It took them hardly two hours. But trail ahead to Marsar was steeper. There is a great view of the lake, with its discharge leading to the Dachigam forest. The lake can be viewed from the ridge but the descent to its shore is steep and full of scree. And of course, one has to climb back up the steep slope! Fun awaited the youth on their return. A lovely snow slope next to the camp offered a good slope to glissade. Shanaya and Shreya undertook many rounds up and down, putting the seniors to shame.

Now we were to go across the watershed from the Lidder (Pahelgam) to Sind (Sonâmarg) valley. Adjacent to our camp was the Sonamus pass (pass of gold-beautiful grass). At first it appeared impossibly difficult but once our mules went down comfortably it was encouraging. After some hard work and exposure, we reached the grassland at its foot. From there on it was a long but easy descent to the Sonamarg valley after a night halt at Sonmasti. The trail ahead was now full of the beauty for which Kashmir is known. A single slope was crowded with chinar, fur, pine, deodar and even the occasional birch. Rajan and Sonal, both trained singers, gave a fitting tribute to the beauty by bursting into song! What a great way to end the walk. We eased ourselves to the river valley floor – with me staggering in later as always.

Our waiting bus took us to a highway restaurant for an early dinner. The youth got busy in demolishing vast amounts of food. My eyes lighted up and without reading the long menu, I ordered a plate of cutlets! "What is that? Never heard of it before", said the waiter. In one ignorant sentence he had dismissed the British Raj, their culinary gift and my desire to celebrate my 76th birthday in style!! I could see Shreya and others giving me sympathetic smiles.

We stayed on the banks of the Nagin lake at the beautiful Dar-es-salam hotel. Here, I could educate my new companions on the continuing pleasures of good old days by ordering traditional Kashmiri Wazwan items of meat – gushtaba, rista, and tabakmas, with dishes for vegetarians; dum aloo, ruangan chaman, and waza palak. All to be enjoyed with saffron-laced kahwa.

Au revior, Kashmir, till next time.

"Don't walk in front of me, I may not follow.
Don't walk behind me, I may not lead.
Walk beside me, and be my friend."

– Albert Camus

Kolahoi peak, Kashmir (Geeta Kapadia).

6

Two Walks in the Kishtwar

The Kablas Lakes and Bhut Nala

(Harish Kapadia with Amrita Dhar)

THE KABLAS LAKES

Our man in Bhaderwah assured us that all was currently peaceful in their part of Jammu and Kashmir. The 2014 floods had been terrible, but Jammu had been spared. So, there we were one sunny morning in Patnitop. Vikas Manhas sipped his kahwa with relish and addressed the nine plainspeople in front of him: "We will let the horses take the main trail up from Nalthy. But with three children in the group, we will make a shorter day of walking ourselves. We can approach the Kablas lakes from Chhettra Gala, from that direction it should be no more than 6 km to the lakes." In this first part of a three-week trip to Jammu, we were planning to trek to a high plateau of snowmelt lakes – the Kablas lakes (3810 m) to the south of the Bhaderwah valley – and it sounded like a good idea to allow a short day to ease ourselves into the high terrain. With three Kumaunis and Vikas, we rattled down by bus from Patnitop to Batote, and up from Batote to Bhaderwah, where we stocked up on groceries. Another hour's drive brought us to the lovely little village of Nalthy (1853 m).

The *Gazetteer of Jammu, Kashmir and Ladak* mentions that Bhaderwah was called 'Badrawar', or variably 'Budar', by the locals, and 'Bubríkar' by the Kashmiris, meaning 'Stronghold of Badha' (a local tribe). During Mughal rule, Muslims of Kashmir migrated to Kishtwar and Bhaderwah via the Sinthen Top. After conquering the district, Mughal emperor, Aurangzeb, visited the area. His first Begum died en route, and she was buried at the Mughal Maidan near the Sinthen Top.[1]

In 1821, Shah Shuja, then ruler of Afghanistan, took refuge with Maharaja Ranjit Singh, king of Punjab. Shuja presented the famed Kohinoor diamond to Ranjit Singh but later they fell out. To save himself from the wrath of Ranjit Singh, Shuja defected to Kishtwar and was given asylum by the ruler Mohamed Tej Singh. This infuriated Ranjit Singh, who marched his large army to Kishtwar, conquering Bhaderwah, Doda and Kishtwar, bringing them under Punjab rule.[2]

Zorawar Singh (1786–1841), a general of the Punjab army, was appointed Raja of Kishtwar in 1821 and he carried out two major expeditions through the valleys of Kishtwar to Ladakh and Baltistan. The first was through the Warwan valley, crossing Bhotkol pass or Lanvilad gully. The second expedition was from the east crossing the Umasi la.

Almost a century later, the British visited the area. Arthur Neve recorded his extensive travels in a book, which was revised later by his brother E F Neve.[3] The Kishtwar mountainous region enjoyed relative peace and prosperity for about a century leading up to India's independence in 1947. In independent India, Bhaderwah became part of the state of Jammu and Kashmir with its strategic geographical and political importance. Matters came to head in the late 1980s when militancy and terrorism threw the state into turmoil. For over the better part of a decade, the Indian army proceeded to 'sanitise' the area. 2008 saw a degree of normalcy return – although it was a few years yet before trekkers and climbers began to trickle in again.

It is a short distance to Chhettra Gala from Nalthy (10 km, but the drive over the winding dirt roads took a good hour). At Chhettra Gala, a gracious young army Captain oversaw the inspection of our papers and

---

1. *Gazetteer of Jammu, Kashmir and Ladak*, Government of India, p. 183. (First published in 1890. Reprint 1974. Vivek Publishing House, Delhi).
2. Drew, Frederic, *The Jammoo and Kashmir Territories*, published in 1875, reprinted by Capital Publishing House, Delhi, 1997, p. 121.
3. *The Tourist's Guide to Kashmir, Skardoo, etc*, Edited by The Late Major Arthur Neve, FRCS, Ed, RAMC Surgeon to The Kashmir Medical Mission. Revised by Dr E F Neve, FRCS (Lahore, 1933, Price Rs. 10). When published in 1933 it ran into fifteen editions in one year.

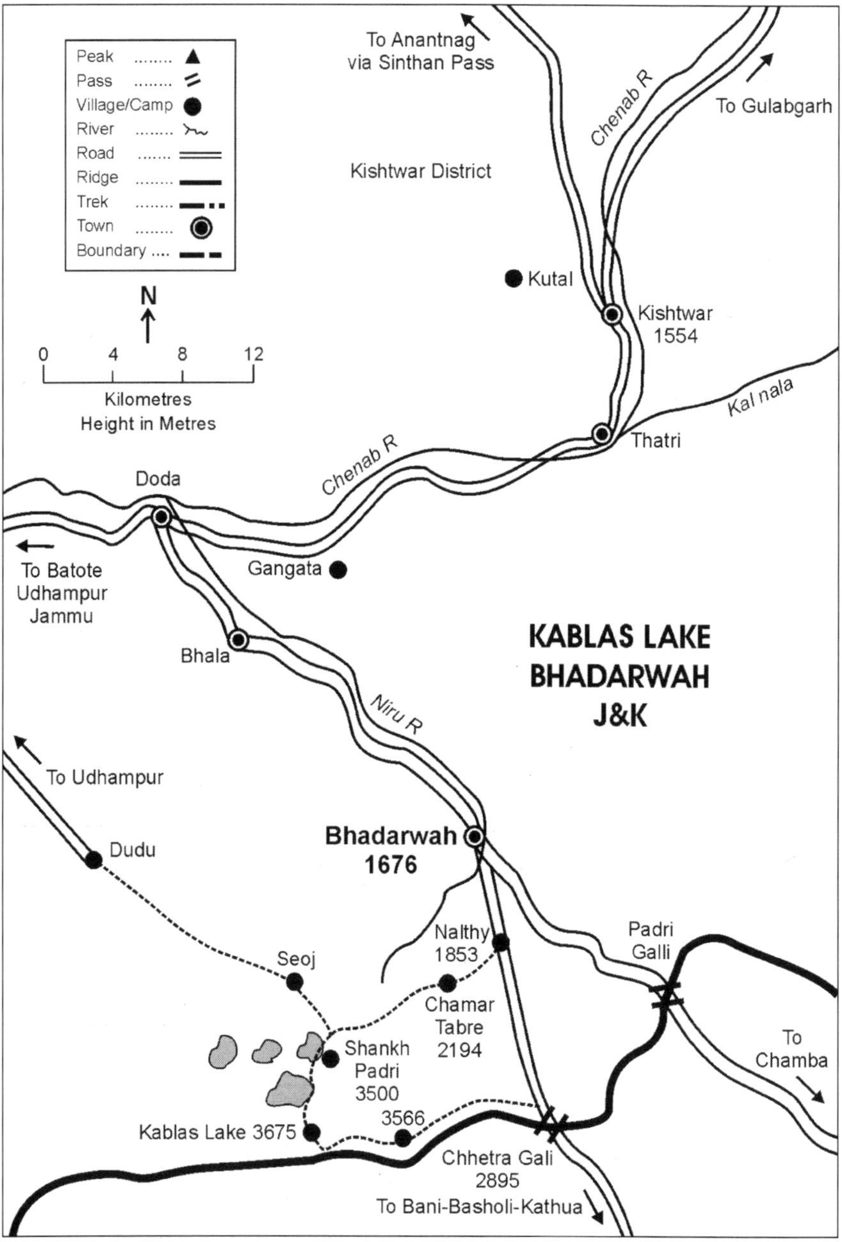

Kablas lake, Kishtwar.

stood us steaming glasses of chai as we unloaded our bags from the bus and strapped on our respective rucksacks. A grassy alpine path from Chhettra Gala climbs up to meet the ridge to its west, then crosses it in a long and gradually climbing traverse – taking in a good number of small ridges on the way – until it comes up, in some eight hours of good walking, against the rim of the bowl of mountains containing the lakes.

The prospect was magnificent. The Kishtwar ranges to our distant north looked resplendent. But by afternoon, it was clear that the lakes were much farther than 6 km from Chhettra Gala. If pace and time were to be any indication, they had to be at about twice that distance! So, as we approached an airy ridge on which was perched a shepherd's tiny shelter, Harish decided to call a night's halt. Vikas and a couple of others went on to the lakes to fetch tents from the party of horses who must by now have reached by the regular trail. The sounds of concerned consultation in the hut gave way to laughter and song and soon, the congenial conversation that takes over any warm campfire. As dusk fell and Vikas and a couple of horsemen returned with tents and food for the night, a cheer went up from the three youngest members of our party.

By lunchtime next day, everyone was assembled at Lake Camp (3675 m). Our tents stood like little patches of colour in a crumpled grey landscape. From slightly higher ground, the two lakes lowest in the bowl came into view. One of the horsemen, Irshad Ahmed, pointed west to say that two more lakes lay in that general direction. A spot of lunch later, Amrita and Irshad set out from camp for an afternoon's scramble.

The ostensible destination for this scramble was a dramatic granite pinnacle directly behind our campsite. But, both in order to avoid a gradient of 60–70 degrees, and to explore further, we headed left and just a little higher towards what was called Trisul lake. This nomenclature, as we would soon find out, was by virtue of an iron trident stuck in the ground near the lake,. The final rise to the pinnacle (4110 m) consisted of about twenty feet of phenomenal exposure involving, however, delightful fourth class climbing. As we stood waving down to the minuscule dots of colour on the valley floor in the hope that someone in camp might spot us, we could see directly across the huge bowl to the rim we had crossed yesterday. A shelter was built on the banks of the higher lake for pilgrims when they visit in thousands in August, for yatra. Carrying blankets and food, most stay for a night and go down the next day.

A few days later, when we walked down by the main trail to Nalthy, evidence of the yatris was everywhere. It is easy to identify with the mystical and emotional pull towards pilgrimage that such an amazing landscape doubtlessly inspires, but less easy to understand the piles of styrofoam, plastic bags and general debris along the trail. It is important to realize that the mountains exist in exceedingly fragile ecologies, and that if travel in these places is to be sustained, the onus is on all of us to keep these areas clean, to meticulously pick up and pack *all* non-biodegradable waste, to respect trails and thus, avoid undue erosion, and to leave behind only the lightest possible footprints.

At dusk, a hailstorm pelted the campsite and turned the world white. But as the barometer held from evening to night, it was not unreasonable to imagine that a bit of good sun in the morning would dry the rock enough to enable a venture to the beautiful three-summited peak we could see from our campsite. Behind the lake stood Chhota Kablas (4270 m) and further behind, invisible from either Trisul or Kablas lake but following the same high ridge, Kablas itself, or Bara Kablas (*c.* 4400 m), and we wanted to head that way.

The next day dawned cold and sparkling. We walked to the temple and shelter that had looked so tiny from the vantage of the pinnacle the day before. Up close, Kablas lake was even more impressive, and some indication of the age of pilgrimage to this spot was obtained in the form of a quarter-anna coin from 1939 we found on the lakeshore. By the time we were back in camp, Irshad had packed a lunch of a few parathas and a couple of apples for himself and Amrita to take to Chhota Kablas.

This time, instead of going right from Trisul lake, as we had done yesterday, we branched off left to a near-circumnavigation of the lake as we gained a tiny corridor of tumbled granite between the permanent snow and ice patches lining some of the higher but relatively more gradual slopes of the mountain. Since we were ill-equipped in terms shoes and waterproof wear to walk in snow, we stayed on the rocks. Last night's hail had left pockets of snow in tiny ledges all over Chhota Kablas, but we were glad that the rock, at any rate, was already bone dry. The sun beat down on us whenever the flying clouds allowed. As one, then two, then three hours fell away into silence, at the start of a glorious afternoon we found ourselves at the upper reaches of this scrambler's paradise. Irshad went one way, Amrita another. Before long, the two of us were smiling at each other from two of the three summits of the mountain.

We completed a circumnavigation of Trisul lake by virtue of the route we took on our way down. From the summit of Chhota Kablas, it is possible to look down almost directly at Kablas lake. But descending that way is not a safe option without the means to set up a couple of full-length abseils. So, we went down again in the general direction of Trisul lake. As the afternoon grew chillier with wind, we started an intricate series of advancements and retreats as slowly, over consistent fourth class climbing that sometimes verged on fifth class, we lost height. It was a relief, finally, to be standing on the banks of Trisul lake again.

We were late for lunch, and we knew we had earned it; but not yet – for Mallik had been scouting that morning for climbing possibilities. Even as the rest of camp moved to Shankh Padri (3500 m), he was waiting for us with ropes and harnesses at the foot of a magnificent bit of slab a little way down. So we raced on, hastily gulping down lunch as we debated anchors for setting up a top rope. We didn't do much more than finish a single short climb, but were tired and happy as we walked down to meet the rest of the team at Shankh Padri. The setting sun leached the final light from the sky, and our three summits of Chhota Kablas receded again into distance and mystery.

The following morning brought us a clear sunrise over a stupendous panorama of Kishtwar peaks. The centerpiece was Sickle Moon (6574 m), flanked by Chomiochor (6322 m), Agyasol (6200 m), Arjuna (6230 m), Brahmma II (6416 m), Barnaj (6250 m) and others. We were already looking forward to the next leg of our trip, which would take us closer to some of these mountains.

UP THE BHUT NALA

A busfull of waving hands pulled away in Nalthy. Our paths bifurcated here. For most of us, the road led home. But for Vikas, Harish and Amrita, it led to Kishtwar town (1554 m) on the way to Gulabgarh village (1786 m), on the way to a walk up by the stream of the Bhut nala in a beautiful little gorge of eastern Kishtwar. We arrived in Kishtwar town – via Thatri, which possibly has the world's best pears – on the last day of Dussehra and found the town's central maidan full of crowds and annual festivities.

The next morning, a drive through Karthai (1800 m) and Atholi (1800 m) – both on the banks of the Chandrabhaga – brought us to Padar district, and in it, the village of Gulabgarh. Vikas asked around to locate a house that had a reputation for accommodating pilgrims on the Machail yatra.

Machail (2740 m) is the village at the head of the Bhut nala. To all appearances standing guard over this village, the craggy peak of Raul (6135 m), locally called Shiv Parvat, oversees the meeting of the Bhujas and Dharlang valleys. The temple at Machail has been seeing increasing yatra traffic in recent times. Signs telling of the 5-day yatra are visible in the market square of Gulabgarh in both Hindi and Urdu. Unfortunately, so is the trash that this peculiar kind of tourism seems to engender in great bulk. In an idyllically beautiful valley such as carved by the Bhut nala, here a flutter of plastic bag and there a glint of white styrofoam catch the eye rudely. As chance would have it, we had an opportunity to discuss the state of things with the sub-divisional magistrate currently posted at Gulabgarh, for Vikas discovered that the man in question was an old friend from university.

Sanjeev Rana, the sub-divisional magistrate, proved to be a man of great hospitality and generous conversation. He enlightened us about the history of the area. The valleys are called the Padar, bounded by the Buddhist kingdom of Zanskar in the north, Muslim valleys of Kishtwar to the west, while the south and further east are part of the Hindu kingdom of Chamba. Due to Rajput invasions from Chamba, Atholi was the only Muslim village left in the eastern section. Gulabgarh is on the right bank of Chenab. It changed hands, and its name, on several occasions, taking on the names of local kings (Shital Garh and Chhatra Garh for example). The Dogra General Zorawar Singh conquered the valley and annexed it to the Jammu state, extending the boundaries till Sansari nala, the present demarcation. He named the place Gulabgarh, after the king of Jammu, Gulab Singh.

Over dinner we talked of efforts to minimise and eliminate trash on the trails, the role played by the Indian army in these remote areas of the country, the weird and wonderful history of migrations and settlements that had

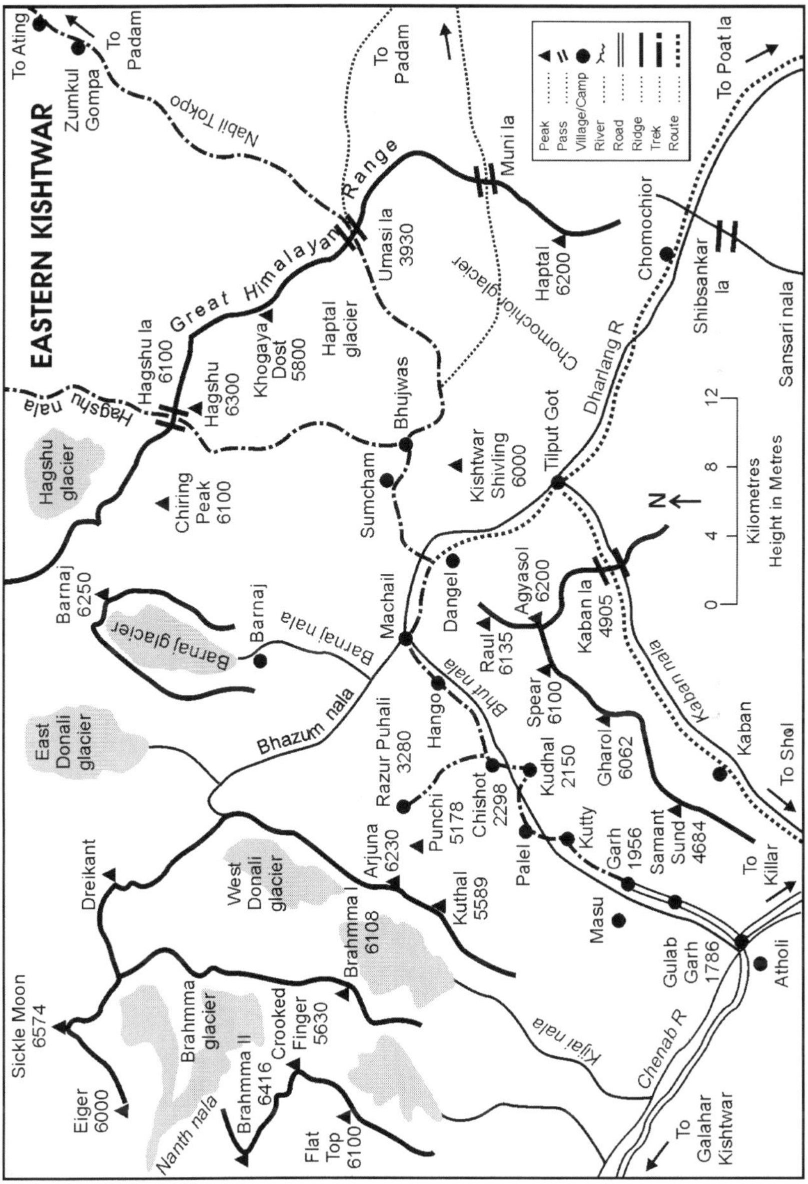

Eastern Kishtwar.

created the currently inhabited regions of the Kishtwar and the terrifying years of militancy in Jammu and Kashmir. For the hundred-thousandth time, the thought crossed our minds about the pity of such beautiful country being under political unrest. Thankfully, eastern Kishtwar is now a peaceful land. Long may it remain so!

Our journey started the following day with a dramatic jeep ride over a stone and dirt road for about 6 km. Once we reached Garh village (1956 m) we made ourselves comfortable in the local schoolhouse balcony. Harish walked into the village to ask around for the right puhali, or grazing ground, to take photographs of the mountains from both sides of the gorge. Our maps told us that although we could not see them, we were standing in the shadow of the mighty Arjuna (6230 m) and the Brahmmas I (6108 m) and II (6416 m) to our northwest, and the uprearing Agyasol (6200 m), Spear (6100 m) and Gharol (6062 m) on the true left of the Bhut nala. An hour of conversation and laughter later, it looked as though our destination would be a high grazing ground called Razur puhali (3280 m). Nothing grazed there this late in the year, and the only people we might meet, if we met any at all, would be a couple of hunters after small game – strangely, no regulations seemed to exist to protect the fauna of the land, or if they did, the villagers seemed to be unaware of them – but Razur seemed to promise an unobstructed view to the southeast. From Chishot village (2298 m) our route would take us up and away from the Bhut nala to one of its constitutive streams, the Chachal nala, for an encounter with one of those charmed places where water is born.

The next two days were a blur of sunshine. The Bhut nala grew younger and more boisterous as we walked. Every few kilometres, there would be the curious sight of someone whacking at stone with a smaller stone, and it was only when we found out that our paths were frequently lined with walnut trees that we realised that this was an effort to first crack the hard seed out of the soft green fruit, and then crack open the shell in order to get at the nut. We soon took to doing this ourselves. Then, one golden afternoon, we arrived at the beautiful village of Chishot, which would effectively be our base for a couple of nights.

Harish and Amrita left for a day's walk up the Chachal nala the next day. The path leading to the grazing ground of Razur faded in and out of forest as a few hundred metres fell away beneath us. We were effectively creeping up the grassy and wooded hillside clinging to a tremendous granite monolith and, by the time we reached Razur puhali, the woods had ended and we had an unobstructed view of the appallingly beautiful rocky Zagal (5210 m). While approaching Chishot, we had marvelled at the east face of Zagal, which had towered some 600 m above the valley floor. Now, it loomed to our right as much forbidding as inviting. A couple of traditional rock-climbers with a weakness for clean, high, sunned-upon granite could spend an entire season playing here, and Zagal alone would justify the long walk-in.

Across the Chachal nala and to our left, another magnificent vertical solicitation of rock currently lay dusted with snow along its many mini ledges. This rocky ridge, called Punchi (5178 m) stood as a massive barrier between us and the mountains that we knew lay beyond: Arjuna, the Brahmmas, Crooked Finger (5630 m). But we drew in our breaths most sharply at what lay directly behind us and to which we now had a ringside view: the slanted sharpness of Gharol (6062 m), and the unmistakable upward thrust of Spear (6100 m). Stretched out against a deep blue sky and newly whitened with snow, they looked close enough to touch.

Although we never did see beyond Punchi – that ridge remained solidly between us and any glimpse of Arjuna or its neighbours in the northwest – Agyasol soon came into view (6200 m) to our southeast. As the Zagal ridge we were on flattened out and dropped off in front of us and to our right rose sheer flanks of rock, the north lay spread out in a serious series of dense ridges and passes that opened in the unseen distance on the Barnaj and Donali glaciers. A few hours later, it started to snow again, but by now we were nearing Chishot and it came down on us as rain.

The mountaineering history of Kishtwar goes back to 1946 with visits of Fritz Kolb and L Krenek. They explored eastern Kishtwar, corrected available maps and attempted several peaks near Muni la. This started sporadic visits of mountaineers which continued till about 1989 when militancy and terrorism closed the area. Details of early climbs are well documented in two articles by Simon Richardson.[4]

4. Richardson, Simon. 'A peak baggers guide to the eastern Kishtwar', *The Himalayan Journal*, Vol 45 1989, p. 90 and Vol 50 1994, p. 202.

Our walk back to the roadhead of Garh village began with a partial walk further into the Bhut nala gorge. While Harish scouted out and oversaw the pitching of camp at Kudhal (2150 m) on a ravishingly beautiful sandy bank of the Bhut nala, Vikas and Amrita walked to Machail (9 km from Chishot). On the way, deodar forests relented to make space for the Buddhist villages of Hamori (2580 m) and Halot (2850 m), before a bridge across the river led the path into Machail. Machail is located at the junction of the Dharlang, Bhut and Bhajun and that has a temple of Goddess Kali. In 1985 Kuldip Singh, a policeman was posted here to guard her ornaments. After retirement he visited the temple every year and this was the start of the yatra that attracts many pilgrims now. The area is known as 'asurbhumi' or land of the devil. The goddess killed one of the chief asurs named 'Agyasur' and now he stands as peak Agyasol opposite the temple. Most other devils escaped and settled on top of different steep peaks and spires.

Despite its brilliant setting, the village of Machail itself is somewhat unprepossessing, All paths lead to the temple, and are often liberally strewn with rubbish. But looking up, one could see Raul in full state. As also the last glimpses, still, of Bion (4985 m), a rocky peak that stands across the Bhut nala from Zagal. Sometime, another day, Machail will be the point of departure for forays into the Dharlang and/or Bhujas valleys. At the moment, it was the point of return for the lovely walk back, over the next two days, to Garh, and eventually Gulabgarh.

Our travels were rounded out by two unreal car rides: on roads that just barely accommodate wheels. Harish and his radio were by now aware of the massive cyclone Hudhud flying in from the Andaman Sea onto the southeastern coast of India. Hudhud would go on to ravage Andhra Pradesh and – since nothing really lay in its way until the high Himalaya – hit the mountains. We were nearing mid-October, and combined with the effects of a storm, our passes for crossing from Jammu and Kashmir into Himachal Pradesh might close for the year if we didn't get a move on. So, we loaded a battered-looking Sumo, driven by one Shashi in Gulabgarh, and set out for Killar (2591 m) a couple of days ahead of our original schedule.

The 'road' from Gulabgarh to Killar (55 km) is an absurd dirt track carved out of sheer rock faces, and there were several heart-stopping instances

1. Kangchenjunga massif and Zemu peak in foreground, from Mangan.

2. Simvu twin peaks from Mangan.

3. Siniolchu from Mangan.

4. Tholung monastery (Kartik Bhagat).

5. Tholung monastery with faded, ancient paintings at bottom.

6. Pauhunri peaks, the highest peaks on 'The Plateau' in North Sikkim.

7. Dongkhya Ri, 6190 m.

8. Khangchenjau with Yulehkang seen from Lachen.

9. Chomo Yummo above Gigong, North Sikkim.

10. Kolahoi north face above Dodsar lake (Mukund R.).

11. Kolahoi group, Kashmir.

12. A Gujjar lady, Kashmir.

13. A Shepherd girl helping a trekker to cross bridge.

14. Madhav Rigo peak above Machail, Bhut nala, Kishtwar (Amrita Dhar).

15. Gharol peak in Bhut nala.

16. Agyasol and Spear peaks, Bhut nala (Amrita Dhar).

17. Arjuna peak from about 5000 meters across the valley (Ranjit Jakli).

18. Road carved out from rock-wall fron Gulabgarh to Killar.

19. Spear peak, Bhut nala (Ranjit Jakli).

20. Phabrang peak viewed from Killar in the Pangi valley.

21. Mules crosing the Shyok river.

22. Sultan Chushku stream.

23. On historic Karakoram Pass.

24. Yurgolak ancient fort, the Shyok valley.

25. Chhongtash camp, the Shyok valley.

26. Peaks of Aksai Chin plateau from the Depsang plains.

27. Two 'Polu Stone Shelters', near D. B. O. Karakoram. In foreground, memorial stones to Ph. C. Visser 1935, (left) and Kaivan Mistry 2002.

when the total width of the track exceeding the width of our car by mere inches. Shashi laughed at our appalled faces, and hearing of Harish's plans to go over Sach Pass (4385 m) into Himachal, said that we must try and locate his friend, Bipin, for there was indeed a road that made this one look tame by comparison, and of the few who plied it by car, Bipin was one of the best. As we sat there gulping silently, the track passed through villages that betrayed no real reason for their existence, so tenuously did they cling to the hillsides containing them: Shol (1835 m), Tayari, Ishtayari (2200 m), Sansari nala (2014 m).

We found and loaded ourselves into Bipin's Sumo in Killar. Soon we were on a road that cut ever deeper into the mountains through a warren of connecting ridges and troughs. The unpaved 'road' was both a marvel of engineering, and a terror. Harish had climbed up to Sach pass in 1971 from the Chamba side, and even the thought of a motorable pathway in this labyrinth had been inconceivable. Yet here we were in 2014. Before long, we had traversed the 43 kilometres from Killar to Sach Pass and were straddling the high ground looking into Himachal. Tier upon tier of mountains stretched away in every direction. As always, our trip was ending with a sense of many more beginnings to come.

About an hour from the pass, we drove into and had our IDs checked at the army post of Satrundi (3800 m), where in 1998 fifteen labourers had been killed by militants. But our passage to Chamba was peaceful, hemmed around as we were by smiles and nods of welcome, and the gathering dusk.

7

Younghusband: 'Damned Rum Name'

The Life and Times of Sir Frances Younghusband

Sir Frances Younghusband was one of the prominent founding members of The Himalayan Club. Though his explorations were conducted in the late nineteenth century and early twentieth century, he was an important explorer, and someone who had to be consulted by Kenneth Mason when he formed The Himalayan Club in 1928.

Many things about Francis Younghusband were unique, including his name. There were hardly any in English society with the name Younghusband. He was born in 1863 in Muree, a hill station now in Pakistan. His father, Lt General Younghusband, and two of his uncles were high-ranking army officers of the British Raj in India. The circumstances of his childhood left a permanent impression on Younghusband. When he was three, his mother moved him to Dorset in England, to the family home. He was left in the charge of two aunts who were to bring him up for almost two decades. They were very religious and enforced strict discipline on young Younghusband. His uncle, Robert Shaw, was a well-known explorer, a player in the 'Great Game' in the North West Frontier of India. Young Francis grew up with frontier tales and Shaw became his mentor.

Hailing from an army family, Younghusband was sent to Sandhurst in 1881, and in 1884, at the young age of 19, he was commissioned into the 1st King's Dragoon Guards. Soon, he was sent to India to be stationed at the Meerut cantonment. His military career started in the intelligence unit of the army under Commandant Colonel Charles Bell, a well-known explorer and an expert on Tibet, who had won the Victoria Cross. Younghusband wrote that Bell "possessed a great physical hardihood and cared for nothing so much as making a secret military reconnaissance"[1]. His superior officer, Sir Charles Macgregor had distinguished himself in the Afghan war. He was an ambitious man and the author of *The Defence of India,* a book that influenced the shaping of the Empire's military. Between these two personalities, Frances was trained in the art of soldiering in the NW Frontier and Tibet, and in the tenets of diplomacy.

> Sir Charles Macgregor was a big, bluff, gruff man. When I was first introduced to him, all he had said was: 'Damned rum name that is'. Now, however he was interested in me. He at least listened to what I had to say. I asked to be sent on duty to China and Manchuria for eighteen months.[2]

His unusual name was many times a point of confusion and sometimes, ridicule. 'Rum name' was typical British slang meaning strange, peculiar, odd or little funny at the same time. During his years of travel, he was addressed by various forms – sometimes on the edge of absurdity: Young, Husband, Houng Husband, House Husband, Loving Husband, Yang-ta-jen, or in Manchuria as 'Yang-hasi-pan'. It seems the name originally derived from Oshan (a variation of Oswald). Oswald's son was known as Young Oshan which somehow transmuted into Younghusband![3]

In 1887, at the age of 22, he was sent to Peking with a brief to cross the Gobi Desert. It was decided that he would return to India by a different route from the rest of his party and present a separate report. The journey was to take him seven months and ended with a dramatic winter crossing of the then unexplored Mustagh pass leading over the Karakoram – a formidable achievement for someone ill-equipped for climbing and with no previous mountaineering experience. It was little short of a miracle that the party came down alive.

Lord Curzon, then Viceroy, was impressed, and referred to him as 'moulded in the frontier school of character'. Younghusband was sent to

---

1. Younghusband, Sir Francis, *The Light of Experience,* Constable and Co. Ltd, London, 1927, p. 13.
2. Younghusband, Sir Francis, op. cit., p. 14.
3. French, Patrick, *Younghusband,* Penguin Books, London, 1994, p. 4.

London to lecture at the Royal Geographic Society (RGS) on the scientific results of his journey. He was elected a member of the RGS at 24, the youngest-ever.

On his return to India on duty, he was selected to go on a mission to Central Asia and the Karakoram. The British had a long-standing problem with the Afghans that had claimed many lives. The foreign Secretary, Sir Mortimer Durand,[4] had finally been able to bring the Afghans to the negotiating table and a border between Afghanistan and the British India, known as 'The Durand Line', was drawn.

During the nineteenth century, a political and diplomatic confrontation developed between Britain and Russia over Afghanistan and Karakoram, at the western border of the Indian sub-continent. There were reports that the Russians were interested in pushing down the western Karakoram with the intention of reaching the warm waters of the Arabian Sea. This alarmed the British and they started counter measures by way of cultivating friendship with the Mir of Hunza and other tribal heads in the region. Intelligence gathered suggested that a Russian Colonel was reconnoitring the area accompanied by soldiers. Not much was known about the northern limits of the area nor about the various passes through which the Russians could invade. Many locals trained by the British were regularly sent to the area to garner information in a strategy, immortalised by Rudyard Kipling in his famous novel *Kim,* known as the 'Great Game'.

There were quite a few 'Great Gamers', as British officers involved in these explorations were called. Now, with his Muztagh Pass crossing noted as a mountaineering feat, Younghusband was to join their ranks. It was decided that he be sent on a wider mission lasting a few months and covering a vast area.

During his second Karakoram journey in 1889, Younghusband travelled from Srinagar to Leh and reached the Karakoram Pass rather quickly. The trail

---

4. Sir Mortimer was also an excellent footballer. In 1888, he started a football tournament in India by contributing a generous sum to establish a trophy, known as the 'Durand Cup'. The match was played at Shimla. The tournament is played even today and is the oldest football tournament in Asia and the third oldest in the world. (The oldest football tournament in the world being 'The Football Association Challenge Cup', 1871, popularly known as the FA Cup, followed by The Scottish Football Association Challenge Cup, commonly known as the Scottish Cup, 1874.)

was good and known as it had been visited by British officers earlier. After the pass, he branched off to enter the unexplored Shaksgam valley. The valley was part of the Kashmir kingdom – which was why, when the Maharaja signed the instrument of accession with India, it technically belonged to India. Kashmir state also included most of the western Karakoram and the area till its northern borders, which extended till the Shaksgam valley's northern limits. This was why the viceroy was keen to know all about this valley.

Entering the valley from the east, Younghusband travelled with double-humped Bactrian camels to cross the Aghil pass and proceeded along the Shaksgam river. He saw the northern face of K2 and the north faces of many peaks bordering the Siachen glacier such as the Teram Kangri and Apsarasas. With a smaller party from the camp at Durbin Jangal he turned south, following the Shaksgam river, proceeding slowly 'like a tortoise', along the long Urdok (Yarkandi name for a tortoise) glacier to reach the northern foot of the 'Indira col'. He saw its forbidding wall and turned further east to reach foot of the 'Turkestan la' (later Dr Longstaff called it 'Younghusband's Saddle') on the eastern ridge of the Siachen. He was hardly about 500 metres below the pass from where he would have seen the entire Siachen glacier. A lack of supplies and the danger of avalanches made him turn back. But his explorer's instinct led him to believe that hidden beyond these two passes was a large glacier – the Siachen Glacier.

On his return to England, he shared his notes and views with another British explorer, Dr Tom G Longstaff and encouraged him to explore the Siachen. Longstaff investigated the Siachen in 1910 from two sides, west and south, and reached the conclusion that the Siachen does not end at the Bilafond la, as it was believed to, but extends till the Indira Col and Turkestan la. He wrote:

> Younghusband was a true prophet. Colonel Burrard of the Survey had suspected the truth. The avalanche-swept pass, whose foot Younghusband had reached twenty years before, *was* on the main axis of the Karakorum range, which thus lay miles farther north than had been believed. We had stolen some 500 square miles from the Yarkand river system of Chinese Turkestan and joined it to the waters of Indus and Kingdom of Kashmir.[5]

---

5. Longstaff, Tom, *This My Voyage*, John Murray, London,1950, p. 192.

Younghusband returned to the central Shaksgam valley and crossed the Shimshal pass, which he thought was a 'fit place for robbers'. This was the 'gateway to Hunza' and the ruler was informed in advance of the Britisher's arrival. As Younghusband came down from the pass, he met Safdar Ali and his band of local militia, all heavily armed. But Safdar Ali brought a message of welcome from the ruler of Hunza and told him he could go anywhere in the Hunza state. He also brought news of and an invitation from a Russian Colonel, Gromchevsky, who was camping in the lower valley. Younghusband was keen to meet him as he was also part of the 'Great Game'. As he reached the Russian camp, he writes, "a tall, fine looking bearded man in Russian uniform came out to meet me". He was with seven tall Cossacks who arranged a grand meal. Younghusband's Gurkhas were conscious of their boss meeting the taller Russian, so they arranged a platform, standing on which Younghusband could meet Gromchevsky at equal height! They covered up their secret by their standing on all sides of the platform.

Both men got on very well and after much vodka, the Russian opened up. He said all that the Russian army was thinking of was the up-coming invasion of India. Russia was ready for the 'Great Game', and he mentioned that a French explorer was also in the area.

In 1888, Younghusband met Major Cumberland, Lieutenant Bower, Frenchmen M Dauvergne and German naturalist Herr Conrad with Col Gromchevsky. It is a curious commentary upon the political state of affairs of that time, that in a 'no man's land', a Russian, a Frenchman, a German and no less than three Britishers should meet as friendly, if rival, explorers without any official passport![6]

Few days later, both men prepared to go their own way, the Russian to Tibet and Sir Frances to India. The Gurkhas saluted the Russian officer by presenting arms, shocking him by the precision of their drill. The Cossacks were sturdy, but irregulars and could not match the Gurkhas. Cossacks presented 'carry swords', their equivalent. When the Russian congratulated them, the Gurkha havildar whispered that Russians should know that they were unusually small and that in their regiment most Gurkhas were even taller than the Russian colonel, who was 6.5 feet! The colonel was amused

6. Mason, Kenneth, *Abode of Snow*, Diadem Books, London, 1955, reprint 1987, p. 102.

when Francis, as a friend, told him of this ingenuous attempt to deceive him, for the average Gurkha is around 5.5 feet! Both explorers gave each other a cordial farewell. The Russian said that he hoped that one day they would meet in peace at St Petersburg, or in the war at the frontier – in either case, Sir Frances should be sure of a warm welcome.

By now Younghusband had enough information for his bosses in India, so he made a rapid return after spending few days at Attock Fort, a British stronghold. The Viceroy was pleased with his report. Younghusband had, through the intelligence branch of the army, by now explored Kashmir, China and returned via the Karakoram to Shimla. He had been in the field from almost 1887 to 1892 and so, was sent to England on well-deserved leave, and to be debriefed by the ministry. He was awarded the coveted 'Patron's Medal of the Royal Geographical Society' in 1890.

COLONEL GROMCHEVSKY[7]

The Russian colonel, representing his country was equally enthusiastic about exploration as his counterpart Sir Frances. On his return to Russia and after the Russian revolution in 1917, he was stripped of all his powers and was arrested, all his property seized and he was sent to prison in Siberia. After few years he managed to escape, thanks to the Japanese, and reached his home country, Poland. He wrote a small book on his Central Asian and Karakoram adventures and sent a copy to Sir Frances.

The contrast between the two explorers was stark. Sir Frances was at height of his honours. He was laden with awards and honours and had a private audience with the King. Col Gromchevsky, who had once struck fear into the hearts of India's defence chiefs, passed away at Warsaw in 1926, destitute, sick and alone.

Younghusband, apart from his own explorations, was creating a legacy for future explorations: Dr Tom Longstaff's expedition to the Siachen (1910) after him was based on his information; the Shaksgam Valley was thoroughly explored in 1926 by a team led by geographer and surveyor Kenneth Mason, who later became the first editor of *The Himalayan Journal* in 1929. Many such as Michael Spender, J B Auden, and even Eric Shipton and Bill Tilman, followed Younghusband's footsteps.

---

7. The name 'Gromchevsky' is spelled in different ways in English. This seems to be most accepted spelling.

YOUNGHUSBAND: TIBET MISSION 1903–1904

Lord Curzon, the Viceroy of India, had a phobia about the Russians advancing into India. It was brought to his attention that the Russians may have reached Lhasa, the capital of Tibet and were building armed stores there. Tibet was an important buffer state between India and Russia. So, he decided to send a 'mission' to investigate this possibility, to reach Lhasa and, if Tibetans would object, to put them down by force. He selected Younghusband, who with his military background and diplomatic acumen, was by now a well-known name, to lead this expedition. He was recalled to India and a mission was planned for late 1903.

Preparations began in the earnest and Younghusband selected a team of officers and units of Gurkha Rifles and Sikhs to accompany him. As opposition by Tibetans was unknown so far, more force than required was on its way. He selected two important officers, one being F M Bailey, nicknamed 'the hatter Bailey', who had much experience trekking in the unknown mountains. The other was L A Waddell who spoke Tibetan and was keen to gather as many antiquities of Tibet as he could on the mission. The army deputed General Macdonald with his band of officers, as the military head of the mission, which, unfortunately, did not sit well with Younghusband. Many conflicting situations developed but, as the overall leader, Younghusband always prevailed.

To cross into Tibet, Younghusband selected Jelep la, a pass close to Nathu la, which was in Sikkim. Jelep la was a well-known trading pass through which caravans of mules carried the much-fancied Tibetan wool to India, to be processed and sold at faraway places like Amritsar and Bombay.

The main assault force of the 8 Gurkha Rifles assembled at Siliguri on 20 November 1903, as part of the Francis Younghusband Mission to Lhasa. They reached Gangtok on 8 December and on 20 December crossed Jelep la to the Chumbi valley, with the full mission. They passed villages such as Yatung (also known as Chumbi). Almost entire villages gathered to witness such a large and disciplined force make its way into Tibet. In fact, Tibet had never seen anything like this. The guns drawn on a large wheel carriage were novelty to them, as the wheel revolution had almost missed them. At Yatung, they met Annie Memsahib, a middle-aged British lady dressed in Tibetan costume. She was a Scottish spinster whose mission was to convert Tibetans to Christianity and she had come closer to Lhasa than any westerner in fifty years. However, she had made only one convert and the officers thought she was an 'intolerable nuisance'.

The mission proceeded along the Amo Chu river, passed a few gorges and a major camp was made on the plains of Phari, below the fort and in sight of the majestic Chomololahri peak.

By now they had information that the Tibetans had sent an army, under a general from Lhasa to intercept them. As they moved through Chumik Shenko to Guru, they could see a large sangar – defensive rock wall – built by the Tibetans. A note was sent with Bailey to the Tibetan general explaining their mission, that they had come in peace and the military power they were carrying, was for defence only. The general refused to accept the note. So, a confrontation was inevitable. The Tibetan army, if you could call it that, had almost no guns and bore primitive weapons – they had come armed with charms from the Dalai Lama. Both armies came face to face.

Suddenly, the Tibetan general fired his pistol, injuring an Indian soldier and was heard ordering his troops to attack. General Macdonald ordered his troops to open fire and the Tibetans were no match against the modern weaponry, the training of the British soldiers and rapid firing from maxims (forerunner of modern machine guns). Within five to seven minutes, almost 700 Tibetans were killed, hundreds more injured, left without limbs, and many ran away. This was a rather uneven display of power and the overpowering of a primitive army. Tibetans mentioned that 'the sound of firing continued for the time it would take for six successive cups of hot tea to cool'.

Such brute, one-sided force was given the name – 'Massacre at Guru'.[8]

The mission marched ahead and soon reached the walled fort of Gyantse, which was reported to be occupied by several hundred Tibetans. After some rest and reconnaissance, General Macdonald decided on a plan of action.

---

8. The phrase entered the old English language to describe extreme one-sided events, in nature or even in sports. For those who follow cricket, once an English team was bowled out for a meagre total in short time by two tall West Indian fast bowlers. The erudite commentator, John Arlott, noted that, "It was like the massacre at Guru, but here the British were at the receiving end!"

Artillery fired relentlessly and the fort wall was breached. The final storming of the fort began at 3.30 am on 6 July 1904. Lt J D Grant and Havildar Karbir Pun led the assault. They tried to climb the cliff as the Tibetans threw stones and mud down on them. They got nearer the wall, but many climbers slipped. Finally, at 6 pm, Grant and Pun reached the top, followed by others. As the Gurkhas made a charge with their khukris, the Tibetans ran to the top and many jumped off the cliff to their deaths – they had heard stories about the savagery of the Gurkha soldiers and the expertise of their khukri charge; of how they chopped off noses and ears of opponents before killing them. More than 500 Tibetans died, and the fort was with the British. For this bravery, 8 Gurkha Rifles received a special citation. Lt J D Grant was awarded the Victoria Cross and Havildar Karbir Pun was awarded the First-Class Order of Merit (as 'Other Ranks' were not eligible for a VC.).

These men had climbed to and fought at an altitude in excess of 5,600 m, which Perceval Landon reckoned to be 'probably the highest point on the earth's surface at which engagement has ever taken place'.[9]

Today, the Chinese have built a museum at Gyantse fort for tourists. Called 'The British Hate Museum', it depicts how bravely the Tibetans fought and forced Younghusband to sign a treaty!

The road to Lhasa was now clear. The troops made steady progress, camping at the foot of the huge glacier at Karo la. The Gurkhas marched ahead across Karo la, Yamdrok tso and reached the entrance to Lhasa without any resistance.

Major Bailey, noticed Tibetan blue-poppy, flowering abundantly in a meadow above the Field of Milk, the army's camp site below the Karo la, and the flower now carries his name, *Meconopsis bectonicifolia baile.* He became a distinguished explorer, naturalist and plant hunter. Exploring the ranges north of Arunachal Pradesh with H T Moreshead, he brought back survey information that was used to draw the famous 'McMahon Line'. Claude White (who later became a well-known administrator of

9. This record was equalled and broken only by the war on the Siachen Glacier, 1984 to 2003, between the Indian and Pakistani armies. Younghusband was the pioneer who had charted the Siachen glacier in 1889 as a part of the British Empire.

Bhutan) and he share joint honours as pioneer breeders of the Lhasa Apso.[10]

On 3 August 1904, Sir Francis Younghusband and his troops marched through a giant chorten to enter and 'unveil Lhasa'. With this physical conquering, the Younghusband Mission was officially over. They camped in front of the Potala Palace, the seat of the Dalai Lama, who had gone far away. There was no one to negotiate with! After a few months, the British arranged to get 'Amban' a high official from surrounding area, who came with many officials and a treaty was signed. No Russian presence was found at Lhasa and only about 22 Russian rifles were found in some private houses. Thus, the major purpose of the mission was a failure.[11]

As soon as the agreement was reached, the atmosphere in Lhasa and the surrounding monasteries changed.

The British decided to free all Tibetan prisoners-of-war and each was presented with five rupees before being released. The Tibetans on their part set free several men gaoled for helping foreigners enter Tibet. One of them was the elderly steward of the Palla estate at Gyantse. He had been sentenced to life imprisonment for showing hospitality to the Bengali explorer-spy Sarat Chandra Das back in 1884.

His first moment of freedom was witnessed by Edmund Candler: "The old man's chains had been removed from his limbs that morning for the first time in twenty years, and he came in blinking at the unaccustomed light like a blind man miraculously restored to sight".

Few celebratory-cum-farewell dinners were held for the departing force of Younghusband. The meal consisted of "Potage Potala, followed by Dalai Lama Cutlets, Penelope Poulet and Oeufs a la Shape, ending with Amban Apricots".[12]

The mission returned to Calcutta without much fanfare. The government in England had changed, and the new Labour government did not appreciate the mission as much as the earlier one. Perhaps the massacres, the uneven

---

10. Allen, Charles, *Duels in the Snows*, John Murray, London, 2004, p. 305.
11. Some of us reached Lhasa on 3 August 2004, exactly a hundred years to the date, after Younghusband. The chorten stands at the same place, but with a major road going around it. Lhasa has now turned into a modern city.
12. Allen, Charles, Ibid., pp. 286 and 290.

treaty signed only with lower officials and stringent rules of the treaty were not appreciated.

The Younghusband Mission and Dr L Augustine Waddell displayed four hundred mule-loads of 'rare and valuable manuscripts of Lamaist sacred works, images, religious paraphernalia of all descriptions, armour, weapons, paintings and porcelain at the Indian Museum in Calcutta. Later, these were lodged at the museums in London.

The majority of these items are today stored at the Victoria and Albert Museum, London. Individual army units also took many objects and displayed them in their museums, such as 'Tibet Campaign collections display at 1st Royal Fusiliers Museum, Tower of London'. Many other museums in London also have Younghusband Tibetan collections, which made some critics call it the 'Looting of Tibet'.[13]

Younghusband was now side-lined from active political and military matters, almost forced into retirement at the age of 42! He was keen to remain a player in the 'Great Game', but the powers to be deputed him to quieter pursuits as a political officer in Hunza, Chitral and then to various places in India. Why Younghusband was thus side-lined has never been satisfactorily explained. But the 'Great Game' had its penalties as well as rewards.

Honours were bestowed on him in plenty. He was made the Resident Commissioner at Kashmir (1906–1909). He invited his Ladakhi and Balti friends to come and stay with him many times. He was knighted in 1905 and received a private audience with the king. He was President of the Royal Geographical Society (1919–1922), Chairman of Mount Everest Foundation (1921) and a Founder Member of The Himalayan Club (1928). He received many doctorates.

Later in life, he took to philosophy and religion, to which he was exposed as a child. He formed the 'Universal World Faith Congress' (1912–1922) and counted leading philosophers, including Bertrand Russel and India's (later President) S. Radhakrishnan, amongst his friends. When he died in 1942, as per his wishes, he was buried in Dorset, England, with a bronze statue of Buddha presented to him by T Rimpoche at Lhasa. His is mentioned as a:

---

13. See Myatt, Tim, "Looting Tibet: Conflicting Narratives and Representations of Tibetan Material Culture from the 1904 British Mission to Tibet", University of Oxford, London, 2012.

Life most honourably lived, the world of his youth gone, which had been ebbing even as he was removed from its centre of affairs.[14]

Younghusband was a pioneering soldier-explorer, whose his deeds made his 'Damned Rum Name' shine in history, and even after more than a century since his explorations, it continues to be well known.

Nobody ever dies, as long as they
Live in memory of those alive.
Particularly those, who live in the
Pages of history.

"Not dead, but living in deeds : such lives inspire"

– On Jesse Owen, the legendary athlete.
A tribute motto on the World War II plaque

14. Verrier, Anthony, *Frances Younghusband and the Great Game*, Jonathan Cape, London,1991, p. 4.

8

On the 'Death Trail'

A Journey across the Shyok and Nubra Valleys

It was 17 May 2002, we were at Shyok village, starting on a long Karakoram journey covering the two large valleys of the Shyok and the Nubra rivers in Ladakh, East Karakoram. It was an ambitious plan, traversing this forbidding terrain, first along the Shyok, crossing it more than 24 times, visiting Karakoram pass, crossing Col Italia, exploring the Teram Shehr plateau and finally, descending via the Siachen glacier. In between all this, we planned to climb the 7030 m virgin peak Padmanabh. Ambitious enough. We were six Indian and five Japanese mountaineers accompanied by an army liaison officer.

Fortunately, we were in the nick of time, for water levels in the Shyok were rising and within a week the route would be closed. This trail from Shyok village to Karakoram pass is a 'Winter Trail', used only in the cold months when the Shyok is crossable. The trail runs along the Shyok river, quite literally a 'river of death' (*shi*-death, *yok*-river, in Ladakhi), as the river has killed many travellers by floods. It's no wonder the trail is also named after the river.

Way back in nineteenth century, the British had tried to build a formal trail here by blasting rocks on the left bank so that crossings could be minimised. One can still see the blast charges on the rocks and at many places a trail could be seen on the opposite bank. But the plans to build it were later abandoned, Ladakhi caravans follow the traditional route, crossing and re-crossing the Shyok more than 5 to 6 times a day, as they have done for generations. Sometimes, in the earlier part of the journey, the water reaches waist level or higher and the horses cross with some difficulty and much prodding by their owners. The owners would always jump on a horse loaded with luggage and cross safely. The hardy mountaineers of our party held hands and, mastering the technique, managed to get across the Shyok. It was fun, as somebody said, but rather cold and very tiring by the time we finished with it.

This route came into prominence during the India–China war in 1962. The area along the watershed immediately to the east of it was taken over by Chinese troops and today the watershed remains a *de facto* border. This was why the route had remained out of bounds for Indians and foreigners alike, and we were one of the few parties to trek it.

ALONG THE SHYOK

The first day of the trek was a disaster. The first few crossings were difficult and our group was divided and stranded. A tired and haggard party arrived at the camp only early the next morning in time for breakfast. Half a day of rest was declared and then we made a short journey to Burma (3760 m). The first crossing was that of the Chang Chenmo river. The Chang Chenmo (Ororotse) gorge flows in from the east and is one of the deep valleys leading from the Shyok valley to the Aksai Chin plateau. A prominent track traverses the Chang Chenmo and, crossing Lanak la (5486 m), reaches the Kun Lun plains and western Tibet plateau. This was an old trade route used by traders from the Tibet.

Staying at Burma for the night and by now a little accustomed to cold crossings, we set off very early the next day. Our aim was to reach Chumed and Char Bagh. We were assured that after Chumed, the crossings would be easier and the water level would be low. True to this assurance, after the third day, at Char Bagh (3920 m), the water level was low. But the final crossing was a terror in itself. One of the porters was heard lamenting, "What sins have I committed in my past life to be crossing the Shyok so many times?! Never again!" and that thought was echoed by almost everyone! But the trail had its rewards too, as we were to discover soon.

A day ahead of Char Bagh, we camped at foot of the Yurgolak fort (4050 m), which was located on a ridge about 100 m above. Though the fort walls were dilapidated, what remained was still solid and one could see the rooms and the courtyards. From the fort, looking across the Shyok valley, was the North Shukpa Kunchang nala, locally known as Nortot. Traversing this glacier and crossing an easy pass, a trail crossed to Sumur in the Nubra valley. This was the old route used by traders from Karakoram pass to the Nubra valley when Saser la was closed. The exact reason the fort was built is not known but, one legend has it that it was to protect against the invasion by Chengiz Khan of Mongolia, known in Ladakh as 'Tsogpo Galden Chhang'. The Ladakhi king also built another fort at Sumur to completely secure his kingdom.

The next day, on our way to Thangnyer (4130 m) (Thang-plain, nyer-in the middle of: *a camp in the middle of plains*) we were to pass through some historical places. The first was Mandalthang on the western shore, gateway to North Shukpa Kunchang glacier. Traversing this glacier, a team had climbed Saser Kangri peaks, as was done during its first ascent in 1973. After their ascent, the rising waters of the Shyok made it impossible to cross downstream and trapped the team. They had to go northwards, undertaking several dangerous crossings to return via Saser la. Fording the Shyok river is a major challenge when attempting any of the peaks in this area.

To our east rose the Kugrung group of peaks (6568 m, 6556 m and 6541 m were the highest of this group) – prominent and formidable. To the east it drained into the Kugrung river which flowed to the Chang Chenmo at Tsongtsalu Hot Springs (north of Phobrang). Peaks such as these suggest the wealth of mountain peaks and opportunities available when it will become possible to approach these areas.

THE GALWAN RIVER

Soon we were standing at the mouth of the Galwan nala, which has a long history – a historic beginning and disastrous end. This is the nala named after Rasool Galwan, one of the great native explorers. Gulam Rasool Galwan was one of the pony-men taken by Lord Dunmore to the Pamirs in 1890. He served a host of other explorers and travellers: Younghusband, Longstaff, Phelps, Church, Wellby and Littledale, particularly on the route along the Shyok. In 1914, he was appointed caravan leader (a very prestigious post) for the big Italian scientific

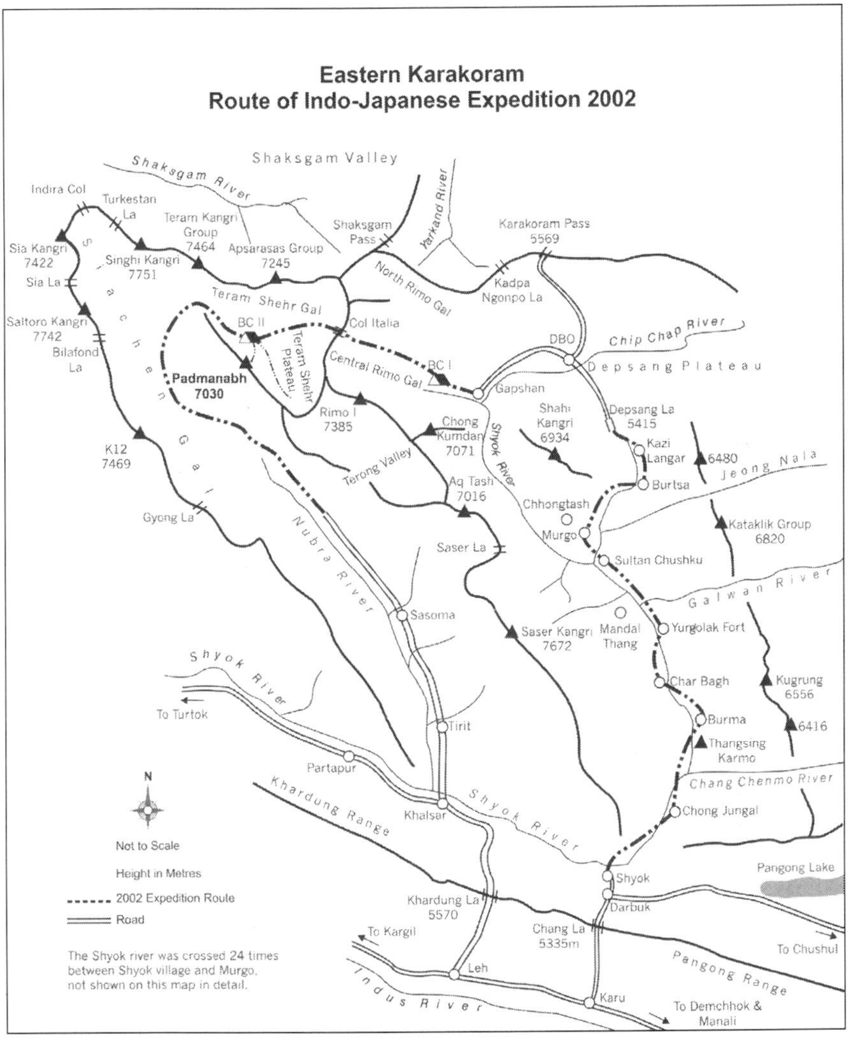

Eastern Karakoram.

expedition of Filippo de Filippi, which explored the Rimo glacier systems and spent several months in the area.[1]

His claim to fame came from an earlier expedition with the British joint commissioner when he explored a large unknown river valley little to the north of the Chang Chenmo. This is the valley that now bears his name, 'the

1. Rasool Galwan was an Arghon. For full details see, Kapadia, Harish, 'In the Land of Argans', *The Himalayan Journal* Vol 58 2002, pp. 99–100.

Galwan valley'. This is a rare instance of a major geographical feature being given the name of the native explorer who put it on a Western map. Other than the Pundit explorers, native explorers have received far less recognition in the survey of the higher ranges. Undoubtedly, native travellers certainly knew most of the routes before they were incorporated in maps.

Looking into this valley with sharp eyes or through binoculars, one could see the remains of an army post, built about 40 years earlier. Three valleys join the Galwan nala at this point. Those who have read books on the 1962 Indo-China war, will find this familiar. It was in this valley, in pursuance of the 'forward policy' followed by the Indian government at the time, that the Indian army set up a post at an almost indefensible spot.[2] The post was surrounded by Chinese troops right from its establishment in July 1962. It was one of the first casualties of the 1962 war, which was triggered on 20 October, when the post was overwhelmed and many were killed, injured and captured. The Galwan valley was one of the routes of attack by the Chinese troops.

From here on the Shyok valley was wide and to avoid some river crossings we went across the small Kalkatra la (4400 m). The route to Kataklik (4240 m) was a gentle and simple walk and the camp was at a beautiful spot on the eastern bank. The nala led eastwards to Kataklik Kangri, a peak of 6917 m. The peaks and groups that we were now to observe are completely unknown, They have never been attempted nor explored. The next day, after a short walk, we camped at Sultan Chushku (4330 m) (sultan-king, chusku-stream: *stream of kings*) where the Shyok took a sharp turn to the west. On the opposite bank in the west was the Sultan Chusku group, with more than four peaks rising above 6700 m. The Sultan Chusku nala and the Murgo nala met at this camping ground and we were only 5 kilometres away from the *de facto* Chinese border. This was the reason why the area was well protected and restricted.

From here we left the Shyok river and followed the Murgo nala from Sultan Chusku stream. We crossed the Jeong nala flowing from the Aksai

2. In 1960, the government of India, as part of policy, ordered the army to establish posts as near to the border as possible to physically occupy land. This was irrespective of its strategic value or possibilitiy of defending it. This policy led to disasters.

Chin plains in the east. The Murgo nala had to be crossed not less than 20 times before we could reach the open plains leading to the Murgo camp (4650 m). The line of control between the Indian and the Chinese forces is not more than 15 km from here and there is a permanent army camp here – the first one we came across on this trail.

To stay the night we went off to Chhongtash, 6 km to the west, in an army truck. Chhongtash is a vast plain with a big stone in centre, and that is what the name implies (chhong-big, tash-stone). A board at the helipad indicated the altitude sensibly, 'You are 15,800 ft nearer to God'! Now that we had joined the summer trade route from Karakoram Pass to Sasoma (across Saser la) the trail being used was well built. At least three of us had travelled this trail before. On 26 May we passed Murgo, Kalon Chumik, to reach Burtsa (4600 m). Passing Kazi langar (4950 m) the next day, we climbed on to Depsang la (5415 m) where our walk and horse rides ended. Indian army personnel were waiting for us with welcoming handshakes, tea and trucks. Depsang la is a vast plain and stretches almost 20 by 20 km, controlled in the east by the Chinese. This historic plain had seen hundreds of caravans pass by and in 1962, had seen attacks by Chinese aggressors.[3]

THE KARAKORAM PASS

We spent the night at Daulat Beg Oldi (5180 m), the famous ground known simply as DBO. Next day on the way up to Karakoram Pass we halted at Polu shelters, where two mud huts mark the place where many Yarkandi traders have taken shelter during bad weather. At this Polu, one of the early explorers, the Dutch doctor, P H C Visser, left a small tablet stating simply 'Visser 1935', which is still enshrined here. Next to it we erected another tablet in memory of Kaivan Mistry, an explorer and mountaineering friend, who died in the Shyok river on 27 August 2000 while on an Indo-French expedition. It was a seemingly innocuous accident where four of us fell into the Shyok. While three survived, pulled by his heavy rucksack Kaivan unfortunately, fell on his back and it appears his head hit a rock. He died instantly.

3. For photos and details of Depsang la area see, Kapadia, Harish, 'The High Altitude Golf Courses!', *The Himalayan Journal* Vol 57 2001, p. 111.

We reached Karakoram Pass on 28 May 2002, a historic day for us as the first foreign expedition to stand on this international border with China. For some of us this was the second visit to the Karakoram Pass but our friends were the first Japanese to reach this pass after 93 years. From the pass itself there is almost no view, because both sides are blocked by small but long mountain ranges. What it has is a bone structure lined with prayer flags and of course, the flag of India.[4]

CROSSING COL ITALIA

Finally on 30 May, our caravan of 55 mules deposited us at Base Camp 1 (4850 m), seven km west of Gapshan, at foot of the Central Rimo glacier. We sorted out food and gear, and started ferries on the Central Rimo glacier to establish our further camps. It was going to be hard work from now on. More than 2000 kg of luggage was to be borne on the shoulders of members and available porters.

We passed near the snout of the North Rimo glacier, which is one of the quietest international boundaries in the Karakoram. From here one can cross the Shaksgam pass (to the Shaksgam valley), which could be seen in the distance. Many caravans had passed through here too. Turning west and going towards head of the Central Rimo glacier, the route was snow covered but luckily, devoid of too many crevasses. We established our Camp IV (5750 m) about three km before Col Italia.[5]

---

4. Karakoram Pass (5569 m). KKP, as it is known in Indian Army slang, is perhaps the best- known historic pass in the region. The entire range of mountains from the borders of Afghanistan till Aksai Chin is known as the Karakoram Range. It is named after 'black gravel' found here. The pass is located at the eastern most point of the range and is on the famous Central Asia Trade Route, which linked India (Kashmir–Leh) in South Asia with Central Asia (Yarkand-Kashgar). No records are available on who pioneered the route. Windswept, isolated and featureless, it stands as a monument to the historic events and caravans that crossed it. After the 1962 Indo-China war, visitors to KKP were banned. It was only in 1997 that two civilian parties visited the pass; when we made it there in 2000, we were the third visitors to have been permitted.
5. For a full description of this route and photos see, Kapadia, Harish, 'The High Altitude Golf Courses!', *The Himalayan Journal* Vol 57 2001, p.118.

This pass, at the head of Central Rimo glacier, crosses to Teram Shehr glacier, which descends to the Siachen glacier, thus linking the Shyok and the Nubra valleys. About a kilometre to the north of Col Italia, were many ridges and depressions, which overlooked the Shaksgam valley (which was part of the Kashmir state, now under Chinese control) and mountains of Shaksgam were clearly seen. Towards the south rose the Rimo peaks, which we were familiar with, having climbed or attempted at least three of them on past expeditions.

In 1930, Prof Giotto Dainelli, who had been the geographer on the 1913–14 expedition of Filippo de Filippi to the Rimo glaciers, had entered the Siachen glacier in June, before the Nubra rose sufficiently to stop him. He spent two months on the glacier, establishing his base at the junction of the Teram Shehr glacier. Later, as the passage through the Nubra valley was blocked due to flooding, he decided to return over a 6000 m pass to the Rimo glacier system, which he knew well, to join the main Karakoram route. He named this 'Col Italia', dedicated to Italian explorers.[6]

This is the only recorded crossing of the pass (5920 m). In 2000, 70 years later, I had stood here with Huzefa Electricwala and Kaivan Mistry. Now our entire team was camped here, and it was 72 years since the first crossing that our party descended towards the west. Col Italia is vast plateau almost 7 x 7 km where someone could get lost (as our porters did in bad weather while ferrying luggage).

We descended to the foot of a giant, 7030 m peak, which we had named Padmanabh and established base Camp 2 (5650 m) at its foot.[7]

From base Camp 2 we had two projects in hand. One was the ascent of Padmanabh. A team of climbers led by Hiroshi Sakai, the climbing

6. Dainelli, G, 'My expedition in the eastern Karakoram 1930' *The Himalayan Journal* Vol 4 1932, p. 46.
7. Grant Peterkin, a surveyor with the Workman Expedition, named most peaks and passes in this area between 1911–12. The only peak named (by Bullock Workman, in 1912) on the Teram Shehr Plateau was Laxmi (6850 m), wife of Vishnu and goddess of wealth. For peak 7030 m, we proposed the name Padmanabh (literally, 'the one who is born from the navel') a name of Lord Vishnu, the preserver of the Universe. Other peaks surrounding the plateau were given various names of Vishnu. It is hoped that he will protect the area and prevent further destruction.

leader, prepared for the ascent.[8] Ryuji Hayashibara and I took up the second project: to explore the Teram Shehr plateau.

EXPLORATION OF TERAM SHEHR PLATEAU

We owe the first views of this great plateau to Stephen Venables. He had observed it while attempting Rimo I in 1985. His pictures of the plateau, which ia around more than 10 sq km, with the peaks of the Siachen glacier and K2 in background, look very inviting.[9] This plateau is one of the unique features of the Siachen, East Karakoram, or possibly any place in the world. It is amazing that such a huge, high plateau exists at 6200 m, surrounded by several peaks, many of them rising up to 6500 m (but only 300 m above the plateau!). From the gaps and cols between these peaks one could look down to the Siachen glacier. I had noted this plateau in 1985 for a future trip, but it remained unvisited until today and finally, after 17 years I was renewing my affair with it.

On 21 June, Lingen (Ryuji Hayashibara), three porters and myself formed an independent party and left for five days of exploration of the Teram Shehr plateau. It was not difficult technically but, conscious that we were going over huge and deep crevasses, we covered ground slowly, about 4–8 kms per day, and established two camps to reach the head of the plateau. Reaching a high col between Mahashrung (6940 m) and Sheshnag (6855 m) peaks revealed great views to the Siachen glacier and across to the Karakoram peaks. Walking around the plateau to different cols we observed peaks we were familiar with through photographs, with Rimo I (7385 m) dominating in the south. The best views were towards the north where the wall of the Apsarasas peaks (I (7245 m), II (7239 m), III (7236 m), IV (7140 m) were seen to a great advantage. Only Apsarasas I has been climbed. To the northwest peaks of the Teram Kangri group (I (7495 m), II (7407 m), III (7382 m) were visible. It was an historical moment for us to stand on this high plateau and look around this vast vista of peaks.

8. Sakai, Hiroshi, 'First ascent of Padmanabh', *The Himalayan Journal*, Vol 59 2003.
9. See *The Himalayan Journal*, Vol 42, photo facing page 88. Later Yoshio Ogata and Doug Scott published similar photographs from higher camps on Rimo.

We returned to base camp 2 satisfied. We could see climbers on Padmanabh. The teams had established a high camp and fixed the route with ropes. On 25 June, Hiroshi Sakai and Yasushi Tanahashi climbed Padmanabh (7030 m). It was a difficult climb according to them – they found some sections on this climb more difficult than the ascent of Nanga Parbat, which both had achieved. There was jubilation, happiness and plenty of camaraderie as we shared Indian and Japanese food and celebrated.

THE SIACHEN GLACIER

On 27 June we wound up our camp and proceeded to descend to Siachen glacier. Crevasses at the edge of the Teram Shehr glacier were deep, open and scary but once we reached the lower moraine, it was a long and tiring walk. Finally, we reached a vast open meadow and were surprised to see flowers and droppings of ibex. We camped near a huge lake, which the army had named 'Forward Logistic Base' (FLB) and were warmly welcomed by the army. This was where the Bullock-Workman and Prof Dainelli teams had camped. It offered wonderful views of the vast, long Siachen glacier running from south to north and across rose the peaks dominated by K12 (7428 m) Saltoro Kangri I and II, (7742 m) and (7705 m) and others. We spent a rest day witnessing with amazement and pride how the army defended the glacier throughout the year.

Satisfied but tired we were now reaching the end of our journey. Over the next three days we stayed with the army and then walked down their well-used trail to reach the base camp of the Siachen glacier on 1 July. It was end of the journey for us as we bowed at the temple. In this journey we had traversed formidable terrain for 460 km, crossed five passes and climbed a peak of 7030 m, the first ascent of Padmanabh. What more did one want than to see this as the blessings of God.

9

Prisoners of the Himalaya

'YOL – Your Own Locations'

During the Second World War, as Britain declared war against Germany in 1939, people of German and Italian origins became 'enemies of the nation' and were interned in countries ruled by Britain as well. Among them were nationals of enemy countries who were in India at the time, including members of a few mountaineering expeditions who were then climbing in the Indian Himalaya. The most well-known case is that of members of the German expedition exploring the slopes of Nanga Parbat, then part of the British Empire. All of them, including Heinrich Harrer and Peter Aufschneiter were interned by the British. They tried to escape to Persia from Karachi but were caught while waiting for a ship. They were then taken to a camp in central India and later, one in Dehra Dun.

Another German expedition, comprising German-Swiss climbers Ludwig Schmaderer, H Paidar and E Grob had spent six weeks in Sikkim in 1937, on the Zemu glacier investigating the approaches of Kangchenjunga. On 26 September, they had made the second ascent of the nearby peak of Siniolchu, which Doug Freshfield called 'the most beautiful mountain in the world'. The three climbers returned in 1939 and made the first ascent of Tent Peak.

They were returning from the high mountains around the Zemu glacier, oblivious of what was happening in the world outside. Grob, who was Swiss, was allowed to leave for Europe, but the other two, being Germans, had to be detained. This was the start of a great saga that introduced Tibet and Spiti to the world through the stories of Harrer and Schmaderer. The strange events that followed were almost like a surreal dream. The events are well documented, but at the same time, the story of the large number of Italians who were brought to India as prisoners of war is less known.

THE PRISONERS AT YOL

When the Second World War broke out in Europe, India's involvement was total. Indian soldiers were sent by the British to fight for the Allied troops, just as they had been during the First World War. All cantonments in India were busy with the preparations.

Over the years of the War, many opposition soldiers surrendered to the Allied Forces, notably Italian soldiers fighting in the hot, almost desert-like regions of North Africa. The numbers of these prisoners grew, and it was getting difficult to house and keep a watchful eye on them in Africa. It seemed irrational to spare valuable men and resources to house so many prisoners.

So it was decided to transport the prisoners to India. They would be away from the theatre of war, and there would be no need for elaborate security measures for them and there would be no stress on food supplies. The Italians were loaded onto a ship on its way to India that served the purpose. From Bombay (now Mumbai) they were transported to the foothills of the Himalaya – near Palampur at the foot of Dharamsala. Most of the prisoners had never been to Asia and would not have survived the heat of the Indian plains. They had no means of escape and not knowing the terrain or language, they had no option but to stay within the camp.

Facilities were created at the camp for thousands of prisoners: a series of bunkers with beds, toilets and a kitchen, to be run by cooks helped by the Italians. The Italian officers were housed separately and in more comfort. A small hospital was established, and a workshop was set up to craft furniture as wood was available in plenty. There were no villages in the vicinity and all supplies were brought in by army trucks. The British called the cantonment 'Young Officers Living' (YOL). But the Italian prisoners mocked at this as they were neither young nor was the place worth living for!

Some special innovations were introduced at the camp. A special currency for the inmates was introduced. Lowest was *one-Ana* and the highest Rs 25. They were printed in bright colours and designed very differently from normal currencies. They could be used to buy items within the camp and in some small shops outside the camp. The receiver had to gather these notes, like coupons, and exchange them for actual currency from the prison office. Lists were created, such as a 'Movement Order' for men and a detailed list of materials purchased was maintained – all managed by the Italians as it 'benefitted' them.

Some of the Italians were artists and artisans, apart from being soldiers. They created statues of mud and wood, painted and made stonework which has lasted beyond their stay here. Overall, they led an easy life, but one desire always remained in them – that of freedom. The area is surrounded by the Dhaula Dhar range. Many peaks and passes here rise from the plains to about 4,500 m. The attraction of these hills lured them and a handful did try to escape by climbing the peaks and attempting to cross the passes to the north. But they would eventually be caught by the local police, who were helped by the villagers, and be brought back to the camp. Heinrich Harrer was amongst the few fortunate ones who did escape – to Tibet from a similar camp in Dehra Dun. Unfortunately, none could escape from YOL. The Dhaula Dhar range has no direct access to Tibet. Moreover, there were two major army cantonments, one at McLeod Ganj above Dharamasala and the other at Dalhousie, and the hills were always well patrolled.

The camp was a free place, and the prisoners were allowed to roam around the camp and the surrounding areas. There were no security check points except beyond a certain distance, as the prisoners had nowhere to go. If a prisoner did try to go beyond the jurisdiction, the villagers would almost certainly 'arrest' him and bring him back to the camp. The Italians could never understand why the Indian villagers were completely loyal to the British even though they had been subjugated by them.

In their memoirs, prisoners noted that the Indian guards would march in orderly fashion even off duty while going for food or leisure. They were never lazy. Here's what Poesio notes in his diary : "Our soldiers mock the Indians that they are on duty even if alone. Our enemies have managed to inculcate their discipline in the Indian soldiers, so we should understand what our enemy's strength is."

The prisoners were free to organise gatherings and discussions amongst themselves in the camp. The most discussed debates were on modern politics. Doctor Scardoni spoke about modern corporate influences, Lieutenant Piolanti, on his part, addressed an original topic: food conditions in Fascist controlled Europe. A brilliant conference held by Nino Nutrizio, commemorative of The Duke of Aosta, made the audience cry, but his lecture on Winston Churchill met the hostility of the most ardent fascists. Some of them signed a report in which they accused him of treason for having shown too much admiration towards the British statesman.

The patriotic spirit of the Italians did not fail, and they observed the Giarabub Festival, a well-known event in Italy, with touching songs.

> Colonel, I do not want water, give me the fire-destroyer,
> with the blood of his heart my thirst will go out
> Colonel, I do not want bread, give me lead to my musket,
> I have lead in my bag that for today will be enough for me.
> Colonel, I do not want the change, here nobody comes back,
> you do not give even a meter, if death will not pass.

Death in the play really arrived, and the Giarabub Festival ended like this:

> Colonel, I do not want praises, I died for my land,
> but the end of England begins with Giarabub!

The Italians worked to make wine and whisky for themselves as well as for the British.

Normally seven prisoners worked for a whole night to get a bottle of pure alcohol, which then was sold to the British. Giorgio Vuxani tell us that the British were not happy with the perfect transparency of the clear spirit, so we gave it colour leaving for a few days a piece of boot sole, rotten and decayed, to soak and the precious drink assumed the colour of the whiskey. The British were enthusiastic by (about) it!

Theatrical performances were often organised by some prisoners using makeshift costumes. It kept them alive and in tune with the culture of their country. Almost every evening a film was projected, missed only when weather conditions made it impossible as it took place outdoors.

After their return some prisoners wrote in the Italian press:

Nowadays, whoever hears of war imprisonment thinks of the mistreatment of prisoners and the hostages of Islamic terrorists or to the cruel images of people locked up in detention camps in the former Yugoslavia from three decades ago.

Yet this conflict has also left us with some glimpses of humanity and loyal behaviour such as the surrender of the honours of weapons to a defeated brave enemy or the application of chivalrous behavioural codes which today, unfortunately we are losing memory of.

An example of captivity 'on human scale' comes to us from distant India where between 1941 and 1947 the British held, on the slopes of the Himalayas, a large group of Italian officers captured from various fronts of war.

One of the many British concentration camps in World War II was in YOL Northern India, at the foot of the Himalayas, not far from Tibet. In that same camp, where hundreds of German prisoners had been locked up during the First World War, about ten thousand Italian Officers were deported (12,000 according to some sources) that 'stayed' there from 1941 and others from 1942 until their repatriation.

The British, far from tender regarding prisoners (as many unfortunate survivors of internment in Kenya and South Africa have experienced), could afford the luxury of using their vast colonial holdings all over the world to organize concentration camps very far from the operational theatres, in such a way that their unfortunate guests' ambitions and possibility of escape were reduced to almost zero.

The cemetery, on the other hand, was about ten kilometres away, in Dharmsala, a place much more comfortable than the one intended for the living. In five years, ninety-eight times that road was unfortunately crossed by funerals. The funeral details included: the procession was opened by an English Guard of honour in arms, a laurel wreath from the camp leader, the blank shots and the trumpeters played "Il Silenzio".

HIMALAYAN CLIMBS AND EXTRAORDINARY TREKS

The prisoners at YOL were by far the lucky ones as they were granted the biggest prize that one would covet – that of the freedom to roam and climb various peaks in the nearby ranges. Starting from the Dhaula Dhar in their backyard, up to Lahaul and even borders of Zanskar. These climbs are well recorded in mountaineering history.

The prisoners, who were allowed to leave the camp temporarily, had to commit themselves to not escape and had to do it in writing. Here is what the bond looked like:

I promise that in the period in which I am authorized to leave the camp, I shall not attempt to escape. I will not have any communication with individuals or components other camps or wings, either European or Indian. I will not do any trades, I will not enter any house or shop without prior authorization, I will not send any correspondence and I will not commit any hostile act towards the British Empire and its allies.

The sight of the majestic Himalayan peaks was what strongly attracted some of the officers, especially those from the Alpine troops, who asked their jailers to give them leave to explore the surrounding mountains, so rich in majestic peaks. They obtained what can be considered, perhaps, unique in the history of the Second World War, permission to go out 'on their word of honour' from the concentration camp to climb some peaks of Himachal Pradesh.

At first, there were just a few but later, more and more joined the groups to ask for permits to climb. They had great enthusiasm but faulty and primitive mountaineering equipment. They climbed Dhar Narwana (4690 m, slightly lower than Mont Blanc, Alps, western Europe) in October 1943. Returning to the prison camp after the first ascent, a detailed report was given to the British authorities, while the protagonists' story, in addition to the photographs and drawings, aroused enthusiasm in the other colleagues, and soon another ascent was organised for Punta Lena (4807 m), renamed 'Dhaula Cervino' for its resemblance to the original and on 23 November, a group numbed by the cold, planted a small Italian flag on the peak.

The following spring Guarjunda (5287 m) was climbed, a beautiful peak, the highest of Dhaula Dhar with views till Kashmir and Karakoram. It was climbed on 6 June 1944 (on the same day in Normandy, on the other side of the world, the Anglo-Americans landed and in Rome the first print of 'Il tempo' was printed). This was achieved by a group of brave climbers equipped only with a rope and a nail.

After the Two Gun Peak (4570 m) (*in Dhaula Dhar, near Indrahar pass*), in June 1944, the mountaineering activity resumed in the spring of 1945. While the war in Europe was coming to an end, the prisoners in YOL climbed Kuja-ka-Tilla (5447 m) in May–June, Mulkila in June, that was the highest peak climbed (6517 m) in July, Cima Italia (6163 m) peak until then inviolate, Kailas of Chamba (5656 m) between June and October and Cima Otto (4981 m) in October 1945. In the same period, an extraordinary trekking expedition was carried out and in between September 6th, and October 8th, 1945, three officers (Gualtiero Bernardelli, Giovanni Battista Mazzolini and Luciano D'Avanzo) carried out a large-scale trek up to Lake Tso Moriri in the Little Tibet. 550 kilometers were walked in 27 days overcoming several hills between 4,000 and 6,000 meters of altitude, in an uncontaminated environment of wild beauty.

In 1946, although the World War was over since a year, the Italians were still held in YOL, and in May a team managed to climb the Kundli Got (4581 m). These mountaineering missions are unbelievable if we take into account the poor equipment available to the protagonists. The results obtained were certainly important: in addition to climbing peaks up to then inviolate in precarious conditions, they contributed abundantly towards a scientific repository of information such as topographic survey of little known mountains, the verification and updating of cartographic material, the observation of phenomena of snow and glaciation, the collection of numerous panoramic sketches and news on the anthropic environment.

But beyond the mountaineering or scientific results, what appears particularly important is the transcendental motivation that encouraged those officers to want to leave the camps: the irrepressible yearning for freedom, the will to maintain and activate their professionalism, a sense of attachment to values of the mountain, in a word that 'spirit of body' that does not fail even in difficult conditions thousands of kilometres away from the homeland.

The names of three Europeans were given to them by another climber-prisoner, Giacinto Ferrero, who writes in his diary: "We met a Romanian Jew, Mundi Ettinger, an Austrian from Vienna, Kreneck, and a German, Gutman. Kreneck, a geography teacher in a school in a small Indian state, was a keen mountaineer, who came to India in 1939 with a German expedition to Lahaul. At the outbreak of war, he was interned and was unable to obtain freedom and to teach again, given his status as a Nazi. He gave us very useful information about the area and the interesting peaks, he also promised us to show us a photobook of Manali".

In the evening it was football time, which the Italians loved the most. Most matches were held between Italian teams only, sometimes challenged by a British team. The local population never participated. After a long day and playing in the strong sun, the British security would blow a whistle and give orders to the prisoners to return to 'Your Own Locations', directing them to proceed to their respective bunkers. Most Italians could not follow English so an Italian officer would whistle and abbreviate the order: 'YOL, YOL, YOL', and the prisoners knew that the day was over. The officer was mocking their jailer, but at the same time creating a new, fascinating name.

RELEASE FROM YOL

By September 1945, the Second World War had ended in Europe and technically the Italians were no longer prisoners in true sense of the word. But because of the distance and problems of transportation, their return to Italy was gradual. Between 1945 and the first half of 1946, only a couple of prisoners were released. The bulk of releases began at the end of June 1946: 90 per cent in the second half of 1946 and the remaining 10 per cent in 1947.

With the conflict over, YOL's prisoners were granted a gradual freedom, and although it was within precise territorial borders, they could meet the locals, the villages and their inhabitants, visit monasteries and Buddhist monks, survey plants and hills. It was a bitter freedom, conditioned by thoughts of returning home, which in fact, still seemed far away, linked to the interminable wait for a steamer. So, they began attempts to try to connect with their motherland by other means. For example, someone worked on the details of arrears of salary accumulated in the years of imprisonment. And soldiers listed out what they would like to do with the accumulated money. Many thoughts of family and relations and what gifts they would take for each of them, as if they were normal tourists!

In the first months of 1947, trucks arrived for the last 'guests', who were transported first to the railway station of Nagrota: from there the journey continued by train to Bombay and then by steamer until Napoli.

But even after kissing the soil of the homeland the problems for the former prisoners did not cease abruptly and their reintegration into society was not a simple 'war within' them. The Italian flag was no longer the one for which they had fought, fascists no longer found fascism, the monarchists did not find monarchy, the antifascists and the antimonarchists found a system that they had not helped to build, the brothers no longer found the brothers devoured by the war (including the worst one the civil-war), the children no longer found the parents, fathers found children who they had not seen and from which they could hardly be recognized. There were also those who regretted leaving YOL.

LATER VISIT

The first Italian journalist who visited YOl in the post-war period was Gino Tomajuoli, correspondent for the weekly *Il Tempo*, who wrote an interesting article in May 1949.

"India was now independent and had already started 'eternal war' with Pakistan for the possession of Kashmir, Gandhi was killed and since a month Italy had joined the Atlantic Alliance."

Tomajuoli had a permit to visit the camp for five minutes but through various subterfuges managed to stay for a whole day. He saw the colossal work that Italian prisoners had to do to level the mountain, a stony cliff, to build the soccer field supported by an embankment of seven or eight meters high.

Only one camp, no. 28, was still in use, this time the prisoners were the enemies of the new India: Indian dissidents, communists, two British officers who were advisers to the Pakistani army, captured in Kashmir. The camp director, a Sikh captain, still remembered the Italians with benevolence and hoped for their return, of course as tourists. The chaperone remarked on the difference in the behaviour between the current guests, who did nothing and the Italians who 'never gave up', worked, studied and produced.

"Everywhere in India" the captain told Tomajuoli, "one discovers a lively sympathy and a polite curiosity for Italy and the Italians. Indians have been educated by the English for five generations, who instilled in them the conviction that Europe is constituted by a powerful, immense and industrious England. The Italian prisoners were the first to generate doubts in the Indians, although absolutely involuntarily, they contributed to the slow liberation of India from English superiority".

As a farewell, the Italian prisoners created an unusual monument which today stands at the YOL Cantonment. The narration under is as follows:

BORN TO BE FREE

The rather uncommon stone relic was made by the Italian prisoners housed in the YOL PSW camp from 1941 to 1945. That topmost pair of stones are symbolic of Man's unsatiated thirst for freedom, depicted here as a pair of wings of a bird, struggling to free itself from captivity. The rest of the structure represents prison walls.

This beautiful idea enshrines the tribute which this band of Italians, although captives, left behind, this emblem of the human spirit, for posterity, to uphold and emulate.

To this day it stands undisturbed by fellow soldiers, and spared even by the unforgiving fury, of both nature and time.

There are two other monuments: one, a large size worn-out shoe, representing hard work, captioned "I am a soldier and defending my Nation is my Dharma". The other, a little above, is a vast beautifully constructed stone remembrance wall in the Rajput chattri style. It is titled 'Shraddha-Tara' and stands "in memory of the gallant martyrs of the Rising Star Corps, who set out to serve the Nation's cause but did not return." Both were renovated in 2015.

The Italian Prisoner of War camp in those days was located in a wilderness with no village or landmark to give it a name. Ultimately, following the recall order post the war, the Italian prisoners returned home, but the village and the cantonment, is now known as, YOL!

The Italian prisoners have published some books (in Italian) about their prison experiences and displayed relevant pictures of their work and the monuments they built. It is not known if any of the soldiers ever returned to visit the area they helped name – YOL!

In a way, aren't we all lovers of mountains; 'prisoners of the Himalaya'– always thinking and dreaming about to this great range, and some of us do manage to 'escape' to the Himalaya, to return soon!

Note: Quotes from Marizza, Giovanni, *Ten Thousand Italians forgotten in India The fascist Republic of Himalaya 1941–1947,* in Italian translated into English.

The Himalayan germ, once caught, works inside like a relapsing fever; it is ever biding its time before breaking out again with renewed virulence.

Once a man has found the road, he can never keep away for long. It is certain you will return.

We become Prisoner of Himalaya

– *Peaks and Lamas,* by Marco Pallis.

Monument created by the Itailan prisoners at Yol Cannt. (Geeta Kapadia).

10

Ramblings in Chhota Bangahal

Kullu Valley

No scenery, in my opinion, presents such sublime and delightful contrasts. Below lies plains, a picture of rural loveliness and repose; the surface is covered with the richest cultivation irrigated by streams which descend from perennial snows, and interspersed with homesteads buried in the midst of groves and fruit trees. Turning from this scene of peaceful beauty, the stern majestic hills confront us; their sides are furrowed with precipitous water-courses; forests of oak clothe their flanks, and higher up give place to gloomy and funereal pines; above all are wastes of snow, or pyramidal masses of granite too perpendicular for the snow to rest on.[1]

The Dhaula Dhar range, from its junction with the Pir Panjal range, proceeds east-northeast, defining the Ravi and the Beas river watersheds. The range meets the Bara Bangahal ridge and continues northeast till Dainasar peak (4602 m) at the foot of which lies the historic Dainasar lake. This part of the range is crossed by the old Bajauri pass to a point below the Sari pass to form a boundary between Bangahal and Kullu. From Dainasar peak, the range takes an almost 90-degree turn to the north to be called 'the Beas Kundi Dhar' and ends near Taintu pass or Mukerbeh peak. Down below in the plains, the road from Mandi to Kullu-Manali also takes a sharp northerly turn, almost parallel to the range.

This range was recognised by General Cunningham, in his account of *The Great Mountain Chains of the Punjab* as the first part of the chain which designates the outer Himalaya.

1. Mr Barnes, on Dhaula Dhar and Chhota Bangahal in *Gazetteer of the Kangra District*, Part I, Kangra (1883–84) p. 9.

"Geography makes history all the world over, and nowhere is this more palpably true than in the Himalaya", wrote Captain Todd, mentioning legends and history of the Kullu, Mandi and Kangra kings who ruled the states of the region.[2] As the history stretches into centuries it is futile to recall all the kings and rajas, but some salient aspects of the history of these high valleys explain few events.

One of the many valleys ruled by Kullu rajas was the Bangahali kingdom. Today, little is known about how these valleys were given the unusual name of Bangahal. The *Gazetteer* mentions that 'progenitor of the family (that ruled Kullu) is stated to have been one Behangamani, brother of a Kulu princ ... whose family ruled for eighty-seven generations till deposed by the Sikhs in 1840.' The 'Behangamani' dynasty was the origin of the title Bangahal. The history of the Rajas and princes is too complicated to be of any use for those interested in its mountains.[3]

Just as several queens were beheaded in European history, the Bangahali kingdom has a history of many queens forced to perform 'sati' (self-immolation on the funeral pyre the husband). "To these instances of cruelty may be added others, fairly numerous according to tradition, where queens were condemned to be buried alive on the faintest suspicion of infidelity". [4]

We can safely get away from this gory history with an edict from Mr Louis Dane (former commissioner of Kullu and the one who pioneered the Pin-Parvati pass trail to Spiti). He writes that "there is a large flat stone below Nagar in rice lands which was used as place for decapitation, and according to all accounts it did not often remain long unused".[5]

The Bara Bangahal (larger Bangahal) is an enclosed valley covered by high ridges on three sides, where a passage is possible only through a high pass when it not snowbound. The Ravi river originates from many large and small glaciers in the valley and drains west to Chamba, cutting a deep

2. Bruce, Lt Col. The Hon. C G, *Kulu and Lahoul,* Edward Arnold, London, 1914, p. 203.
3. *Gazetteer of the Kangra District, Part II,* Kulu, Lahul and Spiti (1899), reprint Indus Publishing Co, New Delhi, 1994, p. 16.
4. *Gazetteer of the Kangra District, Part I,* Kangra (1883–84), reprint Indus Publishing Co, New Delhi, 1994, p. 28.
5. Ibid., p. 28.

gorge. Till date no route exists here other than a scary foot track high above on the walls of the gorge.

To the south of the Bara Bangahal wall is the Chhota Bangahal, (smaller Bangahal), drained by the river valleys of Uhl and Lambadag. It contains several villages with Kothi Sowar (present day Kothi-Kud) as the principle village. Pirthi Pal, the last raja of Bangahal was treacherously murdered at Mandi by his father-in-law, Sudh Sen, Raja of Mandi. That was the end of a separate kingdom, and Bara, Chhota and Bir Bangahal became parts of the kingdoms of Kullu, Mandi and Kangra.[6]

Chhota Bangahal has several valuable metal and ore mines. The early *Gazetteers*, in 1882–83, mention eight iron mines yielding 90 'mounds' a year. The mining extended for several kilometres along the banks of the Uhl river. In 1858, some of the ore from these mines was sent to England and was found to be as excellent as the product of the best mines of Sweden. In the lower valleys there were salt mines at Drang and Komadh.

The legendary soldier-mountaineer Lt Col The Hon Charles G Bruce was one of the first mountaineers to travel in Mandi and Kullu in 1912, with his wife and 'Fuhrer' (oh, no, this was far too early for Adolf Hitler, he was accompanied by a Swiss guide named Heinrich Fuhrer!). Being on leave, Bruce travelled leisurely through the foothills observing the Dhaula Dhar and Bangahal range. He complained though, "How often I felt like the retired colonel who used to engage a bugler to play the *reveille* outside his door every morning at six o'clock, and then cuss him freely and go to sleep again."[7]

In 2004 I had been to the inner parts of the Bara Bangahal.[8] Quite rightfully scared to cross the Ravi gorge, we exited by challenging the Nikora pass to Kugti and making a long trudge to reach Chamba. Now, nine years later, in September 2013, I was back. This time with two companions, Kanu Pomal (69) and Vijay Kothari (70), older, but fitter than 68-year-old me!

We decided to explore the charms of Chhota Bangahal. At first, we entered the Uhl river valley from the Baragram to Thamser pass, quite literally crossing thousands of sheep returning from higher pastures. A gaddi

6. Op. cit., *Gazetteer II*, p. 20.
7. Op. cit., Bruce, p. 2.
8. Kapadia, Harish, 'Bara Bangahal: The Land of Passes', in *Into the Untravelled Himalaya*, Indus Publishing Co., New Delhi, 2005, p. 149.

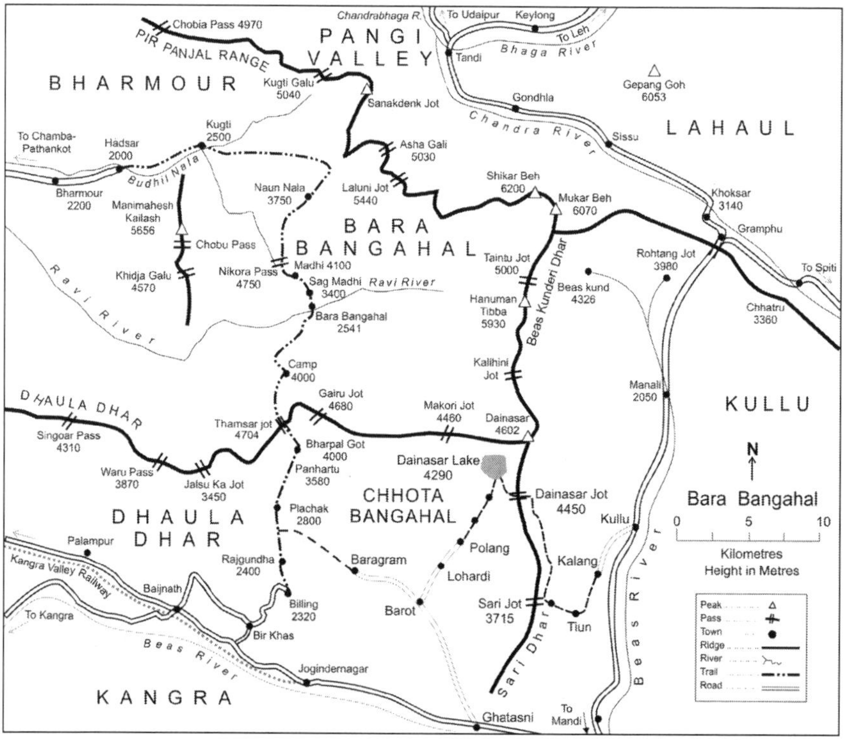

Bara and Chhota Bangahal.

coming from opposite direction will delay your walk as they always have the right of passage! It rained every evening but not enough to be threatening. We discussed a plan of traversing from the high pastureland of Panhartu to Lohardi over a high route. It proved impossible to get a guide who would lead us over the complicated maze of valleys. Returning to Rajgundha (2450 m), the former seat of the Bangahali kings, we enjoyed few days at the lovely forest rest house and explored a two-day walk across the high ridge in the west to the hot springs at Tarwani, at the foot of Jalsu pass.

We retreated to Baragram (2370 m) and by bus to Barot. Barot with Multhan, across a bridge, is developing into a tourist resort for vacation hungry people from the plains. Trout fishing here is in plenty. Now we entered the Lambadag river valley. Lohardi (6 km) was large village, but due to a hydro project, the road carried on ahead till the foot of Polang. As we stood on the road with all our luggage, some ladies returning home enquired, and went out of their way to help us to get mules organised for our trek. At head of this valley were the Gairu Jot (4680 m) and Makori Jot (4460 m) passes crossing into the Bara Bangahal because of which the traffic of returning gaddis continued. On the west, near the villages of Chherna and Shatyar, is a beautiful forest rest house which many shikaris and trout fishing parties have enjoyed.

While they were helping us, the ladies narrated the legend of Dainasar lake where we were headed. The lake is at 4290 m and on the divide between Chhota Bangahal and Kullu. Once a year in September the locals make a pilgrimage to it for a ritual bath associated with fertility. The legend tells of a man from Polang who reached the lake having left his pregnant wife at home. While taking a dip in the lake, he prayed for twins and deposited two golden earrings as offering. His wish was granted and after a few months, he was blessed with two boys. But then, the thought occurred to him that his wife had been pregnant even before he went to Dainasar, so the gods had not played a major role at all! So, he went back to the lake to reclaim the gold earrings. He found them easily enough but they were blood red in colour – and then reached home to find the twins dead. Since then, Dainasar lake is a place for fertility prayers, even if you have not taken any action before going there! However, the true importance of the lake and the peak lies in its location at the end of the Dhaula Dhar knot, where the Kullu range starts.

On 3 October 2013, we walked leisurely through Polang observing activities and the three-day celebrations of Mahatma Gandhi's birth anniversary, which falls on 2 October. Soon we we found ourselves in wilderness and proceeded along a nala. After a camp, we crossed a bridge and from here it was a steep, 1000 m (five hours) climb, mercifully on a zig-zag trail. The mules had to be unloaded at two places so that they could cross. At the top of the ridge was the vast camping ground of Panyali Got (3320 m) but water was some distance away.

The trail continued, still climbing but now gently. As we gained altitude, trees gradually disappeared, and vast open valleys allowed for a great view. Without overly stretching ourselves, we reached Marhi camp (4000 m), one of the many possible camps before reaching the lake. That evening nature presented a grand show of clouds, fog, distant mountain views and deep valleys.

We knew 6 October was going to be a long day, but it turned out far longer than we had anticipated. At first, we climbed to the lake, a lovely bowl at foot of the Dainasar peak. There was a small temple and place to worship. There is another, higher lake up across the ridge but we chose not to visit it. Soon, we turned southeast and crossed Dainasar pass (4450 m) to the Sari Dhar in the east. This ridge descends south to Sari Jot, forming the boundary between Kullu and Bangahal. As the ridge has a steep drop, the trail proceeds in a roundabout way. The huge rock slabs near the Dainasar pass would keep rock climbers busy for months if they ever came. Soon thick fog enveloped us and the confusion began.

The mules had followed another route from the lower camp and we were to meet up at Sari Jot (3715 m). Our guide now sheepishly told us that he had not been on this trail before but had discussed it with a gaddi well before embarking. Soon we were lost and Vijay, as he is known to do, separated from the party and rushed ahead. Exposed traverses, steep rocky descents and shouting for Vijay was the order of the day. Finally, we hit the trail but by then Vijay was shouting almost halfway down the valley. Our guide showed lots of energy and finally, almost at dusk, got us all together again. We decided to wait at a safe place and eventually at about 8 pm, in pitch darkness, the guide returned with our porters, some torches and water. It was a long (13 hour) day. Tea, hot food and a tent had never sounded better.

As observed, Sari Jot and Dainasar pass are on the same ridge, which is the divide between Bangahal and Kullu, so it was a grand view of the Kullu peaks that opened out the next day. Indrasan, Deo Tibba, Inder Killa, Parvati Parvat, and several other peaks could be seen. Sari Jot, on a sharp ridge, also offered a range of 'Brocken Spectre' (see p. 14) as the strong sun of Bangahal projected us from the clouds in Kullu. To see ourselves projected in a circular rainbow and move with it is, if you pardon the pun, a moving experience.

On 9 October we descended 1500 m on a far better trail to Kullu, passing gorgeous forest and grazing grounds into a deep valley. Night was spent at Tiun and we continued our descent along with children on their way to school at Kalang, a further 1000 m down.

As we reached the road head, a *reveille* was playing in our mind, calling us to civilisation and fleshpots.

11

Mobile with a Mobile in the Himalaya

A Ringing Revolution

A revolution is taking place in the Himalaya. The slow progress of last few decades has gained momentum and lives of both villagers and visitors are changing fast. There are roads now, often extending up to the borders, deep inside the ranges. These have allowed easier access to the plains and therefore, for goods available in towns to reach villages. This development has brought prosperity at the price of the environment, with hordes of pilgrims, visitors and security forces. Everyone is using transport instead of walking across a pass to meet a relative, and that too by 'share a taxi' where you pay for a seat in an over-crowded taxi. Buses are fewer and private cars rule the road as young people with good earnings from government jobs come home to meet parents who are farmers.

Roads have brought many benefits too, for example, in the fields of education and communications. There are schools even at Milam, in the eastern Kumaun which is a five-day walk away from the roadhead, Munsiary. Many children are sent to boarding schools in the foothills to study. Children of my friends from Kumaun stay at Almora, learn computers, English and send e-mails. To arrange a trek, I can send an e-mail and the children communicate the message to their parents, who will then do the needful! Even postal departments accept 'E-mail telegrams' – you send a telegram from Mumbai, which will be e-mailed to the nearest post office and a printout sent to the village in a day or two. On an expedition to the Nanda Devi Sanctuary five years ago, most of the porters signed for their wages. Hardly anyone used their thumb impression as a signature, as they would in earlier days. There are banks at bigger villages leading to wise saving and investment – many villagers have more money than we can imagine. Shepherds sometime sell off their livestock, put the money in a bank and live comfortably on the interest that they earn.

There are hydro-electric projects so, even in remote villages, you will find lights. With it comes television and the 'Direct to Home Service' which beams a couple of dozen channels, including foreign ones. I once watched the Wimbledon finals with snow peaks just outside my window. Lifestyle changes are evident too. Educated youngsters do not want to follow goats and cows for days on end, or till the land. They would prefer to work in an office, earn a disposable income and buy requirements and luxuries. Nowadays, shepherds and farmers seem to be either from poor families or of a lower caste. The long-term impact of this remains to be seen as finally there is no substitute for meat, milk and food grain! Laws are also changing to overcome caste barriers.

There is awareness that democracy, now in India for almost 70 years, has brought. People know their rights, can talk to local officials and magistrates and elect their local Pradhan in village (Panchayat) elections. In my friends' village, a lady was elected boss in the last elections! In 1952, the election of the first President of India was challenged as ballot boxes from the remote Spiti area had not been counted. Courts ordered an election, which was held no sooner snow on the passes melted. Ballot boxes were carried for 10 days on mules to some of the most difficult areas, before the highest office in India could be legitimised.[1]

However, we do not live in Pluto's Republic hence all these developments have their side effects too. Villagers now resort to costly court cases to settle disputes instead of looking for amicable solutions at home. Education and the desire for prosperity are accompanied by frustrations caused by a shortage of jobs and relative poverty in comparison with people in the plains. This is the basis for the 'Maoist movement' in these areas. On a trek in Kinnaur I could see so-called development happening around Chhitkul. Hotels and guest houses were coming up. That afternoon there were a few buses and at least thirty cars that brought tourists. Little dhabas were springing up. Sangla

1. Sharma, Parmananda *Men and Mules on Mission of Democracy*, Asia Publishing House, Bombay, 1960.

was also witnessing hectic development to cater to tourists. It was the same case in other small or remote villages which had any tourist potential.

Technology has always been part of Himalayan expeditions, used by many climbers in various forms. Satellite phones, wireless walkie-talkies and internet at the Everest base camp have long replaced mail-runners. I remember a senior bank executive on a conference call with New York from the Tibetan plateau while yaks were grazing around him. Sir Chris Bonington has, for many years now, carried several gadgets on our lovely expeditions. At base camp he would set up e-mail accounts for all of us, imploring us to rush to his shaded tent to check the latest scolding we had received from our wives! One of earliest computer lessons that I received was at the base camp of an expedition to Kinnaur where Chris enthusiastically started teaching me how to print an address on an envelope – after ten failed attempts, I ultimately wrote it out by hand. Almost two decades ago, he was working on a computer at a roadside dhaba while women were carrying fodder and water home. Perhaps a difference of a generation! But it took little less than a decade for the villages to catch up. Now the 'reverse swing' is taking place as the villagers are into these technologies in a major way and are highly technologically literate.

MOBILE WITH MOBILE

Of all the revolutions, a not so silent one is the increased telephony deep inside the valleys. In fact, this year a climber talked from the summit of Everest on a cell phone (popularly known in this part of the world as a 'mobile')!

Instead of laying wires for landline connections in these remote Himalayan villages, the Indian government created a policy that allowed any company to erect mobile towers in different valleys. These towers would provide telephone facilities in these remote areas without the hassle of laying wires. Suddenly villagers, who had never seen or used a telephone, saw a paradigm shift in their lives and went straight into the mobile age. With such connectivity they learnt to use internet and other facilities such as short messaging services (SMS) and, thus, remain in contact with their loved ones down the valleys. Villagers, school teachers, temple priests, shepherds, for that matter anyone living in the valleys has a mobile phone, which is rather cheap in India and has good connectivity. We are witnessing a mini revolution, surrounded by mobile towers, television dishes, electricity and other modern amenities, high in the Himalaya (ugly mobile towers breaking pristine Himalayan views, notwithstanding). Himachal Pradesh is particularly well served by telephone networks as they had a minister from this state in the central government few years ago, who looked after communication portfolio!

Imagine how things have changed. A decade ago, I had to write a letter to my porters at least a month ahead, to fix a place where they could meet me to start the expedition. Now I call the leader on his mobile a week before I leave. His wife tells me that Harsinh has gone to the field, but that she would call him. She dials another mobile number, using a neighbour's mobile and he comes running! Everything is arranged, and we decide to meet at a remote village in the northeast. Instead of deciding on a fixed address we agree that once there, we will connect on our mobiles to coordinate!

Here is a charming example to illustrate what I mean:

We were camping in centre of Janglikh village at 2650 m. This was the end of civilisation in the Pabar valley as there were no villages beyond this. We had travelled from Shimla to Rohru and had driven on a narrow track to Deudi. After a short trek we reached Janglikh with a traditional temple in the Kinnauri style dominating the landscape. The village had a fairly large school as well.

In the evening we came across some ladies in traditional Kinnauri dress climbing above the village with purpose.

"Where are you all going?" we asked.

"To the STD booth" they replied with a smile. In India, the STD (Subscriber's Trunk Dialling) booth is a telephone centre from where you can call nationally and an ISD (International Subscriber's Dialling) is a facility to make international calls.

"Do you have an STD booth so high up in a remote place like this?"

"Come with us, we have the mobile", they laughed.

Above the village, overlooking the approaching valley was a small ledge. The villagers had discovered with experience that, keeping their cell phones at a particular angle at this spot improved connectivity so that they could make calls to anywhere in India or abroad. We saw them merrily chatting with family and friends lower down in the valley and for that matter anywhere in the world. We too learned the technique of standing at a particular spot while making telephone calls and talking.

The next afternoon I met a chirpy girl named Minu in Tagnu village. In an hour we had become friends and she began to ask several questions about life in a city, facilities and what she could expect. I told her about television, telephones, education, transport, water supply and lots of people. She thought for a while and said laughing, "we have all these things here, only instead of people, we have trees". My British friends teased me calling me 'Casanova Kapadia' at this interaction. In India, an elder is called 'uncle'. To give the term more respect, a 'ji' is added as in 'uncle ji'. To the great amusement of my friends I was addressed as 'Kapadia ji'. I had arrived at threshold of a mature age!

We trekked towards Buran Ghati, the pass leading into Kinnaur. After making a camp near the foot of the pass, by noon we were standing at Buran Ghati (4724 m). Immediately, mobiles were brought out, for at this height, we could get mobile signals from Sangla. Many of us could talk and send messages, much to the amazement of our friends in India and abroad. We descended over ice and after a camp reached Sangla in the centre of Kinnaur.

We drove back via Sarahan and Shimla. We travelled in two taxis, one filled with our luggage and the other with us, all talking with a great satisfaction of a trip well made. As we visited the Mahakali temple at Sarahan, several processions of devtas filled the streets to the main temple. People were dancing, priests leading the way and, followers talking on mobiles! By late evening it was dark and the taxi with our luggage had still not arrived. But no cause to worry, for the driver had a mobile and informed us of his whereabouts every half an hour.

Being mobile with a mobile has its advantages and may I add that despite mobiles and other development, these valleys are still enchanting, beautiful and people welcoming. As we had left Tagnu village, Minu asked for my phone number, which I wrote down. "What is this number, it looks weird". She could not understand it because it was a landline number in Mumbai, and she was familiar only with mobile numbers!

Looking seriously at me she asked, "Don't you have mobiles in cities? We have many here."

More such experiences were to follow on my trek with British friends in the Garhwal. Visiting the holy Hindu shrine of Badrinath, we could see mobiles being used everywhere. Inside the temple priest was performing a special puja – for an old gentleman in Delhi who was listening to the proceedings live through a mobile held in the inner sanctum. We had a private audience with the traditional high priest. He ran a school next door, there was a temple where a pre-recorded discourse was being played on a Bose sound system, and there was a community screen to show religious DVDs to aspiring students. We discussed history and the year centuries ago, that, his predessor, Adi Shankracharya would have crossed Mana pass into Tibet, if at all. As we had different points of view, out came his laptop on which he checked ancient Hindu texts which had been scanned and recorded there. Not finding the answers, he picked up his mobile and referred to his library in Delhi! That's the synthesis between traditional thought and modern facilities in the remote Himalaya – the best of east and west!

We were at Auli, a ski resort above Joshimath. Mobiles signals could be recieved only at a point about a kilometre away. Mark Higton, immediately left for the spot with his mobile registered in England but operational here, in front of Nanda Devi. He called the London Police department. The call was diverted to an operator in Scotland. Giving his credit card number, Mark paid the fine for a traffic violation in London, to avoid penalties – it was the last day to do so. At the end of it all, the Scottish operator murmured in amazement, "No one has paid us traffic fines from the high Himalaya, sir!"

12

A Peak, a Pass and a Monastery

Hanle – Hangrang and Gyundi

A WINTER JOURNEY TO HANLE AND CHUSHUL

'We have landed at Leh airport. For your kind information, the outside temperature is minus 10 degrees centigrade.' This was the customary announcement by the airhostess. Passengers rushed to their baggage to pull out and put on warm jackets without waiting to hear anything further. This was in the first week of April (2011) and an exceptionally cold day with strong winds despite bright sunshine outside.

The bazaar was empty, and so were the hotels. One could not imagine that in two months it would be crawling with tourists and there would be no place to stay. But this late winter season had its charms. Very clear views, sharp light, yellow poplar trees swaying in the breeze; and the cold made it enjoyable to walk fast through the empty streets.

After acclimatisation, the three of us (Harish and Geeta Kapadia and Aparna Joshi) left by a sturdy car towards southeast Ladakh. The first stop was at Nyoma for lunch. Life here was as usual with children going to school as if it were summer. These areas are often in the news as borders with China are not properly defined here and there is always talk of intrusion by the Chinese. The airstrip at Nyoma had recently been made functional. We went past the turn to Chumar and after driving for two hours reached Loma, which is situated on the Indus and is a major bifurcation. The road proceeding along the Indus on the left bank leads to the last Indian village on the Chinese border at Demchok. Across the Indus there is another Demchhok in Chinese territory, which tourist can enter with permits from Tibet.

Across the Indus to the south, a good, tarred road led to the vast Hanle plains. We saw quite a few skyangs (wild donkeys), unperturbed by our intrusion. Finally, we turned south, skirting a hill to reach the small and scattered Hanle village. The only place to stay is the Astrophysics Laboratory guest house. This is a major study centre and has scientists staying round the year.

In the morning we looked back and saw the magnificent site of the Hanle monastery perched on a hill. It is an imposing structure but as we found out later, it is empty inside and crumbling. Hanle has a long history.

There is a fine monastery here (*Hanle*) built on a summit of a steep hill which rises abruptly out of the plain. The Hanle plain is about 6 or 8 miles in diameter. Several streams, very tortuous and sluggish, wind over its surface. These were frequently three feet or more in depth, and contained multitudes of small fish, a species of carp.

The streams all converge to a point at the north-east end of the plain, and, uniting into one continue their course down an open valley in a northerly direction towards the Indus. It can scarcely be doubted that it (the plain) has at one time been a lake, which gradually silted up.[1]

Alexander Cunningham called the Hanle plain, Hanle Tso (lake) and described it as the 'largest sheet of fresh water in Ladak.'[2] These wetlands were full of birds and wildlife. According to Rishad Naoroji, a wildlife expert, the wetlands have now dried up and hence there is huge depletion of wildlife. During his many visits Naoroji found birds disappearing (luckily not due to hunting, as Ladakhis respect non-violence).[3]

Hanle will always hold a special place in history, due to its location.

To the south of Hanle lies the Guge kingdom, with its fort and the area of Tsaparang. Tholing Math, established by Adi Shankaracharyya is also situated here. This kingdom, and travellers from here, had a distinct influence on the monastery of Hanle. The first Christian church in Tibet

1. *Gazetteer of Kashmir and Ladak*, p. 354.
2. Cunningham, Alexander, *Ladak, physical, statistical and historical; with notices of the surrounding countries,* W H Allen & Co, London, 1854.
3. Naroji, Rishad, *Birds of Prey of the Indian Subcontinent,* Om Book Service, New Delhi, 2007.

28. On 'Col Italia'. High peaks of Rimo III (right) and Rimo IV seen.

29. Teram Sher plateau. Peak Rimo I at the centre behind.

30. Historic Jesuist church at Leh.

31. Memorial to Ferdinand Stoliczka at Leh cemetery.

32. Camp on Teram Shehr plateau, Peak Padmanabh behind.

33. Kiangs – wild donkeys at Hanle.

34. Black-necked crane at Pangong lake.

35. Hanle monastery, southeast Ladakh.

36. Monument created by the Itailan prisoners at YOL Cannt.

37. Chamba Kailash peak from 'The Jot', Chamba, Himachal Pradesh.

38. Prayers being recited by a Lama over mobile.

39. Author discussing mobile phones (S. Venables).

40. Kinnaur Kailash peak, from Hangrang pass.

41. Traditional dancers at Shailkhar, Kinnaur.

42. Hansbeshan peak from Kedar Kantha.

43. Swargarohini I, II and III (R to L) from Kedar Kantha walk.

44. Rangrik Rang from Kedar Kantha walk.

45. View from the Hangrang pass, Kinnuar. Leo Pargial peak (left) and Rio Purgial peak.

46. View from Valley of Flowers. Rataban Peak in centre and Bhuidhar pass to its right.

47. Nanda Singh Chauhan, guide with Frank Smythe during his two visits to the Valley of Flowers.

48. A young Garhwali girl working with grains.

49. The Valley of Flowers.

50. Harish Kapadia left, with Harsinh Junior and Harsinh Senior.

51. Ladies in a Kumauni carved house in the Saryu valley.

52. Camp at Devkyari. Dhodu peak behind, Obra gad.

53. Ranglana, Obra gad.

54. Villagers dancing at Devkyari to celebrate Obra Devta.

55. Priest dancing with knieves in his mouth.

was founded at Tsaparang on 12 April 1626, and it flourished for four years. Several Jesuit missionaries travelled between Agra to Tasparang across the Mana pass over the next 16 years. In 1630, the king of Guge converted to Christianity and that led to a revolution. The church was ransacked by the lama clergy and four hundred Christian converts were reduced to slavery. Many rushed to Hanle and finally to Leh. In 1631, the Jesuits sent Francisco de Azevedo to Tsaparang and onwards to Hanle. With help from the lamas at Hanle he finally reached Leh on 25 October. "In spite of Azevedo's efforts the Tsaparang mission never fully recovered".[4]

Around the same period, in about 1616, Sengge (Lion) Namgyal, the popular and powerful king of Ladakh, ascended the throne as a minor. As he grew up, he devoted himself to religion and retired to Hanle where he built what is one of the famous and largest monasteries of Ladakh. It also acted as his fort and palace. When the revolt against the Christian missionaries in Guge was at its zenith, 'the Guge king was carried off into honourable exile' to Hanle. Later Guge was under influence of Hanle as it was handed over to a younger son of Namgyal. Sengge Namgyal died at Hanle in 1642, aged 40. In 1647 the kingdom was divided between his three sons and Hanle was ruled by his eldest son Deldan Namgyal.

For the next 200 years Hanle was left in peace and became rich. All that changed in a week when the great Dogra General Zorawar Singh camped at Hanle and plundered the monastery. He went past Guge and Tasparang to Taklakot, where he was killed in battle with the Chinese. At the foot of Hanle, is a statue of Mahakala that grants any wish you may make. It was believed that the prayers of villagers at this statue led to the killing of Zorawar. Many still come to make a wish at Hanle. The main monastery is now dilapidated and as we walked past the ruins we were reminded of the past and the sight of the vast plain was magnificent. To its southeast were several high peaks – the Zongchenmo group, rising above 6000 m, with the highest marked at 6232 m. With a series of intervening hills and valleys, it was an inspiring sight as far as the eye could see.

After two days at Hanle and a leisurely visit to the monastery, we drove back to Loma. Crossing the bridge over the Indus, we proceeded north on the road to Chushul. This road goes all along the Chinese border to its east

4. Mason, Kenneth, *Abode of Snow*, E P Dutton, New York, 1955, p. 57.

and has recently been opened to visitors. Famous landmarks relating to the 1962 India-Chinese war appeared one after the other. We went over Chhaga la, a gentle pass overlooking the border to its east. On the descent from this pass, we entered the Chushul plains. We halted at the army memorial a few kilometres before Chushul. Here the memories of many soldiers who laid down their lives during the 1962 war with Chinese forces are enshrined. The Gurung and Magar hills in the east saw maximum casualties while the plains saw a valiant fight by Major Shaitan Singh who incapacitated several Chinese tanks with a frontal attack. A three-summit hill is named 'Trisul' (the three-pronged weapon of Shiva) and several skirmishes took place across valley here leading to Spanggur lake in Tibet.

The last part of our journey took us along Pangong lake, now made more famous by a recent Bollywood film. It is certainly reeling under the 'attack of tourism'. The Indian territory starts at Thukung (originally Thorung: *spiralling winds/clouds*). The drive along the lake is a pleasure in any season as peak after peak of the Pangong range emerges on the west. The blue waters of the lake and even in this season, some nangpas (Brahmni ducks) swimming in the lake, make it an attractive place. From Lukung at the northern end, Tankse is soon reached. The ancient inscriptions made by the early Jesuit travellers are still etched on the rocks. As we crossed Chang la to the Indus valley, our winter journey was over.

A FORGOTTEN PASS – THE HANGRANG

The Hangrang ridge, as we may conveniently call that mountain range on which the pass of Hangrang is situated, forms the boundary between the districts of Kunawar (*Kinnaur*) and Hangrang. As this range terminates at or close to the point where the Satluj is joined by the Piti river, this division is geographically convenient.[5]

The powerful Rampur Bushaihr kingdom extended till the Shailkhar fort at the edge of Spiti. The British built the famed Hindustan–Tibet road (HT road) through this kingdom. Built mainly for trade, it was immortalised by Rudyard Kipling in his book *Kim*. Apart from this fictional hero, most early

5. Thomson, Thomas, *Western Himalaya and Tibet: A Narrative of a Journey through the Mountains of Northern India, During the Years 1847–48*, Reeve and Co, London, 1852, p. 96.

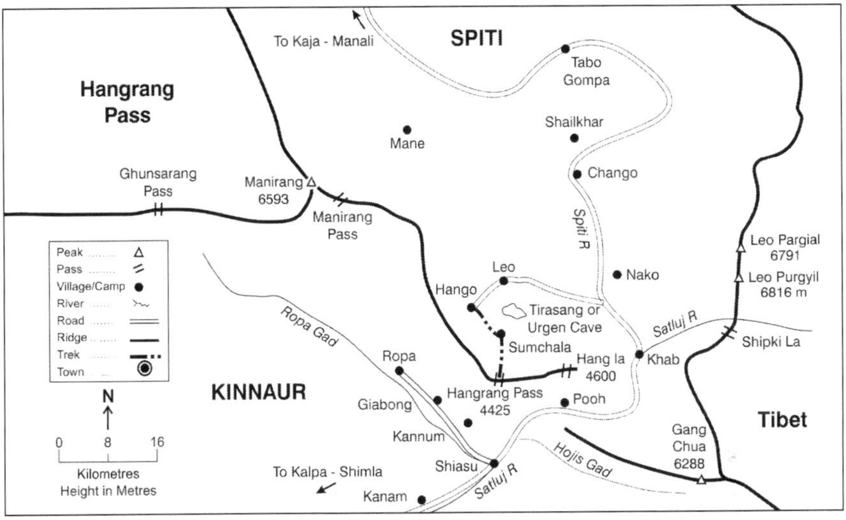

Hangrang Pass, Kinnaur.

explorers travelled along this route. The trail follows the right bank of the Satluj till Pooh village.

From Pooh, the HT road crossed the Satluj to the eastern side and climbed to Namgya, and finally crossed the Shipki la into Tibet. From here it traversed the areas in Tibet to reach Gartok (a trade centre) or Tsaparanag and Guge kingdom. Early travellers proceeded to Hanle and to Leh via this route as it avoided Spiti and higher passes. Often, parties crossed the Satluj near Khab instead of climbing to the Shipki la. The trail then climbed steeply to Tashigong before entering Tibet, a short cut. The part of Hangrang (district of the same name) on the left bank of the Spiti river belonged to the Chinese and was transferred to the Kinnaur kingdom about 200 years ago.

A trail from HT road continued further north on the right bank, from Pooh to Spiti. As the Satluj gorge blocked the way along the river, the trail crossed over the Hangrang pass (4425 m) from Sannum in the Ropa valley to the Hango valley. This pass was regularly crossed by caravans as well as famous travellers such as Moorcroft, Thomas Thomson, the Gerards brothers, Andrew Wilson and many others.[6] But again the route ahead to

6. Wilson, Andrew, *Abode of Snow*, G P Putnam's Sons, New York, 1875, p. 159; Thomson, Thomas, *Western Himalaya and Tibet*, Reeve and Co, London, 1852, p. 96; Gerard, Captain Alexander, *Tours in Himalaya*, 1886, reprinted by Indus Publishing Co, New Delhi, 1998, p. 14.

Tibet was not simple. It crossed the river near Chango and a trail led to Tibet along the Pare Chu river, to Ladakh via Hanle. These became the two major routes for travellers and traders proceeding to Ladakh and Central Asia. Many detailed and sometimes exciting descriptions are narrated in books, of crossing rickety bridges, meeting Drokpas and into Tartar villages (which was what Tibetans were called by them).

After the Chinese aggression in 1962, a road was blasted through the Satluj gorge at Khab. What used to take days could now be covered in a matter of few hours. The road was improved further, and new bridges were built. Now it is a popular 'Jeep safari' route where tourists stop on the Satluj bridge to photograph Reo Purgyil.

So it was that the Hangrang pass fell into disuse and was forgotten. Hardly anyone has crossed it in the past few decades, as the villagers also prefer to use the road. Moreover, the village of Hango district had relations with either people in the east towards Nako or to the north at Shailkhar. Thus, there was no need for them to cross this pass.

Our visit to the pass began with confusion, I dare say, caused by writings of the explorers.[7] They all mentioned starting from 'Sugnam', which is now a famous village in Spiti, the starting point of a popular trek in the Pin valley. The porters as per our instructions reached 'Sugnam' while we reached the original village which is now called 'Sunnam' (only Deepak Sanan in his useful guidebook *Exploring Kinnaur and Spiti* mentions this, correct, name[8]). Moreover, we had difficulties with porters in Sunnam and so we decided to approach the pass from the north, from Leo. The road from Leo now extends to Hango, which is situated in a green bowl and is a very welcoming village. Many explorers have passed this village.

TEA AT HANGO

Alexander Gerard who crossed the Hangrang pass in 1818 spent few days at Hango and in addition to its beauty, he describes brewing of the Tibetan salty tea.

---

7. We were a group of about 15 persons, all young and many first timers to the Himalaya, including many Gujarati Non-Resident Indians from the USA wanting to get to know the country of their families.
8. Sanan, Deepak, *Exploring Kinnaur and Spiti*, Indus Publishing Company, New Delhi, 1998.

The tea is procured from Garoo (Gartok) but it has no flavour, and is otherwise very bad. They prepare it by boiling water and infusion, as we do, but substituting for milk and sugar, salt, ghee and ata (butter and flour).[9]

With tongue firmly in cheek, Gerard quotes from from Bell's *Journey from St Petersburg, which* describes the method of preparation in detail and points out how "the kettle was wiped clean with a horse's tail", and how "the mistress prepared a paste of meal and fresh butter, which was taken out of a clean sheepskin". He approved the usefulness of the tea but added that he "should have liked it much better had it been prepared in a manner a little more cleanly". Bell adds, whether seriously or in jest; "I have given this receipt with a view that some European ladies may improve upon it."[10]

From Hango village, we reached Hangrang pass after a leisurely two-day trek. The pass offered the most magnificent view of Leo Pargial (6791 m) and the Reo Purgyil (6816 m). The first was climbed by Marco Pallis in 1936[11] and the latter stands as the highest peak in the Himachal Pradesh, towering over the Satluj gorge. To the south Jorkanden, Kinnaur Kailash and Phawrarang stood tall, making Hangrang one of the finest passes to reach for views.

As mentioned above, there were two routes to Tibet to and from this area. It is believed that Guru Padmasambhava had meditated at a natural cave below Hango before he started for Tibet along the Satluj to spread Buddhism. This cave known as the Urgen Cave (or Tirasang Cave), is about 500 m below the road to Hango, almost on the banks of Spiti river where it is joined by the Tirasang river. It is believed that one of his disciples reached and expanded the cave after a few centuries when he was attracted there. There are stones with markings and footprints. Several legends are associated with it and it is great testimony to the pure faith of simple villagers that has kept the tradition alive. As usual, apart from in surrounding villages, the cave was not much known.

9. Gerard, Captain Alexander, *Tours in the Himalaya*, 1840, reprinted by Indus Publishing Company, New Delhi, 1998, p. 211.
10. Bell, John, *Travels from St. Petersburg in Russia, to Various Parts of Asia*, Vol 1, R. and A. Foulis, Glasgow, 1763, p. 369.
11. Pallis, Marco, *Peaks and Lamas*, Cassell, London, 1939.

Finally, we reached the Bushaihri fort at Shailkhar where a monastery has now been built. The fort, if you call it that now, was a small building perched on a high ridge. It was certainly located at advantage as one could see far away ranges. In the dilapidated fort wall was a statue of a goddess covered in red cloth. Tradition has it that only woman can lift that veil, a great custom showcasing women's liberation of many ages ago! Nearby at Giu village, a mummy of a lama, believed to have come from Tibet was discovered in the last decade. It is preserved and considered a rarity in dry Spiti area.

Thomas Thomson wanted to follow a route to Hanle, linking the Bushaihri kingdom outpost of Shailkhar with Ladakh.

> A little way above Shailkhar and Chango, two very considerable rivers unite to form Piti river... The other, which flows from the north-east, may be called the Parang river (now Pare Chu), by which name it is known in the upper part of its course... The direct road from Hangarang to the Indus lies up this river, which unfortunately flows for several days' journey through districts which are included within the Chinese frontier. It was our wish to proceed by the most expeditious route, at the same time that nearest line of boundary to Hanle.[12]

However, he was stopped at the frontier just as the party of Captain Gerard and M Jacquemont little before him were. Now with borders sealed completely, these old trails from Shipki la and Pare chu to Hanle are forgotten too.

It was a trek to a forgotten pass as also a visit to a forgotten past.

INTO THE GYUNDI – ALMOST

Gyundi is a relatively large valley in Spiti, with three glaciers draining in as Gyundi east, central and west. To the east of the Gyundi is Spiti and to the west, the great Bara Shigri glacier. This valley had seen one major exploration by Joss Lynam in 1958.[13] He entered the valley from the Losar Pass (in the north) and crossed a pass to the Bara Shigri glacier, both challenging and now, being broken down, more dangerous. A few parties followed this route

12. Op. cit., Thomson, Thomas, p. 113.
13. Lynam, Joss, 'The Gyundi and the Bara Shigri, 1958', *The Himalayan Journal* Vol 21 1958, p. 58.

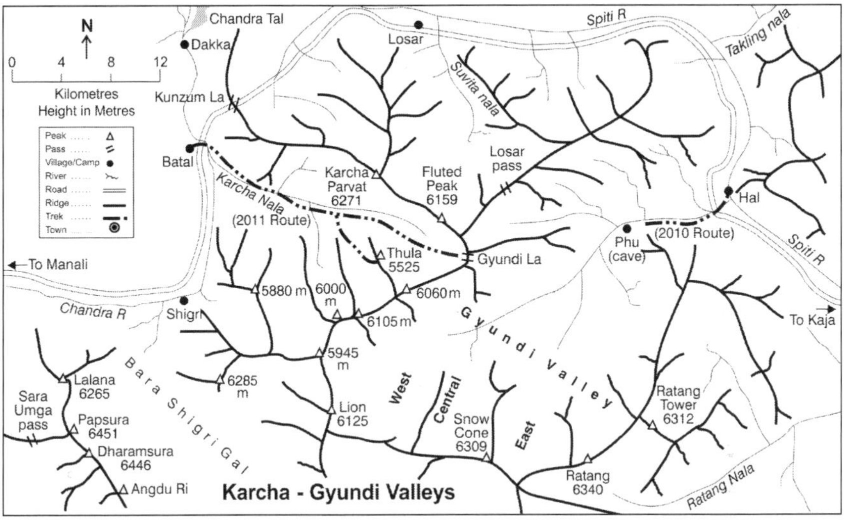

Karcha-Gyundi valleys.

but mostly only till the Loser pass (Arun Samant, 1994[14]) and climbed peaks at the border of these valleys, namely Fluted peak (6139 m).

In 1995, Kaivan Mistry and I made an attempt to cross into the Gyundi from the Ratang valley to its southeast. We could not cross the pass and later in 2010, realised how lucky we were – as the eastern Gyundi, from where we would have crossed, was blocked by steep walls on two sides and it would have been an epic struggle for us to wriggle out of it.

With the Gyundi still at the back of my mind, I tried after 15 years to enter it from Spiti, in 2010. From the village Hal, the first day was an easy walk till the point where the east and central Gyundi valleys meet. The crossing of the river here was too dangerous and we could not proceed. But we heard that the shepherds enter the Gyundi from the Karcha valley which is to its west. But here too we had to cross the Karcha nala, reputed to be a dangerous one.

In July–August 2011, three of us (Harish Kapadia, Kamal and Nandini Limdi) followed the Karcha valley, always wondering why many expeditions did not visit here. From the Rohtang pass we drove along the Chandra river, almost till its head at Batal.

14. Samant, Arun, 'A Spiti Adventure, 1994', *The Himalayan Journal* Vol. 51 1995, p. 100.

The river crossing, especially of the Chandra, is full of danger and deception. The river looks gentle and its flow appears not too strong in many seasons. But it suddenly becomes deep and carries away man or animal trying to go across. It has claimed several lives as people try to cross it to approach the Bara Shigri valley, where it spreads out in channels. The bridge is at Batal, about seven kilometres ahead and by risking a crossing lower down, one could save two days of walking to the Bara Shigri. But alas, many have lost their lives here; Mrs Guha lost her life (there is a memorial at Batal) and later an army team lost two officers while trying to cross. This is an old story too with early explorers.

> One of these bridges – at Kokser on the Chandra river, but now superseded by a wooden bridge – may have accelerated the death of Lord Elgin on his way up to Dharamsala. When crossing it, his coat was caught on the birch twigs; and his progress being thus arrested, he was unable to go over it with that continuous, but not too rapid motion, which is the safest way of dealing with such a passage. To delay on the bridge of this kind, swinging in the wind, is trying to the strongest nerves; and I know, on excellent authority, that the position in which he was thus placed had probably some effect in aggravating the heart disease from which the Governor-General died not many days afterwards.[15]

Except for the first river crossing, the rest of the valley had no difficulties and mules could be used till almost its head.

As we turned the lower Karcha valley, a major peak of the area, Karcha Parvat (6270 m) rose. This peak was first ascended by Trevor Braham and Peter Holmes in 1955 and they gave it this name.[16] Expeditions from Kolkata climbed the peak in 1986 and 1991.[17] Since then the peak has been climbed a few times. The Japanese team (2010) climbed the unnamed peak 6065 m south of Karcha Parvat and while we were there, another Japanese team (2011) climbed Peak 6105 m and named it 'Chemma peak' (meaning twins in Spiti language).

In three days, we reached the head of the Karcha valley with great views of Karcha Parvat, Fluted peaks and many unnamed peaks around. There were

---

15. Wilson, Andrew, *The Abode of Snow*, G P Putnam's Sons, New York, 1875.
16. Braham, Trevor, *Himalayan Odyssey*, Allen & Unwin, London, 1974.
17. *The Himalayan Journal*, Vol 44 1988, p. 106 and Vol 49 1993, p. 229.

no difficulties till here except the first river crossing and our mules reached easily. The pass to Gyundi was not too difficult, except that it required a 12-hour day to cross it as otherwise mules would not find grass to survive. As we were about to do that, a freak storm deposited snow on the pass and to cross it now we would have to wait at least three days for snow to clear, time we could ill-afford – Gyundi was still to remain a mystery for me, though we know the route now.

Not wasting time, we changed valleys and climbed into one to the south where the highest peaks of the valley are located; 'Chemma', 6105 and 6065 m and two other peaks above 6000 m. On 6 August 2011, we climbed steep scree slopes to reach a point 5525 m (18,125 ft) which we named 'Thula' ('great person' after Lynam who was first to explore this area.) From the top we had terrific views and Dr and Mrs Limdi, who had climbed their first peak in the Himalaya, were moved to tears.

On our return, we were unable to cross the Karcha nala, as all the snow bridges that earlier parties had written about had been washed away – another visible effect of global warming. We stayed a night on the left bank of the Karcha nala and early next morning we crossed over to Batal to face our major difficulty – the usual irritating traffic jam on the Rohtang pass (it takes almost 6 hours to cross this small patch) and later, after a torrential downpour washed away bridges and roads, we spent 15 hours on the drive from Manali to Chandigarh.

Enough excitement for two weeks, but there are peaks in the Karcha valley to keep climbers busy for a month or more.

But risk we must, because the greatest hazard in life is to risk nothing.
The man, the woman who risks nothing does nothing, has nothing, is nothing.

– Anonymous

13

A Road Much Travelled

Treks on Trails by Early Explorers

I shall be telling this with a sigh
Somewhere ages and ages hence:
Two roads diverged in a wood, and I -
I took the one less traveled by,
And that has made all the difference.[1]

Kim looked through binoculars. He was awestruck and said to his companion Lama:

"Surely the Gods live here!" said Kim beaten down by silence and appalling sweep and dispersal of the cloud-shadows after rain. "This is no place for men."

(Today the wise Lama with Kim would have lowered his binoculars and quietly said, 'Look down a little. Tourists also live here. This is a place for men too!')

"Who goes to the Hills goes to his mother." They had crossed the Siwaliks and half tropical Doon, left Mussoorie behind them and headed north along the narrow hill-roads. Day after day they struck deeper into the huddled mountains, and day after day Kim watched Lama return to a man's strength.[2]

---

1. The Road Not Taken' is a poem by Robert Frost, published in 1916 in his collection *Mountain Interval.* It is the first poem in the volume. The title is often misremembered as 'The Road Less Traveled', from the penultimate line: 'I took the one less traveled by'.
2. Kipling, Rudyard, *Kim,* Macmillan and co, London, 1901.

This is Rudyard Kipling's legendary novel *Kim*. Kim, a young boy, travels the Hindustan–Tibet road through Shimla and Kinnaur, going through much hardship and finally reaches the present-day border between India and China. Travelling the road in 2008, I wondered what Kim and the wise Lama would have seen today. I have been visiting Spiti and Kinnaur since 1983. Even 25 years ago this was the road 'less travelled by', but today it is the road *much* travelled on, may be even much too travelled.

ON THE ROAD WITH KIM
(if he were travelling today)

Kim spent a day at Shimla with Lama. He found it too expensive to get a decent hotel room – it was peak tourist season after all. They hired a taxi and drove to Narkanda and descended to banks of the now turbulent Satluj. Passing the hot and very crowded Rampur-Bushahr they were soon going past Zhakri village.

"What is this?" Lama exclaimed. "The Satluj has disappeared; its entire course is dry. Look all the stones in its bed can be seen." Confused and shocked they halted the taxi at Jyuri for a tea break. "Nothing to worry, this is not curse of God as you say. This is because of the Naptha–Zhakri project. From Naptha village up stream, the Satluj has been diverted through tunnels into the mountain side. After running its course inside, where large generators are set up, water is released back to the original course of the river at Zkakri. Inside the mountain, at several stages electricity is generated. This is one of the largest power projects in the Himachal state, entirely undertaken by Indian engineers." All along the route, instead of wilderness and rocks Kim observed a two-lane highway, large colonies of residential buildings for the engineers and several taxis parked at every junction.

"Air and water are good, and people are devout enough, but the food is very bad," Kim growled, "and we walk (rather drive) as though we were mad – or English."

"We have to rush to Kalpa to find a good hotel", wise Lama advised. Soon they were settled in one of the many hotels in this crowded town. They spent a lovely evening with many Indian tourists, enjoying the view of the Kinnaur-Kailash range while sipping expensive beer. They were careful to observe and note everything for that was their main mission – spying for the British

Empire. Next day, starting early, they visited the Kanam monastery located in the first major valley to the west. It was a steep ascent to the village – but no problem – a fair-weather road now led to the village, in fact into every major side valley. Csoma de Koros, the Hungarian scholar had spent many months in seclusion and quiet at Kanam. He had deposited many priceless books at the *Kangyur* (library) nearby. As Kim spent few moments there, admiring the view, three trucks arrived with their usual noise and pollution and were quickly loaded with apples to be transported to markets at Chandigadh. The export of this local produce had brought much prosperity to the area.

Permits were checked at the Jangi check post. To obtain a permit from officials at Kalpa/Rekong Peo, foreigners were required to be part of a group of four. Kim could have been denied entry but Lama knew the check post officer and took him aside to do the needful – after all Kim, though he was English, looked like an Indian. They were nearing the climax of their journey. Ahead of Pooh, at Khab, the Satluj enters India from Tibet and the Spiti river joins the Satluj. Kim and Lama climbed up from the Khab bridge, by taxi of course, to reach Namgya, the last village on the Indian side. They could see the Tibetan plateau, but they were not allowed to proceed further as they did not possess the 'Trader's Pass' required to go to Tibet even temporarily. But they had made their observations by now, as demanded by Huree Babu and the mission was complete. Not wanting to arouse suspicion of the forces there, they decided to play volleyball with the troops that evening. And that's where we leave them – enjoying the game!

The road from Khab has to be seen to be believed. High rocks have been blasted and the road passes under several overhanging cliffs. But the view down into the valley of the Satluj is exceedingly gloomy and oppressive; on seeing it, another traveller, Andrew Wislon wrote: "this is Valley of the Shadow of Death, I fear no evil; for Thou art with me ..."[3] Behold, what is that procession in the valley of death? Suddenly in front of us 11 taxis appeared, driving down from Spiti. This was group of foreigners on a Jeep safari from Leh to Shimla via Spiti! They had packed lunches, attendants and expensive cameras which they flashed immediately on seeing the terrific cliffs and the Satluj. How civilised was what we thought.

3. Wilson, Andrew, *Abode of Snow,* (first published 1875) Reprint, Ratna Pustak Bhandar, Kathmandu, 1979, p. 84.

ON THE ROAD WITH MARCO PALLIS

The road climbed up in loops, which are known as the Kah loops after the village at the top. Nako was the highest village and had the only hotel en route. We had sumptuous meal of *dal-bhat*. The friendly hotel owner pointed out a small lake in front. This is where Marco Pallis had camped in 1933. 'They could not drink Coke, as my hotel was not started then", he said with a chuckle. Theirs' was a two-member team from England – Marco Pallis and Charles Warren – who had travelled in many valleys in Sikkim, Gangotri and Kinnaur. They had made the first ascent of Leo Pargial from Nako,[4] visiting the Khunnu and Labrang villages on their way up. These villages have relations with Spiti and are known for their artistic works in silver. Marco Pallis had met a jeweller at Labrang who hailed from Sugnam. He showed them rare pieces of art in silver. Today, observations by Pallis on such artistry sound very true: "The extinction, under the pressure of the modern industrialism that is overrunning the Orient, must be regarded as a social, no less than an artistic, disaster."

Soon we were at a point which has, *unluckily,* not changed, at least for last 30 years since I was first here. The Malling nala landslide blocked the road. In fact, during all my visits here I had to cross this nala at different points, always on foot, and take another vehicle on the opposite side. Road builders have not been able to conquer the force of Malling nala in the summer. But life goes on in these parts and by evening we were at the Chango rest house. Though freshly constructed, it was at a vantage point and Pallis had stayed here.

Staying in those (rest) houses, we gained additional enjoyment from being able to have regular chamber music every evening, playing viols, treble and alto, which had accompanied us so far without our having found an opportunity for using them. ... It often happened that, unperceived by us, little group of porters would gather quietly around us and listen intently. They formed a perfect audience, unobtrusive yet seeming to possess the true faculty for listening. ... We could not help recalling the words of Thomas Mace, in *Musick's Monument.* In the last chapter he speculates on the method of communication that will be used by members of the diverse nationalities there assembled. There must, so he argues, be a common language

4. Pallis, Marco, *Peaks and Lamas,* Cassell, London, 1939.

intelligible to all mankind and the only known language that fulfils that condition is music.[5]

Leaving Chango we drove the final 30 kilometres to Tabo, our first halt in Spiti. Near the bifurcation at Sumdo, a road climbed up to Kaurik, another major crossing point into Tibet where the Pare chu flows in to meet the Spiti river. In June 1945, H Paider and L Schmaderer had returned to Spiti from Tibet, where, like Heinrich Harrer, they had escaped from the British prisoner of war camp at Dehra Dun. On their return, not knowing that the Second World War was over, they decided to travel up the valley to Spiti, past Sumdo. It was somewhere in this area that Schmaderer was murdered as he travelled alone after making some purchases. The cash he carried had been seen and that tempted a rogue to kill him, the first such crime committed in Spiti in many decades. How he would have wished that there were roads and shops to buy provisions as are today![6]

Tabo, a 1000-year old monastery that contains several paintings, is a unique place. Now there are guest houses, hotels and government rest houses. Luckily Tabo and its beautiful paintings were not destroyed by invaders as it was always considered to be part of the powerful kingdom of Rampur-Bushahr.

ON THE ROAD WITH BRAHAM

After visiting the Dankhar monastery, former capital of Spiti, we approached Kaja. Visiting Spiti in 1955, T H Braham had ended his chapter with a question: "In recent years Lahul and Spiti have been closed. One is left wondering what changes will have taken place in those forbidden areas once there is sufficient stability on the borders for resumption of further travel."[7] In 1993, the inner line restrictions were lifted, giving a free access to Spiti. The road from Manali across Kunzum la is covered in hours, instead of the days it took Braham. Traffic is heavy as this is part of the tourist circuit and

5. Pallis, op. cit., p. 64.
6. 'Tabo: A Mountaineer's Destiny', in Kapadia, Harish, *Spiti Adventures in the Trans-Himalaya,* Indus Publishing Co, New Delhi, 1996.
7. Braham, Trevor, *Himalayan Odyssey,* George Allen and Unwin Ltd, London, 1974.

many supplies have to be transported to Kaja during summer months. There are many shops, mostly owned by people from the plains, and bazaar is well stocked with Indian goods, hotels and, of course, a German Bakery.

Braham had written the following about his team member:

> Hey's comments on the country were always refreshing; after a sleepless night encamped outside a Spiti village, bothered at all hours by the chatter and curiosity of the local population impounding around our camp, he peered bleary-eyed out of his tent and muttered, "Can you imagine seven years in Tibet?"[8]

Today, he could have easily spent many months here, staying at good hotels and with the notorious Israeli tourists in the next room! In winter, if he was sick, a helicopter could have been hired to get him to civilisation.

Braham had walked up to Langja, a beautiful village at the base of Chau Chau Kang Nilda (then know as Guan Nilda) in 1955. Now he could hire a taxi and drive-up there! Today Kibber (known as the highest inhabited village) and Langja are popular places to drive to and it is common to see several taxis visiting the place that Braham had climbed to. Braham today would stay at a local guest house that served pizzas, beer and many varieties of cuisine; he could watch television and in the evening, a Spiti troupe would present a local dance in honour of his party. Over the next few days they could climb the summit, with tourists observing them through a telescope. They could observe Shilla peak from the summit. Confirming their position through GPS, they would measure the height of Shilla and would be excited to find that it was far lower than thought at first.[9] As they returned to Langja, Braham would immediately rush for his luggage, flash a mobile and convey

---

8. Braham, op. cit., p. 109.
9. Shilla peak was climbed by an unknown khalasi from Survey of India in 1860. The height of the peak was calculated to be 23,064 ft and thus, this was the highest peak climbed till then. This record remained till 1907 when Dr Longstaff climbed Trisul at 23,360 ft. Later J O M Roberts (1952), and T H Braham and Sir Peter Holmes (1955) suggested a much lower height for Shilla after their observations from nearby Chau Chau Kang Nilda peak. In modern survey Shilla's height is established as 20,120 ft (6132 m) and the legend was demolished. For full details see Kapadia, Harish, *Spiti: Adventures in the Trans-Himalaya,* Indus Publishing Co, New Delhi, 1996, p. 85.

this news to the Alpine Club! Yes, Spiti is covered by mobile towers all along and higher you go, better a reception you get.

At Ki monastery lamas reciting prayers in the courtyard were busy talking on mobiles. Many youngsters, who are pressured to enter monastic life as per local traditions, now run away. They cannot remain there without mobiles and Direct-to-Home television which broadcasts 60 channels! Monasteries now have a rule, imposing a fine of Rs. 25,000 for each child who runs away. Families pay the fine and employ child in tourist industry! In the face of multiple choices in life and its temptations, prayers and ascetic life have little chance.

ON THE ROAD TO FUTURE

We were now acclimatised, and had seen Spiti through the eyes of some of the early explorers and as a tourist would see it today. It was time to do some hard work. We travelled to Sagnam, a large village now connected by road from Kaja. With roads leading in all directions from here, especially one to Kinnaur, this village is heading for status of a town very soon. We were approached by Tashi, a young boy who had khotas (sturdy donkeys). In Spiti it is only yaks and khotas that carry luggage, men are not used to load-carrying and mules/horses are only for riding. Tashi was a graduate (Bachelor of Arts) from the Kullu University but had no qualms about following the khotas, which was the only earning opportunity his family would have.

Our aim was to go south in the Parahio valley and then follow the Killung valley in the east to a pass of the same name. The pass descends to the Larang valley which would then lead us to Kinnaur. It was named Killung–Larang la after both valleys on each side.

We proceeded along the Parahio river to Thidim, making the crossing in an iron-basket on a single wire bridge. Camping at Thango we could see the Killung nala in flood. Our worst fears were confirmed when a shepherd passed our camp and informed us that the river valley could be crossed only at a great risk and that too by yaks, not khotas. Moreover, the crossing of the Parahio here was on a wire bridge which has no basket and one had to tie a harness and pull across. It was prudent to return to Sagnam, which we did via Kah village on the left bank. The view of Ratang Dru from here was stunning.[10]

We reached Mud by taxi (14 km from Sagnam) and our khotas caught up by evening. Our aim was to approach the pass from the Larang valley on the other side (where we would have landed had we crossed the pass). A walk of 8 km on the proposed motor road brought us to the entrance of the Larang valley, which we ascended from a high route, exposed at many places. By evening we were settled at the foot of the pass in a rather uncomfortable camp. The three of us reached Larang la after a strenuous five-hour climb. The view of Shigri Parvat on the northwest was a major compensation while several unknown mountains of various heights surrounded us. Our return from the camp was quick as we followed the nala which was snowbound. Continuing further, we camped at Baldar, where we had to leave the road, under construction, to Bhaba valley.

We were at the junction of three valleys; the eastern valley led to the Pin–Parvati pass to Kullu, the southeastern valley led to Bhaba pass. The motor road goes up this broad valley and is ready till the foot of the pass. The third valley, which we followed, was going south and across the Tari Khango.[11]

Crossing Tari Khango was a long grind with no difficulties and once we descended, we were in paradise, especially after the barren valleys of Spiti. Camping at the beautiful grazing grounds of Phustirang and Mulling we were distressed to see dirty camp sites and garbage left by uncaring trekkers. Two days later we were at Kafnu, where we met the road coming in from the Kinnaur valley. The Bhaba valley is thickly wooded, beautiful and is a part of the Pin-Bhaba National park. The road to Spiti has to travel about 30 km in this valley to link up with the Pin valley and Spiti. As much of the road will cut through the wooded area, permission to build it has not been forthcoming. But the people of Spiti and Kinnaur desperately want this road.

10. Ratang Dru, named after the famous peak in the Alps, is a stunning, 5960 m peak, near the Pin-Ratang valley divide. It was first climbed by Sir Peter Holmes, Trevor Braham and Rinzing in 1955.

11. Locals call this 'Bhaba pass' as, till the road is ready, this is the pass used for going to the Bhaba valley. As per the map, this pass is Tari Khango and the Bhaba pass is further west. See Sanan, Deepak, and Swadi, Dhanu, *Exploring Kinnaur & Spiti in theTrans-Himalaya,* Indus Publishing Co, New Delhi, 1998.

With fuel prices rising, they point out that it makes economic sense to build the road, which will reduce the distance to Kaja by almost 115 km. It will make it possible for local produce to reach Chandigarh markets in a day, which will be beneficial for the local economy. Local villagers voted out a legislator who was against building the road (for other political reasons – not to protect the environment!) and the new representative has promised to fulfil the wishes of the people. It is a classic conflict; men vs environment, with issues of politics, democracy and protection of nature intertwined. Soon, one more *less* travelled road will become a *much* travelled road.

Kim, Marco Pallis and Trevor Braham – all would see that the major changes in Kinnaur and Spiti have been brought by roads which are much travelled. In a way, they facilitate visits to this remote land and bring comfort and prosperity to its people. The question is, will they increase the attraction of this area or take away from it?

The Himalayan germ, once caught, works inside like a relapsing fever; it sits quietly, ever biding its time before breaking out again with renewed virulence. Dr Longstaff had warned us when we set out, "Once a man has found the road, he can never keep away for long." "It is certain you will return," had declared Professor Tucci, over supper, that evening at Namgya: to which I could only answer "Amen" in all sincerity.[12]

12. Pallis, ibid., pp. 102–103.

14

The Valley of Flowers

A Trek to the Bhiundhar Valley, Garhwal

To the southeast of the shrine of Badrinath in the Garhwal, there is a small village called Bhiundhar.[1] Frank Smythe and his team, which included Eric Shipton and R L Holdsworth, had climbed Kamet (7756 m) in 1931. Like true explorers they decided to return by a high pass instead of the usual trade route. They crossed Bhiundhar pass (5150 m) and descended into the northern Bhiundhar valley. The valley, like many valleys of Garhwal in that season, was in full bloom. With its wide meadows and lovely layout it must have appeared as paradise to them after their hard work on the barren slopes of Kamet.

To us the Bhyundar Valley will always remain the Valley of Flowers. It is a place of escape for those wearied of modern civilisation... True, it would be necessary to descend in winter to warmer and less snowy levels, but for half a year the lover of beauty and solitude could find peace in the Valley of Flowers. He would discover joy and laughter in the meadows; the stars would be his nightly canopy; he would watch the slow passing of the clouds; he would share the sunset and dawn with God.

Beyond the hills, nations might fly at one another's throats; Mussolinis rise and fall; anarchy and revolution rot the nations; but in the Valley of Flowers the only strife would be that of the elements, the only sounds the wind in the flowers, the voice of the stream, and the rumble of the avalanches.

---

1. Smythe called this village, the pass and the valley 'Bhyundar'. On the recent maps it has been changed to the correct Indian spelling, 'Bhiundhar'.

Peace and contentment were ours as we sat around the campfire. Felt rather than seen, were the peaks about us. A million stars eyed us. The voice of the mountain torrent lulled us to sleep.[2]

Smythe wrote eloquently about his time in this valley in two books, *Kamet Conquered* and *The Valley of Flowers*. Thus, a legend was born and this sleepy, obscure valley today holds a special place in Himalayan folklore. Most pilgrims visiting the shrine at Badrinath detour to visit this valley, which has now been declared a 'National Park'.

In 1996, we travelled by road from Haridwar to Joshimath (276 km) and Govindghat (18 km). September first, saw two of us trudging our way up from Govindghat (1800 m) to Ghagria (3080 m; 3 km). There were tea-stalls and many pilgrims. But they made colourful company under grey skies that were to accompany us throughout this trip. Bhiundhar village lies halfway up on this route. Originally the village was near a huge cave, hence its name (Bhui – cave, dhar – place). Despite the heavy rush of visitors little seems to have changed for these villagers. But the state of the route and places to stay certainly needed much looking after. Tetra packs, aluminium foil, bottles, plastic and other garbage littered the path. The route to Hem Kund, the well-known place of pilgrimage for Sikhs, also lies along this trail and it has heavy traffic.

Hindus had been visiting a lovely lake, at 4150 m, called Lokpal for centuries. It was believed to be the place where Laxman (the younger brother of Ram, of the epic *Ramayana*) had meditated. His other name is Lokpal, 'protector of the masses'. In the holy scripture of the Sikhs, *Dasham Granth*, Guru Govind Singh mentioned a lake with seven peaks surrounding it as a place where he had meditated in his past life. Scholar Bhai Bir Singh of Amritsar decided to search for such a place. In 1932, he visited Badrinath. He observed many Hindu pilgrims climbing up the Bhiundhar valley to Lokpal. He returned in 1936 to make further inquiries and reached this lake, which is at the foot of seven peaks, marked on the map as Saptashringi. He declared this to be the lake where Guru Govind Singh had obtained Nirvana in his past life and decided to build a gurudwara here. Havildar Sohan Singh, deputed to this task in 1939, built a small place next to the

2. Smythe, Frank, *Kamet Conquered,* Hodder and Stoughton, 1938, pp. 252–253.

ancient Laxman temple, which was expanded in 1974 and wide footpath built leading to it. Today it bears heavy traffic and is called 'Hem Kund' (lake of solace) after the mention in the Sikh scriptures. It is an important place of worship for the Sikhs. It is 6 km and almost 1000 m above Ghangria.

The Valley of Flowers is about eight km from Ghangria. As one enters the valley a vast meadow unfolds. With the backdrop of Rataban and other snow peaks it makes an enchanting sight. Flowers bloom here from August to October and the flora, a wide variety of which has been catalogued by Smythe in his books, changes every few days.

As we walked on the pilgrim trail, we met an old man. In fact, having read about him, we were looking out for the old historian of this area. He was Nanda Singh Chauhan of Bhiundhar village. Aged 82 (in 1996), he walks up to Ghangria everyday to chat with his friends. He narrated stories, telling us of his involvement in the history of this valley and his associations with legendary visitors.

After his first brief visit in 1931, Smythe returned here in 1937 with Holdsworth, and stayed for four months. Plant specimens were collected every week and sent to Joshimath for onward transmission to Edinburgh. A hot-house was created in the Botanical Garden of Edinburgh and the flowers and seeds were nurtured there. Nanda Singh and other villagers carried these specimens to the post office. He vividly remembers 'Dr Smythe' as a pucca British Sahib and talked fondly about his association with him.

"The Sahibs had a very comfortable and huge camp for months. Supplies used to arrive from Ranikhet regularly and everything was well organised."

Not surprising, I thought, for Smythe was known for his taste for the good life.

Most mountaineers have, I think, and affection for 'ruggedness' -- for toughness at all times; a pride in indifference to discomfort and in a capacity to endure in all conditions. Frank (*Smythe*) would have none of this. In face of tradition, and sometimes of ridicule, he preached his faith in 'be comfortable while you can, then stick it when you must'. So at the beginning of an expedition, we would behold an apparently unmuscular, soft and almost pauchy Capuan, appreciative of the lush hospitality of the Planter's Club at Darjeeling and blandly unconscious of such a thing as training. But we saw a different Frank Smythe once we were at the base camp.[3]

But of course Smythe dismissed any suggestions of too much comfort in this valley.

To my mind, the acme of mental and spiritual discomfort would be to live in some super-luxury hotel in the Valley of Flowers. Happiness is best achieved by adapting ourselves to the standards of our environment.

In Garhwal, I met true civilisation, for I found contentment and happiness. I saw life that is not enslaved by the time- factor, that is not obsessed by the idea that happiness is dependent on money and materials. I had never before realised until I camped in the Valley of Flowers how much happiness there is in simple living and simple things.[4]

There was talk of building a helipad and a hut in the valley when a former prime minister of India had decided to visit. Luckily wiser counsel prevailed, simply because the PM could not find time to visit !

The Valley of Flowers had another claim to fame as well. Smythe in 1937 had 'discovered' footprints of a Yeti.

But when I came up to the tracks I saw the imprint of a huge naked foot, apparently of a biped, and in stride closely resembling our own tracks. What was it? I was very interested, and at once proceeded to take some photographs. I was engaged in this work when the porters joined me. It was at once evident when they saw the tracks that they were frightened. Wangdi was first to speak.

"Bad Manshi!" he said, and then "Mirka!" And in case I still did not understand, "Kang Admi (Snowman)."

They were unanimous that the Snowman walked with his toes behind him and the impressions at the heel were in reality the front toes.

---

3. Ruttledge, Hugh, obituary of Frank Smythe in *The Himalayan Journal*, Vol 15 1949, p. 102.
4. Smythe, Frank, *The Valley of Flowers*, Hodder and Stoughton, 1947, p. 90.

In order to descend the face, the beast had made a series of intricate traverses and had zig-zagged down a series of ridges and gullies. An expert mountaineer could not have made a better route and to accomplish it without an ice-axe would have been both difficult and dangerous, whilst the unroped descent of a crevassed snow-covered glacier must be accounted as unjustifiable. Obviously the "Snowman" was well qualified for membership of the Himalayan Club.[5]

He took prints, made affidavits and prepared to shoot the beast upon his return. But the report from England declared it to be the footprints of a bear. Thank God for that. The Himalayan Club would have had a most unusual member on its rolls.

Tragedy befell a member of The Himalayan Club here in 1991. Firdaus Talyerkhan from Bombay, was a reputed lawyer and a charming person. While trekking with friends he intended to descend to the Valley of Flowers from Bhiundhar Khal. As he was standing on the pass, alone and unroped, a crevasse gave way beneath his feet. He fell into it and was wedged in the ice between the walls of the crevasse. His companions tried to rescue him by different modes for few hours and then went down towards Gamsali, leaving him alive in the crevasse. When they returned, it was to find him dead. His body was abstracted after almost two years when the crevasse widened naturally. Locals remember the incident and attribute it to supernatural forces in this valley.

The Valley of Flowers was visited in 1862 by Col Edmund Smith. In 1907 T G Longstaff with Arnold Mumm and Charles G Bruce passed through the valley. But it required Frank Smythe's botanist's eye and philosopher's heart to recognise it as the Valley of Flowers. Since then many have passed through the high passes of this valley and literally thousands visit it every year.

We arrived in the centre of the valley to a place called 'Bamani Dhaur' (cave of Brahmin). As the legend goes a brahmin sat here telling the fortunes of all visitors, drawing up their fortune charts called 'kundali'. This he did by observing shadows on the long meadow across the river. At what day and time to observe the shadow depended on the date of birth of the person and other factors. This meadow is called 'Sri Kundalisen'.

A little ahead of Bamani Dhaur is a small meadow where stands the grave of Joan Margaret Legge. Inspired by Frank Smythe's work here, the Botanical

5. Smythe, op. cit., p. 147.

Garden of Edinburgh deputed her to spend a few months in the Valley of Flowers. She arrived in Ranikhet and met the local representative of The Himalayan Club, Mr Brown. She trekked across the lower foothills with her porters, reached Joshimath and finally Govindghat on 25th June 1939. Together with her porters, Nanda Singh Chauhan had accompanied her as guide from Ranikhet and she, walking up slowly and collecting samples reached Bamani Dhaur in the Valley of Flowers. On 4th July she went up the slopes towards Khulia Garva to collect sample and slipped. She died instantly. The Ranikhet porters brought down the body and with villagers from Bhiundhar informed the local magistrate at Joshimath and Chamoli. A *thanedar* was deputed to visit the site. He ordered all the villagers to gather in the valley and made a panchnama (literally, 'record of the oberservations of five people'). While some villagers stayed with the body, a report was sent by wireless to Ranikhet and England. Legge's sister requested the body be buried in the valley. All the items Legge carried were listed and sent to England and a small grave was erected at the site. The next year, her sister visited and erected a small memorial for Legge, which stands today. It carries the inscription:

I will lift up mine eyes unto the hills
From whence cometh my help.

As this grave is the only point of reference in the valley, most visitors reach here and many believe, rather erroneously, that it was Legge who discovered the valley Perhaps, a memorial to Frank Smythe should stand in this valley for it was he who introduced Himalayan flowers to the multitude. This is what he wrote about last day spent in the valley.

Beauty, health, good comradeship, peace, all these had been mine in the Valley of Flowers. For a while I had lived simply and happily, and I like to think, indeed I know, that those about me had been happy too.

So I spent some of my last hours in the Valley of Flowers, seated by the camp fire, until flames died down and stars brightened beyond hill-tops; and all about me was the serenity of God.[6]

---

6. Smythe, op. cit., p. 286.

It was drizzling as we returned from the valley. A party, including a middle-aged housewife from Bombay, was on its way up. I tried to dissuade them from going up due to the inclement weather.

"We have come this far to see some flowers. We must see them. After all this is the 'Valley of Flowers.' And like true pilgrims, they trudged on, unmindful of any hardship."

This valley is Frank Smythe's tribute to the flowers of the Himalaya. Because of its catchy name and easy access many Indians, non-mountaineers and common pilgrims, now know that there is more to the Himalaya than shrines and snow. The valley is a celebration of Himalayan flowers.

We cannot walk or climb among mountains for long without noticing that our senses are most responsive to external impressions when the fibres of the body are working at their hardest, in harmony with the will.

(G Winthrop Young in *On High Hills*)

There is much comfort in high hills,
and a great easing of the heart.
We look upon them, and our nature fills
With loftier images from their life apart.
They set our feet on curves of freedom, bent
To snap the circles of our discontent.

Mountains are moods; of larger rhythm and line,
Moving between the eternal mode and mine.
Moments in thought, of which I too am part,
I lose in them in instant of brief ills.
There is great easing of the heart.
And cumulance of comfort of high hills.

– Geoffrey Winthrop Young
(From *The Climber's Fireside Book* compiled by Wilfred Noyce (p. 123)

15

The Valley of Friends

My Companions from the Saryu Valley, Kumaun

Some associations in life are lasting. For several decades I have been trekking and climbing with the support of people of a particular valley in the Kumaun, the Saryu valley. They have cheerfully accompanied me to most of the places where I have been in the Himalaya. Be it carrying loads, cooking or climbing peaks with me, they have served me well. Ardent travellers like me, they join me not for money but for the fun of it. As Lawrence of Arabia said about his companions: 'Most of them will fight for money, but the best of them will fight for Lawrence.' I can say the same about my friends from the Saryu valley.

A lot has been written about Sherpas and high-altitude climbing-porters. I would like to pay a tribute to these simple folks, who have not achieved much in terms of peaks and records but have certainly the capacity to take on the best of them. Many peaks would not have been climbed easily without their support. They are as good tigers as any holder of the 'Tiger Badge'.

In 1962, I was a young student on my first visit to the Himalaya. Like many, my choice was to go to Pindari glacier, a formidable trek in those days. Advised by seniors we packed our kitchen utensils in a tea-chest to keep them in shape while the rest of our stuff was packed in kitbags. We reached Bageshwar and Bharadi from where a muleteer was hired to carry our luggage on two mules. Everything went all right on the first day. However, as we climbed up to the Dhakuri pass, the utensils, since they were loosely packed in the tea-chest, were banging and clanging against each other. Suddenly, one of the mules decided enough was enough and upturned the tea-chest, littering kitchen-ware all around. Coincidently, just at that moment, a light-eyed porter was approaching from the other side and he stopped to help our muleteer to gather the utensils.

"I will hire this person to carry the utensils instead of the mule, at my expense", we were told by our muleteer. 'This person' had, by the evening, taken a firm control over the situation and us. He was Pansinh Malgunjar of Chaura village, who proceeded from there on to act as friend, philosopher and guide to us, the youngsters. From that memorable, accidental meeting, people from Chaura and nearby villages of the Saryu valley have accompanied me wherever I went.

Pansinh was a muleteer and he loved to sing. He accompanied us to Rupkund, Milam and all the treks that I undertook till 1968. Then, in 1969, we organised our first climbing expedition to Tharkot peak in the same area. Pansinh with Laxmansinh was leader of our porter team. Close to the summit we were swept down by an avalanche and Zerksis Boga almost died.[1] We spent an uncomfortable night at the last high camp. The sight I most cherish is of Pansinh and Laxmansinh climbing steadily up to the tent the next morning. Once we were in their hands, I collapsed. Slowly but surely, they brought us down. That night as we slept around a large fire without sleeping bags, Pansinh was singing a Kumauni song which, loosely translated meant: "As a bull tied to a rope in centre goes round and round, a man is tied by his desires and he keeps going round and round in this world."

After a decade of trekking, Pansinh was getting old and now could not accompany us. He promised that in his stead he would bring us his relatives when we halted briefly at the Bageshwar bus stand on our way to the Kalabaland glacier in 1979. At Bageshwar, I was surrounded by porters eager to be employed on our trip. Some produced certificates and citations from previous expeditions. I was about to take on some of them when I saw Pansinh in the distance waving at me and shaking his head – I postponed the decision.

As we sat down over a cup of tea he said to me, "These so called experienced chaps are all cheats. I know them too well. I have brought my

---

1. See *The Himalayan Journal*, Vol. 29, p. 123, for story of the Tharkot expedition. Also see Kapadia, Harish, *High Himalaya Unknown Valleys*, Indus Publishing Co, New Delhi, 1993, p. 141.

uncle's sons and their friends to join you. Take them with you, they will be most useful." He pointed to four young boys standing shyly in the distance. I took an immediate liking to them and promptly employed them. This was the beginning of another generation of associations.

One of them was Shersinh of Khaljuni village, which is a little further up the Saryu valley. He was quiet and never complained at all. In fact, whenever we said anything to him, his standard reply was, 'as you say'. Once in the Darma valley we double marched, almost 30 km per day, for four days. Shersinh was the only porter with us carrying heavy loads, but not one word of complaint passed his lips. On the third day he lagged behind. It was then that Muslim Contractor noticed that Shersinh had hurt his back, and that it was badly bruised. We immediately took time off. Shersinh accompanied us for eight years in all. But then the search for greener pastures brought him to Vapi, an industrial complex little to the north of Mumbai. Once there, his attitude changed. Of course, we did not expect him to come to the Himalaya but his greed for more and the disappearance of that Himalayan village contentment was evident. Perhaps that is what civilisation does to us!

By early 1980s, we had a large circle of climbing friends in Bombay whose children had grown up. Hence, we decided to organise a sort of camp in the Himalaya where all of us could enjoy ourselves and some could climb. The group consisted of almost 25 persons, aged 6 to 66 years – membership restricted! A contingent of porters from the Saryu valley met us at Delhi and accompanied us. In that group was Harsinh Mangalsinh (Sr) and Harsinh Balaksinh (Jr). Harsinh Sr was put in charge of the kitchen, the most formidable task on this venture. Breakfast for 25! He would start dishing out hot parathas at 7 am and would continue till noon. By then it was time for lunch! But without a murmur Harsinh Sr would continue tirelessly. Ever since that testing time he has been our chief cook and has served with distinction the likes of Sir Chris Bonington.

I have never known anyone quite like Harsinh Sr – someone almost devoid of material desires. There is nothing you can offer him that appears to tempt him even slightly. On international expeditions, the gift of the best Goretex jacket means nothing and he refuses anything that's not of use to him. Many a time, after an expedition, I have offered him all the leftover food like packed dal and expensive dehydrated foods. He would always refuse stating that they 'smell' in comparison with the fresh potatoes they eat and that no one likes them. The commercial value of the object offered never attracts him.

Once in Manali, as we walked together down the street after a long trip, I noticed fresh sweets being prepared at a stall and suggested we celebrate by feasting on them. Harsinh Sr looked at his watch – it was past noon – looked at the others and firmly passed the verdict: "It is lunch time. We will have simple rice and dal only." Typical of this man. He is unmarried and with a simple lifestyle; he has almost conquered temptation.

The junior Harsinh is another of my favourites. He is a shepherd and spends almost three-fourths of the year with his herd in the high mountains. As a result, he is the strongest of them all and carries the heaviest loads. It is a treat to see him jumping across rivers with a full load and scrambling up slopes like a goat. If there is a difficult section and I stop to look around for a track, a whistle will cut through the air and there is Harsinh J, pointing out the route from a distance. This shepherd's shrill whistle was around at the slightest hint of any difficulty. Harsinh Jr has three brothers. All have now been educated and now work at government jobs. With everyone in the family out of the village, the entire responsibility of the family, herd and fields is on him, a burden he carries philosophically. He quoted a Kumauni saying:

Pahad ka pani aur Pahad ki Jawani
Kabhi Pahad ke kaam nahin aati.

'The water and the youth of the mountains are never useful to the mountains.' (Water, because it flows down to the valley and the youth, because they leave for the city to earn.)

These hardy supporters have seen us through many different terrains. We arrange we meet at Delhi railway station for each trip and from there travel on to our destinations. They have seen Spiti, Ladakh and almost the whole of Himachal Pradesh with us. When we took a flight to get to Ladakh, we were wondering how much excitement that would produce in these porters, who were flying for the first time. As we reached Leh, a relaxed Harsinh Sr summed up their feelings: 'Good show, we reached in an hour instead of three days'. A very prosaic reaction, so typical of the man.

In 1985, I organised an Indo-British expedition to the formidable Siachen glacier. We had three Kumaunis with us. From Ladakh we employed 15 Ladakhi porters, known for their temper and reluctance to work. Three days after we entered the Terong valley, the Ladakhi porters came screaming out. Stephen Venables, who was quietly walking behind them in a green outfit, had frightened them. They thought he was a Pakistani spy! And this was as good an excuse as any to desert us! We were left standing with the entire expedition luggage a little short of our base camp and with only three Kumaunis. We started to ferry loads. Sr and Jr Harsinhs, ably supported by Paratapsinh would do a double ferry in a day. Between the three of them, they carried the entire international expedition's luggage on the Terong glacier. Pratapsinh was toughest of them all. Fair and handsome, he was reputed to eat the meat of an entire sheep, alone, in one sitting. Unlike the others, however, he was temperamental and required special handling.

On our return the Terong river was in flood. There was no way we could cross to the left bank. After an intricate rope fixing, the entire team came out climbing dangerously up and then rappelling down expertly. But the final crossing of the river remained. Our liaison officer had thrown an aluminium ladder across the torrent and as each person crossed, the ladder bent lower and lower at the centre. It almost drowned Dave Wilkinson. As I came near the crossing I saw the incident. Pratapsinh was already on the other side, while Harsinh Jr. was about to cross. I shouted to him to stop and come back. In the confusion and may be out of nervousness. he did not listen and managed to cross with great difficulty. I was furious. Trapped on the other side without food for the whole day, by the time I reached the other side after crossing the glacier from above with heavy loads, my anger had only increased. I vented my rage on poor Harsinh Jr. In response, Pratapsinh ordered a mutiny: he asked all three of them not to carry anything anymore and walked away. Harsinh Sr came forward and lifted his load, but Harsinh Jr walked away in tears. We finally managed to reach the army base camp at the Siachen glacier with great difficulty.

With my ego hurt and my anger out of control I was harsh on the two deserters. They were taken to task and even the army gave them a dressing down. Pratapsinh never came with us again; Harsinh Jr took two years to forget and forgive the incident. This was our first difference and I had failed to understand the simple fears of simple people, something I always regretted.

The one shortcoming these people have is that they do not tolerate altitude too well. Once on snow and above 5500 m (18,000 ft) they start melting. Even with a good deal of equipment and good tents they simply cannot tolerate the height. Once an entire contingent of 10 porters went snow-blind on the Pin-Parvati pass. They did not appreciate the value of wearing dark glasses. This was why for some climbing trips the Kumaunis looked after the kitchen and valley portering, but for the high altitudes we called for climbers from Manali. One of them was Pasang Bodh. He was a fine climber and the higher we went, the better he performed. But such heady stuff is not for everyone. After a few years and a few peaks, his attitude, his level of honesty and loyalty, left much to be desired and we had to call off the partnership. Too much tourist influx in Manali led the Manali porters to a more commercial approach.

Our relationship with the Kumaunis also acts as insurance. These villagers work more for the fun of it. Of course, they are paid all the expenses and normal wages, but more than that, during times of emergency they know that there are friends in Bombay who will respond. In any serious medical emergency, severe financial crisis or whenever they need us, we support them. Thus, it works out well for both of us. The area they come from is called 'Danpur' (area of generosity). The name is derived from the fact that in earlier times, whenever a traveller from Tibet was stranded in these valleys, he was looked after by the people of the villages without any charge till the passes opened once again and he could return safely. They are known to be some of the finest load-carriers amongst Himalayan porters and even Shipton and Tilman, during their explorations of the Garhwal and Kumaun, used porters from this area.

1995 was a special year for our association. During the year we climbed in Rupshu, near Tso Moriri lake in Ladakh. Both Harsinhs were flying out to Leh with us. This year, as we climbed higher, both of them seem to be taking the altitude better. Finally, we roped up to climb Lungser Kangri (6666 m). On the final slopes Kaivan Mistry led across a deep crevasse. Following him, Harsinh Sr suddenly disappeared from view. Holding him on a belay, I shouted anxiously.

'I have fallen', came a calm reply with a straight face. Soon he was up and about and with both these charming people we were standing on the second highest peak of Ladakh.[2]

The Harsinhs had invited us to visit their village many times. This became possible after many years. What better occasion than to celebrate their climb, I thought. So 1995 saw us approaching their village.

Each mountaineer has many friends who, though not mountaineers themselves, are very supportive and interested in what their mountaineer-friend was doing. Sarita and Vinnie Chaudhury in Delhi have been supporting our expeditions for many years. Large teams have been feted in their home and many a dirty mountaineer has taken the first shower after many months in the mountains in their bathroom. Vinnie has a heart as large as his stomach and Sarita has spiritual interests. So, what better group than a mixed bag of friends for a visit to the home of the Kumaunis.

We reached Bageshwar from Delhi and finally arrived at Song, the last roadhead where Harsinh Sr was waiting for us. That night we spent at Loharkhet on the popular Pindari glacier trail. The route to their village, Harkot, bifurcates from here and climbs steeply. Halfway through Diwansinh, who was accompanying us, gave a loud whistle and shouted.

"A signal to them to prepare tea and start warming the sweets as our party is arriving," he explained.

The village postman passed us, smiling. "I deliver your letters to them you know. I read them if they are in English," he told me proudly.

Soon we were there. The entire village had gathered and arrangements for our stay had been made in the village school. There was tea, followed by halva and sweet curd. The entire school was around and the children sang a welcome song.

Come evening, I saw a fit figure approaching the school, swinging his arms in the air and smiling – it was Harsinh Jr. He had been up in the hills with the goats and had walked almost 45 kilometres to meet us! We went to his house and were introduced to the family. He rolled out another round of tea and food which at first, I refused.

"This is Harsinh's swagat (welcome), you cannot refuse." It went on like this in most of the houses and by the end of the day we were bloated.

2. See *The Himalayan Journal*, Vol 52 1996, p. 86.

The next day the schoolteacher visited us – as we were staying in their school, a special holiday had been declared for the kids. He showed us an insignia from the Second World War.

"This is the badge of the Indian National Army. My father Ramsinh served with Netaji Subhash Chandra Bose in Burma." He was referring to the Indian National Army that fought the British. Bose was their charismatic leader.

"Netaji Bose stayed in this valley for six months, hiding from the British," he told me proudly.

We were to hear this story at almost every village in this valley. They showed us the place, Bhenkali, where Bose had stayed. According to the legend, Netaji had appeared in the middle of the night with two companions, Krishna Kant and Radha Kant, They were the only ones allowed to meet him and kept him supplied with essentials. Finally, one night Netaji went out of the valley and said he would not return.[3]

After a day we started on a trek going up the Saryu valley. Passing Supi village, the largest in the valley, we reached Khaljuni. This was Shersinh and Pratapsinh's village. Both were out and we could only meet their families. In the evening came a well-dressed person whom I could not recognise at first. He was Jagatsinh, who had accompanied me for three trips. Armed with some education and luck, he had joined government service as a *patwari*, a revenue official. He had always been totally squint-eyed and on an expedition, he was called 'looking London, going Tokyo', for when he looked to his right he was talking to someone on his left! Jagat always laughed at this.

The next day we approached Juni village. From the fields a worker shouted out to us. It was Charu Ram, who had joined us on a trip to Kinnaur in 1986. He was an artisan, an expert weaver and potter. We saw his work and met the family. Anywhere else his work would have commanded a good price but here, a four day-walk away from civilisation, he had meagre resources. We now left the village track and entered a forest on our way to the upper

---

3. I checked out this story with Netaji Subhash Chandra Bose's son. He wrote back to say that he was tired of such claims about his father made from so many places. For the record Bose never went to this part of the Himalaya and he did not visit Kumaun. That was end of the matter. But I never had the heart to break this news to these simple village folks. Why destroy the simple faith of these simple villagers in their simple story.

Saryu valley, camping amidst forest at Dholibita (huge rock) Rauli (small nala). An ancient temple of Sahastradhara (thousand streams) was situated here. An open ground, about 800 m above the falls is called Rikheshwar. It is believed that during the Vedic ages, the sage Vyas Rishi stayed here. A huge stone marks the site of his meditation. Everyone was in high spirits and as Harsinh and company dished out several great dishes; the happiness was tangible. Sarita busied herself in painting and observing the surroundings, Vinnie was fond of taking baths and meditating. There were campfires and chats which enlivened the group. The villagers were great company. I was learning that there was more to the Himalaya than simply trekking and climbing!

Returning to Juni village we separated to climb steeply to Bhenkali (a tank for buffaloes) where Netaji Bose had supposedly stayed. The steady but steep climb continued the next day till we were on the top of the ridge. This was Ratamati (red sand) camping ground. This ridge was called the Pankhwa dhar. On both sides of the ridge rhododendrons line the slopes. A wide vista now opened out before us, from Nanda Devi, Nanda Kot to Tharkot. In front of us was a *kutiya,* a small house built by Swami Purnanand who had stayed here, meditating for almost seven years. After he left, the place had been regularly used by other holy persons. It had a divine view for sure.

On the last morning on the Pankhwa dhar the sun rose in the clear sky. Far in the distance was Panch Chuli. It was here, in 1992, that we had been climbing with the British. On Panch Chuli V, Stephen Venables sustained a fall and was stranded high on the mountains. He needed food and supplies till a helicopter could pick him up. Steve Sustad, one of the finest alpinists in the world, persuaded Harsinh Jr to accompany him on steep ice, with a heavy load. Fitted with large size climbing boots – the toes stuffed with paper to fit his tiny foot, Harsinh Jr rose to the occasion and climbed brilliantly to help the stranded climber.[4] The British were impressed.

"We will sponsor him for a mountain training course at any of the mountain training institutes in India", the British offered.

---

4. For the full story see *The Himalayan Journal,* Vol 49 1993, p. 71. This event appears in several books and articles on the Panch Chuli Indian–British expedition 1992.

"That will be a little odd. These courses are undertaken by army officers and others. A villager will be a misfit" I replied.

"In that case we will sponsor him to do a course in England at some leading institute. He can be turned into a fine mountaineer with some training. Ask him if he will take a free trip to England for two months?"

After I translated, Harsinh Jr replied quietly, "At present I simply want to return to my village and goats. They have been unattended for a long time. Just let me go."

It was difficult to tempt these simple friends away from their way of life.

Finally, we came down and our nine-day trip was over. It had strengthened memories and enhanced our long association. It was a celebration of our friendship with the people of this valley.

All that survives of a climb is seldom more than a sediment of small incidents. In our exalted valley humour we find them as less in our glass of memory and stir them diluted into a tale with friends.

(G. Winthrop Young)

Flocks of birds have flown high and away.
A solitary drift of cloud, too has gone, wandering on.
And I sit alone with the Ching-Ting Peak, towering beyond.
We never grow tired of each other, the mountain and I.

– Li Po (d. 762)

16

An Autumn Walk to Kedar Kantha

My trek ended before it began – well, almost. My companion, Ashwin Popat, hit his knee against a railing at Taluka rest house and had to return home. Thus, I was left alone for the trek with my faithful porters and mules. This was a first for me – walking alone in the Himalaya. It was a very different experience, spending many hours by oneself on the walk and in the tent.

We started from Taluka (via Dehradun–Sankhri) and a well-made forest trail climbed steeply for next two days. But there was nothing to complain about as the forest was exquisite. I had two contrasting personalities for company: Jeet Singh, our guide, was ahead and had never even heard of a vow of silence. He poured out information about the trek, the villages and even his personal woes. If there was nothing to say he would sing to himself. Walking behind me was Harsinh, who never uttered a word unless spoken to.

On maps of almost all scales and antiquity, you will find Kedar Kantha peak marked. For several years I had wondered why so? At a mere 3812 m it is quite low by Himalayan standards. Moreover, it is named 'Kedar', after Shiva, while his abode, the pilgrim centre of Kedarnath, lies a few valleys away. We were in the Yamuna watershed and the pilgrim centre of Yamnotri was near to us. Then why was this little ridge important enough to be on every map and why it was named after Kedar?

The answers are found in local folklore. They were mystifying to me but the people of these regions believe them. The simplest explanation was geographical. Shiva descended from heaven on Swargarohini peak ('ladder to heaven'), which is clearly seen from here. He assumed the form of a bull and intended to settle on the Kedar Kantha ridge. But he could hear the groan of a cow calling her calf from Sirka village, across the Tons river and decided that the place was not secluded enough. Hence, he went to where today the Kedarnath temple is situated.

The other legend gets a little complicated. When Shiva descended from heaven to earth on the peak Swargarohini, one rung of the ladder he descended on broke, though he was unware of this. Many aeons later, the Pandavs, of the mythological text *Mahabharat*, climbed up to heaven from Swargarohini, via the same ladder. But Bhim, the strongest of the brothers, fell because of that broken rung. In anger, he went looking for Shiva. Afraid of Bhim's wrath, Shiva turned himself into a bull and ran away. Bhim chased the bull, but it buried itself in the earth. Bhim dug him out and that was right on top of the Kedar Kantha peak. He dismembered the bull in five parts and flung them in different directions. A temple was erected at each of the places where the parts fell. Thus, five temples of Shiva (the Panch Kedar) exist, one at each of these places and many make the pilgrimage to each of them.

Soon we were on the upper bugial of Pustara (3440 m). Several routes bifurcated from here: to Saru tal (lake), to Yamnotri temple and one to Kedar Kantha. Each place was at least two days away. Saru tal is known for a profusion of the brahma kamal[1], a rare, high-altitude flower that blooms during the rainy moths of July and August. As we started to traverse the ridge towards Kedar Kantha, the beauty of the entire region opened up. Above the meadows (bugials) were peaks of the western Garhwal. To north and northeast were peaks of Har ki Doon and Swargarohini. To north was the high Kinnaur range led by an old companion, Rangrik Rang, (6593 m) which we had climbed in 1994.[2] To the west rose Hansbeshan ('where sun touches first') on a ridge. Though only 5240 m, it rose sharply into the sky. It was an old friend too – I had been to the peak in the winter of 1996. Now, in the play of autumn light, every aspect of these mountains looked beautiful.[3]

1. Brahma Kamal (*Sausurrea obvalata*) and Fain Kamal (*Sausurrea graminifolia*).
2. Kapadia, Harish, 'Language of Mountains', *Meeting the Mountains,* Indus Publishing, New Delhi, 2009 (2nd edition), p. 133.
3. A very long time ago, when even the sun did not shine in the sky, the sage Ahan rishi meditated in the Himalaya. He acquired mystical powers and

The traverse to Kedar Kantha was long. But on the first night camping on a small bugial I was treated to a rainbow, changing autumn colours and distant thunder. On the second day we started climbing a ridge. Soon, and to my surprise, we were on top of Kedar Kantha with our mules and had crossed over to descend on the other side. This is not a peak but a long ridge. There were some old stones of a broken temple. But the summit offered a priceless view. From the top, seven river valleys were seen – each a major river system of western Garhwal and eastern Himachal, from the Yamuna to Satluj watersheds.

First, to my east, was the Ruinsara valley with a lake of same name and the well-known peaks of Bandarpunch and Kalanag.[4] It drains into the Ruinsara gad which soon joins the Tons at Osla. Flowing from Har ki Doon and from north of Swargarohini massif, the Tons contains waters of Jamdar gad, Hatta gad and Maninda gad.

The next valley was the Obra gad, bordered by peaks of Dhodu, Ranglana, Jairai rocks with Devkayri ground in centre. At Bhancha, Obra meets the Supin river which starts from the watershed of Kinnaur. At Netwar, the Rupin river, flowing below the villages of Dodra and Kwar merges with the Supin. And finally, the Pabar river joins the flow at Tiuni. Each of these rivers – Tons, Ruinsara, Obra, Supin, Rupin and Pabar joins the Yamuna in the plains.

In the far distance, the ridge of Chanshil Ghati was at the head of the Pabar valley. Hansbeshan (5240 m) ridge with peaks of similar heights is

---

could create or destroy almost anything. In heaven, the god Indra grew apprehensive about Ahan's powers and felt threatened. So, he commissioned the most beautiful apsara (celestial fairy) Usha, (Dawn) to descend to earth and break Ahan's concentration. The moment she came down there was morning light and beauty all around after a million years of night. But Ahan, still undisturbed, created the sun and no sooner did its powerful light reach the earth, Usha had to disappear. This celestial play of light has been going on for ever since: Dawn (Usha) descends to the earth after a dark night and vanishes with rising sun. See Kapadia, Harish, 'A Dawn in Winter', *Meeting the Mountains,* Indus Publishing Co, New Delhi, 2009 (2nd edition) p. 140.

4. Kapadia, Harish, 'Youth in Gibson's Garhwal', *High Himalaya Unknown Valley,* Indus Publishing Co, New Delhi, 2001 (4th edition), p. 94.

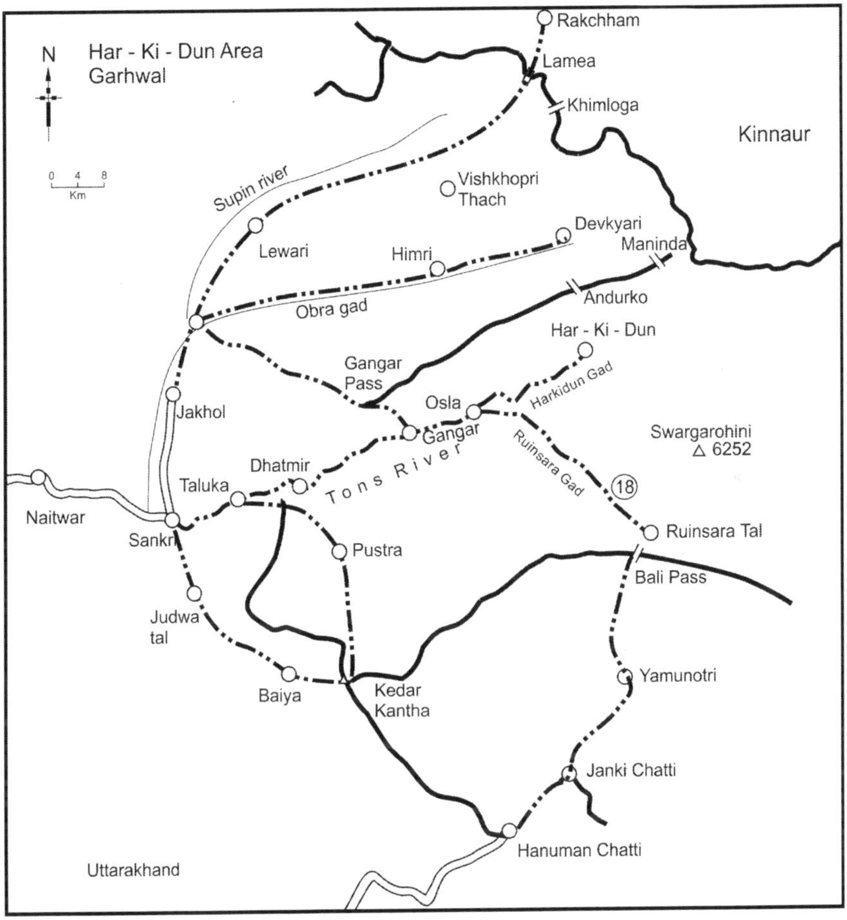

Har ki Doon area – Kedar Kantha.

on the divide with the Satluj valley. This was certainly the playground of the future when climbers are tired of just going high and wish to enjoy another type of 'high'.

To the south-southwest were the lower hills of Mussoorie from where the survey of the Himalayan mountains (and of India) had started. Possibly Kedar Kantha is an important location as a major observation point in the survey of these areas and beyond.

After a night at Baiya bugial, at foot of Kedar Kantha, we descended steeply to Judwa tal, a small tarn in midst of forest, with all its beauty and peace. Just when I thought I had seen all I wanted and heard all there was to hear about Kedar Kantha, came the final edict from an old shepherd, who added a philosophical twist to the tale.

In Garhwal, the traditional method for extracting oil from seeds was to grind them in a stone mill known as a 'kohlu'. The 'kohlu' comprised two round stone slabs placed one on top of the other. The upper stone, which had a hole into which the seeds were fed was rotated continuously by bullocks tied to it by a rope. To prevent the bull from getting dizzy, it were blindfolded.

The pilgrimage to Kedar Kantha is compared to the working of the 'kohlu'. You go round and round in life blindfolded, tied to your desires. When you are here, going around Kedar liberates you and enables you to see the great beauty around you. The sight you behold opens your eyes and you are freed from the burden of your desires – you cut the rope and you are free.

I love the upward ways
To the sun-tipped crest of the mountains
High over the billowy world;
Where the wind sings hymns of praise,
And the snows break into fountains,
And life is a flag unfurled.

– Harriet Monroe (From *Everest : The West Ridge*
by Thomas F. Hornbein, p. 25)

17

We Are the Pilgrims
Mountain Ranges and Temples of Garhwal

We were climbing a steep but well-made trail to Deoria tal near Okimath.

"My name is Jaishankar," a man with a smart moustache introduced himself. "I live in this area and am visiting this lake after a long time with a guest." We sat down under a small canopy made for just such a meeting and exchanged light banter and some information.

His friend called, "Come on Jim, it is time to go." Jaishankar is an orthodox Hindu name, while 'Jim' was truly British. Looking at the query in my eyes he replied, "I am called Jim after the famous shikari, Jim Corbett. I am an official shikari linked with the forest department. When there is a leopard or tiger that turns man-eater, my team is called to eliminate the beast. We try to sedate and shift the animal, but if not, we kill it."

"This is the Corbett area, as you know," he added.

We were to meet many such non-pilgrims visiting the area. Following a regular pilgrim trail along with these experiences made us pilgrims too, though of a different sort.

The area encompassing the middle region of the Himalaya, contains oft-visited ancient temples and villages. Of particular interest is the trail known as the 'Panch Kedar' (five temples of Kedarnath or Shiva) that has been followed by the faithful for hundreds of years. Much has been written about them, more so in vernacular literature. The temples are situated in different valleys so, using them as base, a trekker can look forward to a magnificent experience in the surrounding ridges, peaks and valleys. I have always been fascinated by the variety of trekking opportunities these valleys offer. But, given the fact that these popular pilgrim trails are very crowded when accessible, I had earmarked them for a more appropriate age.

There comes a time for dwellers in the Indian subcontinent, when they have climbed their own particular Everests and are no longer young enough, or perhaps wealthy enough, to take part in a large-scale expedition to one of the few remaining 8000-metre peaks, but when the urge to spend their holiday in the high places is still insistent. For such as these there are still literally hundreds of mountains between 18,000 and 22,000 feet which are accessible without grandiose arrangements for stores, porters or equipment. I have long since reached this age and perhaps a few memories of such moderate mountains will be of interest to some readers of *The Himalayan Journal* who are approaching this stage in their life.[1]

Over the last few years, I have visited some of these temple trails with family and friends. In ancient days, sages situated these temples with great thought and purpose. While it is true that the sanctity of these places draws thousands each year, the grandeur of the surrounding high mountains provides a backdrop to these temples that can definitely attract many more trekkers and mountaineers.

KEDARNATH

The Kedarnath temple (3600 m) is situated in a bowl-like valley, surrounded by a ring of high mountains. If you look away from the temple and the crowds, a majestic range rises within about four km to its north. They are the great south faces of Bhartekhunta (6578 m), Kedarnath (6940 m), Rock Tower (6150 m), Sumeru Parvat (6350 m) and Mandani Parvat (6193 m) ending in the great Chaukhamba massif (6954 m). These south faces provide some great climbing to challengers. The Italians were active here in late 1980s. The first two peaks climbed were Kedarnath in 1988[2] and Rock Tower in 1990[3]. Both climbs were achieved on the second attempt, after their first attempts failed in the previous years. Many peaks situated on the watershed with the

1. Holdsworth R L, 'Moderate Mountains for Middle-aged Mountaineers', *The Himalayan Journal,* Vol 25 1964, p. 85.
2. Mandellin, G, *The Himalayan Journal* Vol 45 1989, pp. 45 & 186.
3. Righetti, Stefano, *The Himalayan Journal* Vol 48 1992, p. 182.

Gangotri glacier in the north of Kedarnath were climbed by approaches from that glacier. Kedarnath valley can also be considered as a centre for serious climbing, as it lies within a day of availability of supplies.

We did a short trek up to Vasuki tal (4300 m) on the west of the valley and camped amidst a field of brahma kamal flowers. It was a beautiful tarn, but its importance to mountaineers lies in the opportunities offered nearby. Numerous peaks between 5400 m to 6000 m and cross-country routes to the Dudhganga and Chorabari glaciers lie here.

There are trekking routes to cross the watershed to Bhilangna valley from Kedarnath valley. You can go across Masar tal to descend to Bhilangna valley, or do a cross-country traverse to cross Auden's Col to the Gangotri valley. For an easier trek, one can follow the trail from Triyugi Narayan in the lower valley and cross over to Panwali Kanta which is renowned for its grand views.[4]

We spent the evening at the temple – a group of sadhus sitting within the precinct were awaiting alms. I happened to get into a conversation with a young sadhu who had been coming there every season for many years and seemed very aware of the geography of that area. The temple bells started pealing loudly and this young sadhu's superior gave him angry looks. I pressed a hundred rupee note into his hand for the knowledge and company he had shared, but his superior now gave me an angry look as if asking 'why not me?'

An excited companion had once remarked that if world class facilities were built in this valley, like hotels, helicopter services, well-marked trails and so on, the Kedarnath valley could be a competitor to Chamonix!

MADHYAMAHESHWAR

Though pilgrims have always visited this temple located northeast of Gupta Kashi, it was brought to the notice of the western world in 1934 by the exploits of Eric Shipton and Bill Tilman.

Shipton and Tilman once followed a legend that said that many hundred years ago the priest at the Badrinath temple would cross a pass in one day to the Kedarnath temple to perform puja, thus serving both the temples on the same day. It is believed that there could be a pass joining the temples, known

4. Kapadia, Harish, *Meeting the Mountains,* Indus Publishing Co, New Delhi, 2009, p. 124.

to the priests. Shipton and Tilman decided to investigate this by crossing from the nearest low point, with near disastrous results. Their trip exemplifies the difference between knowledge and legend, or fact and fiction.[5]

Starting from the Satopanth glacier near Badrinath, they planned to descend to this valley with their Sherpas in four to five days,. After forcing their way through a sheer ice wall, they had to cut through thick forest. As they hacked their way through and crossed and re-crossed many streams, they ran short of food. They lived on bamboo-shoots, but had to compete with bears, for bears also love the shoots. The situation was near hopeless. Finally, one afternoon, they climbed up a ridge to get their first glimpse of a village. The Sherpas were joyous, but Tilman greeted the sight with a characteristically dry comment, the kind for which he was well-known: "We shall be down in time for tea", to which Shipton merely stuttered "Thank heaven for that!"

Two trekkers from Bengal were lost here in 1986 attempting to partially reverse the Shipton-Tilman route and were presumed dead. Martin Moran completed the route in 1999 – starting from Badrinath he followed the route until Kedarnath temple[6]. It would certainly not have been an easy day for a priest!

The five temples in this area are called *Panch Kedar* (five Kedars) based on a legend of Shiva.[7] "What is the significance of Madhyamaheshwar temple?" my companion Jehangir, a renowned Mumbai yoga teacher, enquired of the only priest at the temple. After narrating two different stories, the priest asked Jehangir how he could reduce his belly. To each his own profession!

5. Shipton, Eric, The Second Crossing of the Watershed (Badrinath–Kedamath)', *Nanda Devi* part 4.
6. 'Shipton's Lost Valley', *The Himalayan Journal* Vol 55 1999.
7. Chased by Pandavas of Mahabharata fame. Shiva assumed the form of a bull to escape from them. When the Pandavas discovered his disguise, they held the bull by the tail and swung him around. Different parts of the bull fell at different places, where temples were erected. Kedarnath is where his shoulder fell. Other parts of the bull landed at four other places, the centre at Madhya (centre) Maheshwar (a name of Shiva). Geographically, two rivers flow through here. From the north flows the Markand Ganga, and from the south the Madhyamaheshwar Ganga, on the two sides of the hill on which the temple stands. So one explanation of the name could simply be; 'Shiva temple on the hill in centre of two rivers'.

Considering the route we had come up by, it was a wonder that the priest was fat.

Next day, as we climbed up to Budha Madhyamaheshwar (3500 m; 2 km) clouds gathered and we were denied the supposedly close and excellent view of the Chaukhamba group. From here, a *gaddi* track leads to Kashni tal, a lake at 4730 m. Many other trekking routes are possible in the area. A little above the lake some of the various gullies could lead a qualified party across the watershed to the Panpatia bank and the Badrinath valley. Locals had heard about this route. Perhaps, Shipton's party was one valley to the north (Satopanth bank) of a possible crossing.

Towards the east, Maindgalla tal and Pandosera (5120 m) are visited by the shepherds. Crossing a small watershed ridge, one can descend to Rudranath, which is another temple of Shiva and has an exit to the south.

For two days, near the temple, we observed the rituals. Two assistants looked after the ablutions and preparations for the simple worship. Our friend, the priest, then made an appearance for the *aarti* and did the final perambulations. This activity was certainly not enough to keep him physically fit! Jehangir showed him some yoga *asanas*. When we left, we were firmly convinced that the priest may rise spiritually but would not reduce an inch at the belly!

DEORIA TAL – TUNGNATH

The view that I had missed at Madhyamaheshwar I saw at Tungnath, a few years later. We climbed up to Deoria tal and camped in one of the most beautiful places in Garhwal. In the moonlight, viewing the Chaukhamba peaks reflected in calm waters is a treat. From Deoria tal, the forest department has built a trail from the lake to Tungnath, about 16 km away. If you wish to enjoy a walk in the forest, this is the route to take. We trekked leisurely, admiring birds and trees and, after two camps en route, the trail joined the main route to Tungnath from Chopta (3 km). As we camped near the ancient temple a loud speaker was blaring *bhajans,* unfortunately something you cannot avoid here.

Our eyes, though, were on Chandrashilla ground, about 200 m above the temple. It has an expansive panorama of Garhwal peaks. The panorama is vast and covers almost all peaks of Garhwal. On a sunlit morning in autumn, most peaks of Garhwal and Kumaun can be seen from here.

BANSI NARAYAN

On the trail to Bansi Narayan, I saw a tall and strong person approaching us, carrying a heavy load. He was a German 'pilgrim'.

As we exchanged experiences, he said, "I have been to these parts of the Himalaya often. I love the concept of spirituality mixed with mountains. I return here often as Bansi Narayan is a special place.

"Some peaks are not allowed to be climbed as they are declared holy. Some areas are called holy. But, what is not holy in the Himalaya? You cannot separate feelings in the Himalaya at all". He had imbibed the true spirit of a pilgrim.

Bansi Narayan is a small and isolated temple at about 3200 m. A huge rocky outcrop next to the temple has several fissures and cracks. When a strong wind passes through those cracks it makes a sweet sound that local shepherds associate with the flute played by Lord Krishna. The *bansi* (flute) played by Lord Narayan (another name for Krishna) can move the faithful here, if one is lucky enough to hear the sound. I was introduced to this place by Dr Vasant Desai from Mumbai, who lived till 100. He had visited it from Kalpeshwar (another temple in the valley) about 30 years ago, with a guide as old as he. It had rained and they slept in an apology of a cave next to the temple. He heard the flute but dismissed it as hallucination. But, when his guide and porter both asked about the sound, he enquired further and was told of this phenomenon by local shepherds.

I climbed up to this temple from two different sides, each one steep, with different companions, in 2015 and 2016. One of the benefits of growing old is that you have friends plus their children or grandchildren. My companion on the steep climb from Urgam, was Shanaya, then eight years old. The horses struggled on the steep narrow trail which she walked effortlessly, all the time telling me about her school life and the walks she had done. I borrowed her youthful energy until we reached the temple! A year later, I was to climb from Kalgot, having crossed over to this village from Urgam. It was almost 1000 m of steep climbing. Shreya (10 years) started walking behind me and, without losing breath, narrated the story of a handsome prince and some golden apples. The prince was looking for the apples which were hidden under a throne over which sat a huge bird. The prince managed to reach the throne, and forced the bird to fly – by the time the prince discovered those golden apples, we were on top of the pass.

We arrived at the temple on a rainy day so the peaks were hidden under clouds. As the clouds lifted, Nanda Devi appeared in the blue sky and turned golden. The view of the peaks on each side of Nanda Devi was a joy to behold. To the south, were the twin peaks of Bethartoli Himal, Trisul, Nanda Ghunti, Ronti and the faraway Tharkot. Towards the north stood Dunagiri, Tirsuli West, Hardeol, Hathi and Ghori Parvat and ending with a glimpse of Rataban. The climbing history of each of these peaks speaks volumes and they are the core of exploration of Garhwal. I did not hear the flute that evening as it was still and not windy, but my young companions had already whispered music in my ears with their stories and the view had made it a special place.

RUDRANATH

We descended to Kalgot and crossed to Dumak in two days. The trail crossed a nala and climbed towards the Panar bugial, passing Talli tal (lake) and many beautiful meadows. The forest gradually gave way to grassy meadows as we reached Panar bugial, to link up with the main pilgrim trail. We woke up to a mesmerising morning as sun rose over vast grassy and green meadows. The horizon was lined with peaks of Vishnu Ghar range (Home of Vishnu). These peaks are of moderate altitude as Himalayan heights go, but each is a challenge to climb and the valleys are punctuated by steep glaciers. The Chaukhamba peaks and Kunaling stood to our west. Seen behind the range was Nilkanth peak with its long history. To complete the panorama in the east was Nanda Devi and most of the peaks we had seen from Bansi Narayan, but now from a different angle.

The Vishnu Ghar range symbolises what is left to be climbed in the Himalaya; what I call 'Mountains of the Future'. Climbers, when they are finished with Everest (will they ever be?) could seek challenges in these small but difficult peaks. The future had already begun while we were looking at this range – a team led by explorer-mountaineer Martin Moran was climbing the first peak in this range, approaching it via a trek from Bansi Narayan.

There were many pilgrims now on the trail to Rudranath temple. While admiring their religious fervour and spirit one cannot hlep noticing a complete lack of interest in the peaks and ranges around. The main temple was small but on a ridge at the edge of a valley with vast meadows. Near the temple, there were some white pigeons, supposed to be souls of lucky pilgrims. As we all posed for a photo with the priest; he raised his hand behind our companion Vijay as a blessing. He kept it up for so long that we feared that this blessing would turn Vijay into a pigeon! As we descended steeply to the motor road at Sagar, we met pilgrims, young and old, weak and strong, non-mountaineers mostly, climbing only on the strength of their faith.

These areas of the Himalaya with their temples and forest have loads of mountain history and legend. They allow for great views while walking on well-known trails in relative safety. You can seek your golden apples, or the souls of good people in pigeons in the shadow of some of the highest peaks of the Himalaya, like pilgrims on the golden road to Samarkand.

We are the Pilgrims, Master, we shall go
Always a little further: it may be
Beyond that last blue mountain barred with snow.[8]

Tred softly for this is holy ground;
It maybe, could we look with seeing eyes,
This land we stand upon is paradise.

– Christina Rosetti

8. Flecker, James Elroy, *The Golden Journey to Samarkand,* Act V (ii), Max Goschen, London, 1913.

56. Niti village.

57. Rarely seen Geldhung peak, Niti pass area.

58. Trekker on way to Dayara bugiyal. Peak Jaonli seen behind.

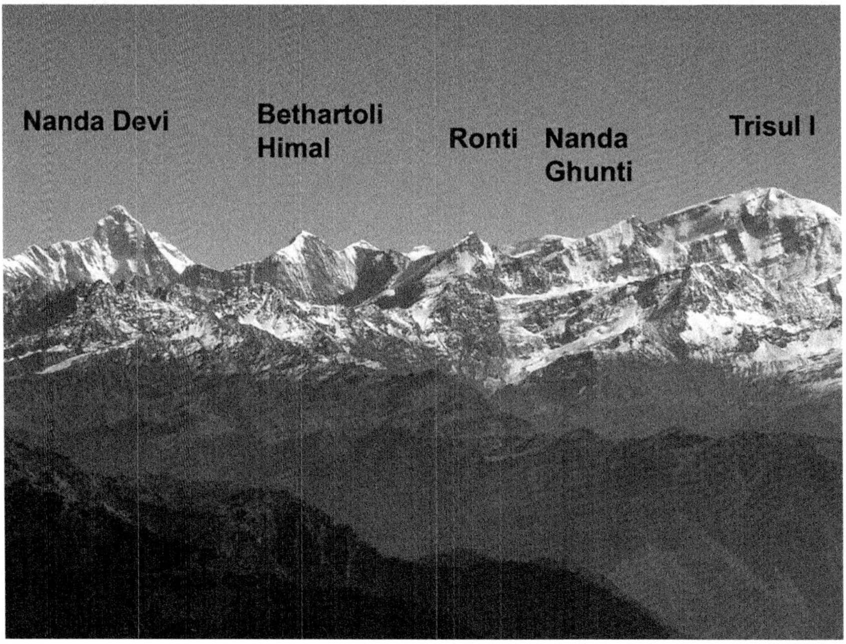

59. View from Chandra Shila, Tungnath (Monesh Devjani).

60. Januhut from Deoria tal (Monesh Devjani).

61. Hardeol peak from Bansi Narayan.

62. Bethartoli Himal main (left) – and South from Bansi Narayan.

63. Nanda Devi from Bansi Narayan.

64. View from Bansi Narayan, Garhwal. Peaks Left to right: Dunagiri, Changabang and Kalanka.

65. Trisul peak from Panar bugyal, Garhwal.

66. Peaks on The Plateau.

67. Hathi Parvat (R) and Ghori Parvat (L) from Bansi Narayan.

68. Kora chorten at Trashiyangtse, Eastern Bhutan.

69. Takstang monastery (Tiger's Nest) near Paro.

70. Punakha dzong, western Bhutan.

71. Trongsa dzong, Central Bhutan.

72. Chomolahri peak (left) and the range, in Bhutan.

73. Jokhang temple, the spiritual centre for Buddhist at Lhasa.

74. Norbulinka, residence of the Dalai Lama at Lhasa.

75. Northern view of Everest peak from Pang La (Kunj Trivedi).

76. Pilgrims with prayer wheels at Jokhang temple, Lhasa.

77. Paryer wheels at Tirthapuri, Tibet.

78. Gyantse fort, Tibet.

79. Karo la pass and glacier, en route to Lhasa.

80. Kailsh peak and Rakastal lake, Tibet.

81. Kailash peak, southern face, Tibet.

18

In the Valleys of Eastern Kumaun

Byans, Johar and Danpur

A thousand, two thousand passes,
Passes in the lands of strangers,
I will cross three thousand passes,
To go to my own country.

– Bhotia Song

As far back as one can remember people have traversed mountain valleys, ranges and passes. They travelled for trade, in search of work or for communication. Today travel continues for defence reasons, government duties or to earn a livelihood. Some of us trek for pleasure, to seek beauty and glean knowledge of these ranges. Motives differ and that, perhaps, leads to a vast change of attitude: for some each step is a discovery of beauty; for others it is unbearable hardship. But, from the earliest times, one of the major reasons for travel in this region is for religious purposes. In a way the entire Himalaya is the 'Abode of Gods', but several places have always been special. This is even more true in Uttarakhand.

The people of the Darma, Byans and Chaudas (Kuthi-Kali) valleys have always been travellers. Every winter they descend to the lower valleys. Formerly, they had almost no connection with the plains of India. For them trade, community interaction and lifestyle were all dominated by the people of Tibet, a region which extends towards their northern borders. They also had close links with Nepal, which lies to the south-southeast. In fact, many still own land in Nepal and continue to till it. It was the British who penetrated these valleys, naming the people who lived here 'Bhotias', a term now commonly accepted for the inhabitants of these valleys or for all those who are Hindu in origin but follow Buddhist customs.

The first thing that impresses a visitor about the Bhotias of these valleys is their appearance. A large part of the population still subsists as shepherds – someone called it 'goat-culture'. But the others, particularly the young, can be seen in the latest brand of jeans and jackets. The education level is high, and the people travel all over the country to earn a livelihood. Most of them take their surnames from the name of their village. One who is from Dar is Daryal; from Garbyang, Garbyal, and so on. So, the next time when you are in a big Indian city look around for a Kutiyal (from Kuti) or a Sonwal (Son) or even a Sipal (Sipu). You will be amazed to learn how far and wide they have travelled.

The remoteness and their unique customs have made the people of these valleys the subject of a quite a few anthropological and social studies, and they still present an interesting subject before 'civilisation' fully takes over. One of the interesting customs we had read about was that of 'rang-bhang'. On a particular day, the marriageable boys and girls of a village would come together, and the festivities would go on till most of them had found a suitable partner. Like many other aspects of their lifestyle, this tradition, though it still exists, is slowly dying out.

The upper Kuthi valley borders Tibet to its east and north, while Darma lies to its west. The Darma valley is bifurcated into Lassar and Darma at the upper reaches. To its west lies Johar or the Kalabaland-Munsiary area. These valleys have many interconnecting passes which are still in use, as well as connecting passes with Tibet leading to Gyanima Mandi or Taklakot, and trade flourished on traditional lines. Bhotia traders have crossed passes to Tibet for trade and religion for generations. While Milam and Niti areas were very popular, they went up till Gyanima Mandi to exchange goods with the Tibetans. Some of them married Tibetan woman. Rich Tibetans were also invited to their homes back in India. This has stopped since the borders were closed in 1962, though some trade, illegal of course, still continues via Tinker la in Nepal.

Today, the river Kali divides India and Nepal, forming a natural border, but the Kali valley has always attracted many visitors and was well-known.

One of the pilgrim routes to Kailash-Manasarovar (over the Lipu Lekh pass) leads through its fold. It is believed that in the Vedic era, sage Vyas stayed here; hence its name 'Byans'. There is a temple dedicated to him at Gunji. The lower valley 'Chaudas' is named either after four followers of the sage or because fourteen villages nestle there.

The major pilgrimage in the Himalaya is to the Kailash peak in Tibet, which many Hindu and Buddhist texts refer to as the centre of the universe. The trail passes the lower valleys of Darma and Byans. To help pilgrims who undertake the arduous journey, Narayan Swami established an ashram here in 1946 that not only provided shelter to the pilgrims but looked after their spiritual needs too. it is interesting to note the beauty of the area where the Narayan Ashram is located and how these areas can truly be said to contain the abode of God. We were lucky to spend a month trekking the two valleys in the area and while they speak of many traditions as well as religious fervour, the main focus is always the beauty of the Himalaya.

The valleys are lined by many high peaks – Panch Chulis, Chiring We, Sangthang to name just a few, which naturally attracted mountaineers to the region. Among the earliest visitors were the geologists, Prof Arnold Heim and Augusto Gansser. They explored the Kuthi and crossed Shin la to Darma in 1936. Cutting across to the west they crossed the Ralam pass. In 1950, the Scottish Himalayan Expedition led by W H Murray, entered from the Ralam pass and attempted Panch Chuli from the Sona glacier. Also in 1950, Kenneth Snelson trekked extensively in the area. His party attempted Panch Chuli, crossed Gangchal Dhura and recorded their travels with a beautiful panorama. Among recent visitors we find reference to an attempt on Panch Chuli (in 1971) by a group led by Prof C K Mitra. The uppermost Lassar, Darma and Kuthi valleys remained unrecorded for many years.

Himalayan exploration, as known to us today, started with the British taking interest in the inner valleys. Their meticulous notes resulted in several books that created a valuable record. But Indian sages and pilgrims had been roaming the inner valleys for generations before them. Unfortunately, because they did not leave many records, they tend to be forgotten. Adi Shankracharyya was one of the earliest travellers to cross the Mana pass at the head of the Alaknanda valley into Tibet. He then trekked the valleys of Tibet till Tsaprang and Guge. A *math* built by him still stands today. Tholing

Math, as it is called, has a proper place for *havan* (puja) and Hindu deities painted on walls. Adi Shankracharyya was followed by Jesuit fathers who travelled till Guge and then proceeded ahead to Hanle and Leh.

Swami Pranvanand trekked to Kailash and Manasarovar in Tibet, passing the site of Narayan Ashram on the way. He stayed at the lake through the severe Tibetan winter and into the summer, and was very active in researching its history and religious significance. He left two classic books that narrate his journey and these books have so much accurate information that for some time the Chinese had banned them.

A classic exploration story by Hindu sages is the crossing of the Kalindi Khal by a party of three sanyasis. Leaving the temple at Gangotri with a guide they proceeded along the glaciers. Along the way, they ate nothing but boiled potatoes, some rotis and rice; their clothes were simple and they wore grass chappals on their feet. They crossed the formidable Kalindi Khal and descended to Badrinath temple where they were met by a German expedition that was climbing in the area. The Germans were impressed by their journey of faith and brought their story to knowledge of all. It was Navneet Parekh who persuaded Swami Anand, the leader of the group, to pen down the journey. It was published and is a rare historical record of travel titled *Across Gangotri Glacier.*

Apart from Hindu sages who walked the Himalaya, there were 'Pundit' explorers employed by the British – natives who were trained in surveying and gathering information. Many of them were from Kumaun and became legends in their lifetime. Names like Pandit Nain Singh, A K, and Kinthup were recorded and given special awards by the Royal Geographical Society. They were responsible for unveiling much of the history of the Himalaya and adjoining Tibet.

This was the area that attracted us in the summer of 1982. We trekked up Darma, climbed around Meola glacier, crossed two passes, visited three valleys and camped near two exquisite lakes. It was a happy and enjoyable summer for us as diary entries indicate.

MAY 13: Dharchula was in darkness and wore a deserted look when we arrived there late in the evening. The 300 km bus journey from Kathgodam via Almora, Didihat, Jauljibi was tiring. But amidst the depressing surroundings we saw the smiling faces of Sher Singh and two other porters, old and trusted friends. In a short while we were settled and had even managed to contact the tehsildar (at the movie-theatre during the interval) to obtain his signature on our permits. Next morning, we surveyed the scene: on the opposite banks of the Kali river lay another Dharchula – with a Nepalese flag!

A welcome lift on an army truck and we were at Tawaghat (1000 m; 16 km), our road-head. On the ridge above Tawaghat a huge pillar can be seen. This pillar is said to have inscriptions in Chinese, on this basis of which the entire Darma valley is claimed by China. As we prepared for the trek, we must have been a curious sight – this area rarely receives visitors. Moreover, we were a varied group in age, ('Age limit 18 to 66 years; membership restricted') and with a similarly wide difference in experience.

Our trek, (initially with 8 porters), started on the 15th. In the first three days we were to reach Duktu, a fairly large village at the entrance of the Panch Chuli valley. The trek was easy, most enjoyable, and the route was sprinkled with empty villages. *Mawasas* were not moving up yet due to a late winter. Nue (1700 m; 16 km) was on a jeepable track; Sela (2500 m; 17 km) was set amidst a most beautiful forest, while Duktu (3260 m; 19 km) was surrounded by some unbelievable mountain scenery. We stayed at dak bungalows, enjoyed easy gradients, admired unspoiled forests and crossed many snow-tongues. But the trek will be remembered for the waterfalls. There were plenty, of various shapes and heights. It was an unforgettable sight. Sometimes you'd see a silver trickle on the opposite bank and sometimes you'd pass underneath a huge downpour. They conducted their own symphony with beauty.

Duktu is at the centre of the valley, adjoining the village Son, with Dantu across the Sona nala. Across the Darma River nestle the villages of Baun and Philam. With the the Panch Chuli range as a backdrop, it was a most impressive sight. No wonder our enthusiastic host at Dharchula was writing to the government to develop Duktu as a 'Five-Star resort'! From here Panch Chuli base camp at 3380 m, was 6 km away. The route was easy and followed a good track till the junction of Meola and Sona glaciers. But we were warned about a major hazard on the way – a mad yak; and the chowkidar added, very softly, that if the yak located us, we were sure to reach the base in record time! We did see this terror, but it seemed that we also held some terror for the animal for, though it chased our porters, it did not bother the sahibs. Good manners?

The five days at base camp were a delight. For the first two, we let loose on snow and ice and practised all possible skills. It was hard work. One day we climbed to the base of Meola icefall to locate Scottish explorer W H Murray's Camp 2 and trace their route of 1950. Sona icefall was sending down thundering avalanches while Meola seemed to accept things quietly. The last day we decided to climb a small peak of 4330 m on the ridge descending from Panch Chuli V in the south. It had a wonderful panorama. Panch Chuli V (6437 m), IV (6334 m), III (6312 m) and the highest, II (6904 m) formed a cirque above the Meola glacier. Panch Chuli I (6355 m) could not be seen. On the horizon above Sona glacier was Ngalaphu (6410 m). Many other peaks lined the sky on all sides. A short rest, some food, a little getting lost on the rocks and we were back at base. Camp was wound up and we rushed back to Duktu.

MAY 23: We shifted our camp to Sipu (4760 m; 16 km). We walked along the Darma. On the opposite bank the village of Go was peculiarly situated on a huge black hole in the mountain side. Anyone would refuse an invitation to lunch there! At Tidang the valleys bifurcate. To the northeast is the main Darma valley while to the northwest lies the Lassar Yankti valley. Lassar Yankti was like a dream, with clear, turquoise-coloured waters. Its banks were lined with multicoloured stones of various shapes and shades. Sipu is situated about 150 m above the riverbed. We camped at the school's volleyball ground. A few families had returned to the village. They were digging out the stock of potatoes they had stored for the winter. We had read a lot about the Sipals and it was fun to be here. One villager demanded dues not paid by a 'white-man's party' (Scotts' or Heim's?). After promising to produce the note from them on the following day, he disappeared. Again, good manners prevailed!

MAY 29: The entire party started out once again towards the upper Lassar Yankti valley. We reached the main valley and proceeded, quite literally, along the riverbed. The map indicated a track on the right bank but, taking advantage of the snow-bound river, we trekked up the river. It was a tired party that camped at Kharsa (3750 m; 10 km) in the evening.

MAY 30: Our most tiring day. Three of us started for Nassa (4270 m; 10 km) in the uppermost Lassar Yankti valley. With heavy loads we crossed

Jhutan glacier, descended to Ralphu and Anchri Tal, then across Ghutan and on, to cross Damolia glacier. All the crossings were very tiring and getting to the final camp was a relief. And, as if ordering a rest, heavy snowfall the ensuing day did not allow us to move from the camp. Through the clearing we could see the great ablation valley bordering Tibet leading to nowhere. To the west there were many peaks, but we were too close to the moraine walls to be able to see the summits.

JUNE 1: We decided to return, but could start only in the afternoon at 3 pm It cleared by evening, and we followed an easier, lower route this time. By 5 pm we were at Anchri Tal (3660 m; 4 km) and could not resist the temptation to stay at such a beautiful spot. For Dhiren (18 years) this was his first encounter with the Himalaya. His excitement about everything ('first time') was infectious. He had a habit of nicknaming everything – potatoes were pats, tea was inty and theplas were theps. But the final touch was when Panch Chulis became Panchus, and now we camped at Anchu!

But without exaggeration, Anchri had a Wordsworthian air about it. A small lake, very quiet and crystal-clear, the rising sun reflected in the cold water, a small bird singing somewhere and our red tent in the background. There were no other human beings in the whole valley. We sat out around a fire till late at night and watched a glowing moon light up the unbelievable beauty of Anchri. I repeated Nandu Jayal's words to (his) my companion; '(John) D, in all this beauty I guess God must be pretty close!'

JUNE 3: The three of us moved to stay at Gangchal camping ground. Gangchal Dhura (5051 m) lies on the divide between the Lassar Yankti and Darma valleys. At this time of the year, it was totally snowbound. We had learnt that locally it is also called 'Baisakhiram Jot' after a popular ITBP officer. Baisakhiram, and a few others, were killed while crossing this pass a few years ago. Unlike most passes, this one does not cross the ridge at a lowest point but at one of the high points. This leads to the deathtrap with a deep gorge on both sides. The apparently alluring Dhura was dangerous ground.

JUNE 4: By 6 am we were making our way out under a bright and clear sky. The route climbed up steeply. Far too steeply to relax or enjoy the view. Soon grass gave way to rocks and we ran into hard snow, Dhiren kicked steps through a wide gully, and we rested mid-way. Slowly a beautiful panorama unfolded. A quick cup of tea and some food, and we deliberately left that alluring lower gorge to climb a steep ridge full of scree. A deep soft snow ground near the top thoroughly exhausted Muslim who was opening the route. At last, at 3 pm we hit the high point. Traversing the ridge, we reached the lowest point. This was Gangchal Dhura. Both sides were lined with the most famous series of mountains one can come across. It was like looking at a crowd of people and finding familiar figures. Some were old friends with whom we had rubbed noses: Chiring We, Bamba Dhura or the recent Panch Chulis. There were many whom we had seen before: Suli Top, Rajrambha, Lalla We. And then there were famous figures: Api, Nampa, Chaudhara. It was a most satisfying place to be in!

But perhaps every white cloud does have a black lining! It was clear that a big storm was developing in the south and we had miles to go before a camp. I led the way down, avoiding obvious traps but even then, regularly sinking right up to the hip – a tiring affair. We lost height fast, and just when it seemed that the slopes would never end, we were on the bank of Darma River and camping little short of Dawe (4390 m; 10 km) in the north. That was the signal for the storm to let loose on the area and we could not move from the tents on the following day.

Dawe is the last outpost on the Indian side. Two passes, Nuwe Dhura (5645 m) and Lowe Dhura (5562 m), lead to Tibet (Gyanima Mandi) from here. It is strategically an important place and witness to the past glory of trade between India and Tibet. But the Darma valley, in marked contrast with the Lassar valley, is devoid of any vegetation. Even juniper shrubs are missing. The reason – defence. It was evident that many bushes had been dragged out with their roots. An ecological disaster!

Whenever Muslim Contractor (23) was introduced to someone, we got a variety of reactions. 'You have a Hindu Contractor also on the trip?' or 'So what if he is Muslim?' He had trekked widely and now he decided to have a bath in the cold waters of the Darma! He left a little ahead of us to investigate the crossing at a shaky snow-bridge. Unfortunately, as he was about to cross, the bridge broke. He lost his ice-axe and got drenched. Undaunted, he bravely descended into the chilly waters in search of the ice-axe – for the next hours all he managed to do was shiver! We walked along the true right bank for 4 km before wading through the cold waters of the Darma to cross.

We camped at Piungang (4270 m; 8 km). Two porters were sent to bring up the cache of food we had left there. We had food with us but no fuel. For the next day and and a half, we combed the area for little pieces of wood and managed to survive on half-cooked *shyakpa* and luke-warm tea. We would have paid anything for a litre of kerosene. When Sher Singh arrived with that broad smile and load of wood, things immediately appeared better.

JUNE 8: We reached Bidang. The huge camping ground is where Tibetan caravans used to camp. A large quantum of trade took place here. Now an ITBP regiment is all that is seen. But we had no grounds for complaint as they treated us to a sumptuous lunch – so welcome since our appetites had been whetted over the last two days. We rose to the occasion.

Our proposed route now was to cross Shin La (5496 m) in the east, reach Jolingkong lakes, then follow Byans valley down. Inquiries at Bidang about the exact location of the pass were answered casually. We were told that *barats* (marriage processions) go over it in *chappals*. So, we started in the late afternoon and camped 300 m above. The next day we encountered cloudy weather. Not wanting to miss the view, we did not proceed to the pass but shifted the camp another 150 m. There were three gullies to our east but no route clearly apparent. Everything was snowbound and that changed the situation.

JUNE 10: Starting early, we entered the second gully, which rose steeply with crusts of ice and rocks. It led us to a wall, 600-m high, with a wide ramp at its base. The route passed on that ramp. It was a virtual death-trap with stone-falls due to the melting of snow. We branched off on a steep rocky wall a little away from this wall. Mixed ground with ice-rock-scree and snow had to be negotiated. A terrible, nerve-taxing, wet climb! At the top another high rock-wall guarded the route, discharging stones down the slope every now and then. We traversed more loose snow and finally reached a clearing. Our tired party stared and ten steps ahead we saw the welcome cairns 15 m below us. We were at Shin la at 3 pm after an eight-hour climb. Some pass, we thought, for a *barat* in *chappals*! The view to the east was dominated by Sangthang (6480 m), the black rocks of Kunti valley and Tibet. We descended again through the terrible hip-deep snow and later over a moraine ridge. A 6322 m peak adjoining Shin la appeared to be a replica of the famous Kailash. It is locally worshipped as 'Baba Kailash'. In the fading light we climbed up three moraine ridges and 100 m to camp at Jolingkong lake (4630 m; 10 km).

JUNE 11: This was the rest day. We surveyed the surroundings. The lake was about 5 km in circumference and still frozen. A small temple and little cairns separated it from the roaring Kunti river. Jolingkong is also worshipped as 'Chhota Manasarovar'. We had heard about a pair of 'Rajhans' that lived here. But we had also heard that no one can shoot them because the bullets went 'cold' while shooting across the icy lake. But the very thought of shooting was disturbing. The valley up takes a peculiar S turn to Wilsha. Two passes, Lampiya Dhura (5547 m) and Mangsha Dhura (5486 m) leading to Tibet lie a little ahead. A large moraine bed in the Kuthi river was a reminder of the gigantic lake that had once formed but we could not determine when the natural dam had burst.

JUNE 12: This was a day to remember. As we left the lake there was a climb to a prominent ridge in the south. Walking leisurely, we observed three figures on that ridge. We continued and coming a little closer were astonished to see three jawans aiming Light Machine Guns at us! We waved and that led to a scramble among them to the bunkers with LMGs. still pointed at us. We were worried; never trust a khaki brain, particularly as they had no live shooting practice since 1962! Unashamedly hiding behind a huge rock, we let Sher Singh go ahead as he looked the most 'Indian' amongst us. Soon we were waved up. The officer spoke to us but a jawan still kept a gun pointing at us. At last things were sorted out and the jawan, distinctly unhappy, very reluctantly unloaded. Perhaps, he had visions of medals for capturing three Chinese. The patrol had just arrived and they thought we had crossed the Tibetan pass. Shin la is not open till late in the year. Credentials were established and the alarm sent down the lines in the valley was withdrawn. But all along our trek down we encountered curious glances and had a story to tell.

By evening we were at Kuthi village (3760 m; 14 km) which has the most exquisite carved-wood houses. As we were seen off by a local officer, he pointed to a small hill at the outskirts, with ruins 5 ft high. This was Pandu Killa where the Pandavas stayed. According to the legend, a nine-storeyed building on that hill was their home. With a mischievous chuckle he added, 'Since we have come, it has always appeared a little smaller!' In the evening we camped at Nihal and on the next day crossed Gunji.

At Gunji, the Kuthi river merges with the Kali which forms the Indo-Nepal border. As the legend goes, it is the British who interchanged the names of the white Kali and the blackish Kuthi rivers. This ensured a vast area of land as British territory since Kali was accepted as a border. They built a temple dedicated to Kali near Lipu Lekh pass to authenticate the name. A good example of British diplomacy! An old man advised us now to follow *kachhuve-ki-chaal* ('tortoise walk') for the route down the valley involved many ups and was rather tiresome. Here we joined the well described Kailash–Manasarovar pilgrim route from Lipu Lekh pass. We were to suffer that 'curse of Kali'. Because of the narrow gorges it forms, the route climbs up thousands of feet a few times and finally descends at Tawaghat. At certain places the track was wide enough to be motorable. In 1960, a contract was drawn to build the road from Almora to Lipu Lekh pass to facilitate pilgrim traffic. The contractor was persuaded by the Chinese to start the construction from the pass to Almora. This would allow a good deal of strategic advantage to the Chinese to descend to lower valleys. The folly of this plan was soon discovered.

JUNE 15: In three days we reached Narayan Ashram at 2775 m via Garbyang (9 km), Malipa (16 km), Jipti (11 km), Ashram (16 km). The place appears like a building in fantasy land. The location, the construction and the atmosphere it generates is most conducive to spiritual practise. The ashram was built by Narayan Swami in 1946 to help the pilgrims to Manasarovar. With Api-Nampa in the southeast and Panch Chulis in the northwest, it is a place of rare beauty.

We decided to climb up from Tawaghat to the Ashram. There was no road then and one had a steep climb of more than 6000 feet reach there. Many failed to reach in a day and were looked after by local villagers. But we were experienced and fit, so we started at 2 am, climbed up in cool weather and were trooping into the Ashram by 7 am to be welcomed by a young Swami, who we learnt later was Swami Tadrupanandji. He was epitome of knowledge about almost all aspects of Hinduism and the *shashtras*. We stayed three days at the Ashram.

The next day another legendary person dropped in, Gangotriben Garbyal. I have never met a kinder lady and even at her advanced age she had climbed up the slopes. On hearing that we were Gujaratis, the first thing she ordered for us was plenty of tea and pakoras! In evening she performed a long and systematic puja, which was a moving experience. Here was the bhakti that had created humility in her as love for God.

On the last day a young student dropped in. He was son of a shepherd and had learnt about various herbs and their usefulness while roaming the area with his father. A Swiss medicine company had invited him to share his knowledge and sent him to Geneva to study further. He was now back home. "Are you planning to settle in Geneva now that you have been admired in the West", I asked. His answer was clear: "No no, I have to do a lot of service for my people here. They are illiterate and many a times they quarrel with officials also. I must do something for them using the knowledge that I have gained". To me this was the perfect combination of *bhakti* and knowledge inspired by the grace of Narayan Swami! And also a perfect way to complete our trip with his grace.

We now jostled in buses, ate at dhabas and sped home by trains. All that had gone past was already beckoning us. We had finished our travel. But it will be impossible to forget the Panchus, goat-culture, LMGs, Kutiyals, passes and of course Anchu!

19

Obra Gad – the Hidden Valley

Western Garhwal

In September 1999, we came down the steep trail from Lewari and Fetari along the Supin Gad. The descent ended at a small tea stall where we relaxed. A river coming in from the northwest met the Supin River at this point and I eyed a lovely trail going up on the right bank of this river. Sensing my looks of inquiry, the tea stall owner said, "This is the Obra Gad. It goes up for a while and there are beautiful grounds at head of the valley. Initially the river remains hidden and you rarely see it, hence the name Obra, the hidden valley." I stored this information somewhere at the back of my mind for a future date. We often organised short, week-long visits to the Himalaya so that friends who could not take a longer holiday could join us. One such trip was being planned with our friend Maninder, who worked for a leading foreign bank and was always short of time. Despite my suggesting other nearby valleys, he kept insisting on going into the Obra and eventually I said, 'why not'! We were a small party of about eight people and in September 2005, we were walking up the slopes of this hidden valley.

With Maninder came Bhushan, his neighbour in Delhi. Bhushan had travelled in the Himalaya and in the typical Delhi manner and language, he said, "I have seen each *chapa chapa* (corner) of many valleys in the Himalaya". He narrated how he used to trek different valleys in slippers, sustaining on local food and sometimes even on grass (!), trekking without a water bottle, tent or much equipment. As he talked, the Mumbai crowd exchanged glances – he surely must have regaled the ladies at many parties in Delhi with these stories! But he was a great company as we trekked up, full of innocence and enthusiasm.

Camping at Obra Gad temple, going up steeply we tried to go too long a distance on the second day. Unacclimatised as we were, we were forced to camp on a grassy ledge in the middle clearing, as it poured down heavily. The grass was too tall to see the trail and there were many plants that caused scratches and itching. All this had taken three four days and already our banker friends were looking at the calendar and their watches. So next day, despite inclement weather, they decided to make a dash for the upper valley and return straight home. Bhushan also left with them without exploring a single corner of this beautiful valley. The same fate was written for us as it continued to rain. Unfortunately, on such a short trip, one has to accept that if there is bad weather, it means you go home, which is what we did.

But some of our climber friends had managed a tantalizing glimpse of a peak named Ranglana (5554 m). This peak grew in stature and Obra Gad spread its tentacles in our minds. So after just a few months, in May 2006, we were compelled to return to the Obra. Travelling from Mumbai to Dehra Dun, we entered the Govind Pant Wildlife Sanctuary at Naitwar and reached Jakhol (2240 m), where the road ended. Jakhol, named after Jakhand Devta, was home to a beautiful temple and a small forest rest house, a little above the village. Talking to the village elders, we came to know that in few days the local god or Devta would be carried in a procession up Obra Gad to a holy cave which is supposed to be his home. This would be the first time the Devta was travelling there in many years.

This time we decided to go slowly, and camp after walking short distances so as to acclimatize – a better approach if you wish to see the *chapa chapa* of any valley. We camped at Obra temple (2290 m) and then made the steep climb up to Rakhanda (2810 m) where we had been trapped by rain during our last visit. As we climbed the forest trail on the third day, a vast panorama opened to our eyes, something that one could never imagine existed on the upper slopes of this valley. We camped at Himri thach (3400 m) surrounded by small but challenging and beautiful mountains. A short distance up at 3680 m was Jairai, where our porters left us to make a sort of base camp. There were some steep granite rocks up one of the side valleys

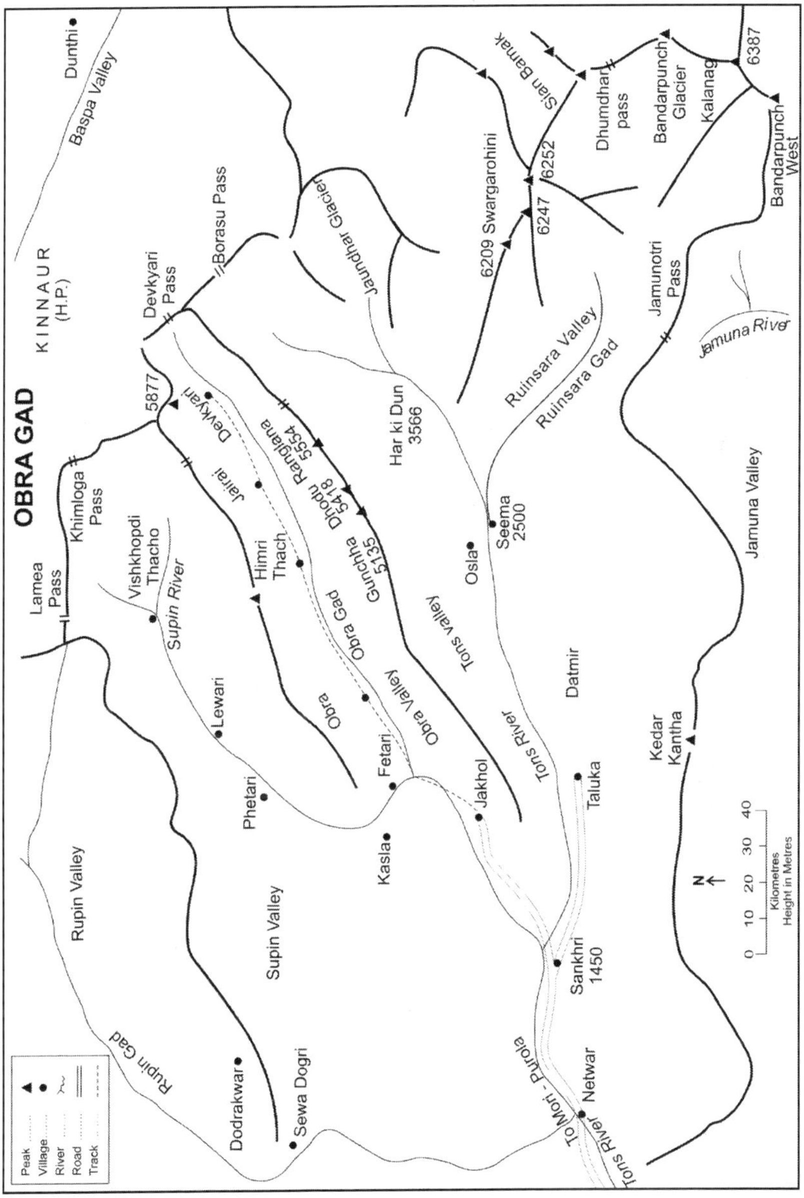

Obra Gad valley.

which our climbing friends eyed. However, what attracted them more was a collection of peaks south of our camp. The group was dominated by Ranglana (5554 m) and the ridge continued to Dhodu (5418 m) and Dhodu ka Gauchha (*c.* 5100 m). Behind this ridge, stood Andurko, the only peak named on the map, and further east lay the famed Har ki Dun valley which is visited by several hundred trekkers every year.

Four of our group left for the Gunchha ridge. The weather was unsettled and as a result the mountain was not in the best condition for a climb. Wisely, opting for a lower peak, on 29 May they climbed Gunchha to a grand view towards east and north amidst gathering clouds. On the 30th we shifted camp. For the next four days we operated from this camp, everyone going in different directions, some reading books and a variety of combinations between these two options. I chose to go 6 km up the valley to Devkyari (4040 m). I would never forget the first view of Devkyari. As I climbed steep jumble of rocks, suddenly a vast open ground surrounded by steep rocky peaks opened up. It was still recovering from winter, but there were large patches of green grass on which some flowers bloomed. Towards the north was the Devkyari glacier, which, after taking a sharp turn led to a pass of the same name and on into Kinnaur (Sangla). The entire area was full of sharp, rocky peaks. Again, as the climbers left for the upper glacier to attempt peaks, some of us made excursions to different sides of the valley. A couple turned west towards a col which would have led them to Vishkhopri thach on the Supin river, through which we had come down four years earlier. Towards the east there were cairns marking an easy route down to Har ki Dun. For an enterprising party, it would make for a grand traverse, starting from Bhardsar lake in the Supin coming across to Obra at Devkyari and crossing over to Har ki Dun. Once again, it was a route to be tucked away in the mind for future.

On 1 June as we woke up, the large procession carrying palanquins made its way to Devkyari. To the sound of trumpets, the beating of drums and chanting of songs, Jakhand Devta arrived in style at his ancient home. He was accompanied by not less than 300 people, all of whom camped about a kilometre away from us on this vast Devkyari plateau. After several ceremonies. Jakhand Devta was taken up the glacier for a ritual bath in the pure waters near the mouth of the glacier. As the god rested in his cave, the villagers gathered in a circle and started performing a simple but rhythmic dance in his honour. They were each carrying a small sword with a thick flat blade, moving it round and round as they danced to the drumbeat. On the vast plateau of Devkyari, the surrounding mountains and green grass made for a beautiful setting. Towards end of the dance, the villagers gathered around two priests who were performing rituals with the Devta in the centre. They moved slowly, as if in a trance with the drums beating in a slow, rhythmic movement. One of the priests gathered a few swords from different people, held them between his teeth and continued dancing in a trance for a while. As the dance ended these swords, now purified with blessings of Jakhand Devta, were handed back to their owners. The villagers stayed quietly near the cave while we retired to our tents nearby.

The next morning, the Devta left early with the same fanfare as he had arrived. By this time our climbers had also returned. They had recceed the peaks surrounding the glacier but had been unable to climb any due to the fresh snow. It was time to return to Jakhol, which we did in only two days.

We had tasted the beauty of this hidden valley, seen its peaks and enjoyed its beauty. Devkyari, the 'square of god', is certainly a blessed place and very inviting for any future party to climb, trek, just enjoy the beauty and flowers or visit the nearby valleys. There is lot to do and I can assure you we still haven't seen the *chapa chapa* of this valley.

20

The Age of Exploration
Dhauli Valley, Niti Pass and Bara Hoti

Dhauli valley in central Garhwal is surrounded by a ring of high and famous mountains: Kamet and Abi Gamin are to the west, Ganesh Parvat to the northwest, Bara Hoti, which saw so much conflict in the 1962 India–China war, is in the northeast. Several passes in the east complete the cirque.

The area has a long history of exploration – by the likes of Frank Smythe, W H Murray, and Alexander Kellas. It is also chased with old trade and pilgrimage routes to and from Tibet across the Niti pass. While in the last few decades, the valley has largely remained out of bounds due to security concerns, the permit situation has eased now. Taking advantage of this, Kanu and Rama Pomal and I, visited its upper reaches and trails in the summer of 2014 and studied the history of the valley. This is an account of our travels and of the rich history of exploration in the area.

WILLIAM MOORCROFT

The age of Western exploration of the Himalaya and Tibet started in earnest in 1811 with a daring journey by William Moorcroft. Moorcroft had trained as an apprentice to a surgeon in Liverpool, studied veterinary science in France, and eventually set up a practice as a horse veterinarian in London. His work patenting improved horseshoes brought him to the notice of the East India Company, for whom he began to buy breeding horses.

In 1807 he sailed for India, and by 1808 was appointed to various posts in Bengal and Bihar. He obtained permission to journey to the Himalaya to buy new strains for horse-breeding and to investigate the possibilities of wool trade with Tibet.[1] Moorcroft was accompanied by Hyder Young Hearsey, an Anglo-Indian explorer. Disguised as fakirs, they called themselves Mayapori and Hargiri. At first, they followed the Ramganga river from the plains to its source. Then, following Captain William Webb's route along the Alaknanda, they reached Joshimath – an achievement in those days. Proceeding further, they entered the Dhauli valley and took Niti pass to Tibet. They were the first Europeans to cross Niti pass, although not the first to cross into Tibet, as the missionary Jesuit Fathers had taken Mana pass to Tibet a decade earlier.[2] Moorcroft became the first European to reach Manasarovar after Ippolito Desideri in 1715. Later he went on to explore Ladakh and Kashmir.[3]

TOM LONGSTAFF

In 1907, the British explorer Dr Tom Longstaff arrived in the Dhauli valley with his Gorkhas, whom the Niti men called 'Katara-dar' (knife-bearers), as they carried their traditional curved *khukris*. Longstaff was keener on exploration than on climbing in the Dhauli valley. A fortnight earlier he had explored the Nanda Devi Sanctuary and made a fast and first ascent of Trisul (7120 m) – at the time, the highest peak ever climbed. He crossed into Tibet via Niti pass, reached Manasarovar, and almost climbed Gurla Mandhata (7694 m), thus achieving both exploration and climbing.

---

1. Mason, Kenneth, *Abode of Snow,* E P Dutton, London, 1955, pp. 65–66.
2. Mason calls Niti the best-known pass (*for explorers as a route to Tibet*) and Mana, which 12 early missionaries had crossed, the most frequented pass. Mason, pp. 24–25.
3. 'Given his career – and it is here, as he would have wished, that his greatness lies – Moorcroft's character may best be seen as approaching that of the erratic genius. He was indeed obstinate, eccentric and controversial, but he was full of infectious energy and invariably ahead of the times. To anyone responsible for his activities he was an unholy terror but to his friends and followers, a guiding light. He should have been safely cloistered in a progressive university rather than let loose in the Himalaya. Empires are created by men of vision, but Moorcroft was visionary' – John Keay on the unconventional Moorcroft. Keay, John, *When Men and Mountains Meet,* John Murray, London, 1977, pp. 18–19.

During his second visit to the area, he crossed the Lipu Lekh (*c*. 5000 m) pass to Tibet. After spending a month travelling in Tibet, he reached Gyanima Mandi, the traditional market where the Niti men and Tibetans exchanged goods. Here, he was laid low by ill-health. After a week of rest, Longstaff started out again, this time on a yak and marched in shorter stages. He decided to cross the little known Shalshal pass (4908 m) just south of Niti pass. Kedyar Singh, an influential trader from Niti, offered to assist him. After four days, the party crossed the Shalshal pass to Bara Hoti, which was 'full of small alpine flowers and whistling marmots'.[4] Here, his Tibetan yak driver deserted him and returned to Tibet fearing that if he carried on to Niti, his yaks would die from the heat. This was break of agreement and caused much inconvenience to Longstaff. With the help of Kedayr Singh's son, Longstaff crossed the Chor Hoti Dhura (5429 m), a direct route, to reach Niti village.[5]

OXYGEN EXPERIMENTS

The Royal Geographical Society had entrusted Dr Alexander Kellas, a Scottish climber, was with the task of conducting experiments on the use of supplemental oxygen by mountaineers at high altitudes, with a possible Everest expedition on the cards after the end of World War I. In 1920, the Society deputed Kellas to conduct experiments in the Dhauli valley. He was to go as high as possible on Kamet (7756 m). The Survey of India deputed Major H T Morshead to accompany Kellas.

The apparatus and cylinders were scheduled to arrive in India by June 1920. Kellas therefore, made his way to the Niti village by easy stages in July. The programme was, however, seriously delayed by the late arrival of the oxygen cylinders. As the cargo was marked 'high explosives', it was held up by customs – the border agency was presumably under the impression that Kellas was about to start a private war! The cylinders reached Niti only

4. Longstaff, Tom, *This My Voyage*, John Murray, London, 1950, p. 139.
5. 'Months later, when staying with Philip Howell, then of the Guides Cavalry, on North-West Frontier, the postman brought me a postal order for six rupees. I never found out what this was for till I returned to Niti with Charles Bruce and Mumm in 1907. It then turned out that it was sent by the Dzongpun of Dhaba as refund for the last day's hire which I had paid; the march his man had burked. Honesty typical of a Tibetan gentleman.' Ibid., p. 140.

on 27 August. This delay prevented the pair from climbing above Meade's Col on Kamet.

Kellas and Morshead found that their Garhwali porters were not all they wanted them to be. But they had nothing but praise for the Bhotias of Niti. 'On rock they can climb like goats, while on ice they readily learn step cutting. It appears very doubtful if the present-day expense of importing Alpine guides can ever justify their employment in future Himalayan exploration.'[6] These experiments with the oxygen cylinders in the Dhauli valley were eventually extremely valuable in designing the oxygen apparatus for subsequent expeditions to Everest.

WE ARRIVE IN JOSHIMATH

Kanu and Rama Pomal and I arrived in the Dhauli valley in June 2014. Much water had flowed in the Dhauli since the explorations by Moorcroft. Bureaucracy had tightened its grip: we had to obtain four types of permits – an Inner Line permit from the local magistrate, as well as permits from the Forest Department and Nanda Devi Bio-Reserve. We also had to pay fees per day to pitch tents in the area. Besides, permission was required from the local district magistrate and the Indo-Tibetan Border Police. But the ultimate winner was the demand for a medical fitness certificate for each member and porter. Such as things stood, the local doctor had printed forms to issue such certificates in reams!

Having read about the Dhauli and Niti passes in historical records, we were looking forward to trekking in these remote valleys. But no sooner had we arrived at Joshimath than we were told of a proper road leading from Joshimath till almost the foot of the Niti pass. The road was lined with bulldozers, road builders' camps, and taxis plying daily to the 'remote' Niti village. One can now be transported from Joshimath (1875 m) to the foot of Niti pass (4420 m) in just a few hours! We travelled on to Malari (2860 m) in three hours from Joshimath to enter the Inner Line.

THE GIRTHI GANGA VALLEY

A little ahead of the Malari police check post was the confluence of the Girthi Ganga with the Dhauli Ganga. Accessing the Girthi Ganga valley still

6. Ibid., p. 186.

remains a challenge although a motorable road now leads partially into the valley that goes north towards the Bara Hoti. The Girthi Ganga originates from two glaciers, both flowing north at first, west of Unta Dhura. Girthi, the eastern valley, is broad and drains the glacier at the foot of Nanda Gond – its waters are black. The western valley drains the glaciers at the foot of the peaks Kholi (6114 m) and Chalab (6160 m) where milky white waters gush from a narrow and highly-crevassed glacier. The Girthi then flows westwards, forcing a way through the gorge to meet Kio Gad at Girthi Dobala and merge with the Dhauli at Malari. This gorge had first been traversed by Dr Kurt Boeckh in 1893.[7]

THE SCOTTISH HIMALAYAN EXPEDITION OF 1950

There seems to have always been some explorer or other in the Dhauli and adjoining valleys. Moreover, the trade with Tibet kept the passes busy. In 1950, four Scotsmen decided to pay detailed attention to the valleys of the Girthi. Led by author and explorer W H Murray, they roamed these valleys at leisure, climbing peaks and observing the local villages. They were near a village – which they called the 'Metropolis of Surai Thota' – when they met Hartwell P Singh and Professor Chowfin of Allahabad University. Singh had a degree in Agriculture from the University of Edinburgh in Scotland. His immediate job was to trek up the Dhauli Ganga to the Niti pass on the Tibetan frontier to test the soil and introduce suitable seeds, potatoes and fruit trees. The Scottish party was happy to learn that potatoes grown here came from Scotland and found the Himalayan potatoes near Niti pass 'white and floury, well formed, and [with a] flavour superior to anything I had tasted in Scotland'. The Scottish party therefore surmised that Himalayan soil must be especially favourable to the growth of potatoes. Indeed, potatoes from upper Garhwal are greatly in demand to this day.

Murray and his team travelled towards the Tibetan frontier. They passed many herds of goats laden with bulging saddle bags driven by wool-clad Tibetans, passing south. The Bhotias of Niti were also on their way up the valley to trade with Tibetan caravans. Each party carried a Singer sewing machine to stitch bags and repair tents. In this remote frontier, the famous British sewing-machine was very popular.

7. Murray, W H, *The Scottish Himalayan Expedition*, J M Dent, London, 1951, p. 203.

As a young mountaineer I had read the accounts of these areas by Bill Murray and Frank Smythe. In 1988, we three trekkers from Mumbai had followed the footsteps of the Scottish team and explored the Girthi western valley. The eastern valley is relatively broad and frequently used by shepherds. Turning south from Topidunga, we had crossed Unta Dhura pass (5360 m) down to Milam and the Gori Ganga.[8]

THE AMRIT GANGA VALLEY

Going up the Dhauli valley, the first villages are Bampa and Gamsali – both at about 3400 m. They are some three kilometres apart, with the Amrit Ganga flowing between them. The Amrit Ganga, draining the 40 km long Bank Kund valley in the northwest, meets the Dhauli near Gamsali village. Going up the Bank Kund valley on a trail along the Amrit Ganga, is Dumsain, a flat open *maidan* with a clear pond.

We went up the Amrit Ganga valley as it turned and twisted in various directions. At the head of this valley lies the Gupt Khal (secret Pass), crossing over to the Alaknanda valley to Mana village. In 1907, A L Mumm suspected the presence of this pass and called it the 'Secret Pass' as it cannot be seen until the last slopes of the glacier are reached. Very few parties have crossed it from the Bank Kund valley. It is also known as the Zaskar pass, as it lies on the dividing line between the Great Himalayan and Zaskar ranges.

One branch of the Amrita Ganga valley leads to the Bhuidhar pass (5090 m; earlier called the Bhuyandar pass) and the trail from the pass descends across to the Valley of Flowers. We continued trudging across the Bank Kund glacier for four days to reach the foot of Gupt Khal (5760 m). We could see some figures on the pass. An exchange of shouts finally established that it was an Indian Army team on a reconnaissance of Mana peak (7272 m). Helped by their fixed rope on the final 200 m, we reached the pass. It was an experience, exchanging notes at that altitude. But an invitation to lunch at their camp on the Alaknanda side had to be reluctantly turned down as the distance would make returning to our camp in the Amrit Ganga valley later in the day impossible.[9]

---

8. Kapadia, Harish, *High Himalaya Unknown Valleys,* Indus Publishing Company, New Delhi, 1993, p. 43.
9. Ibid., p. 44.

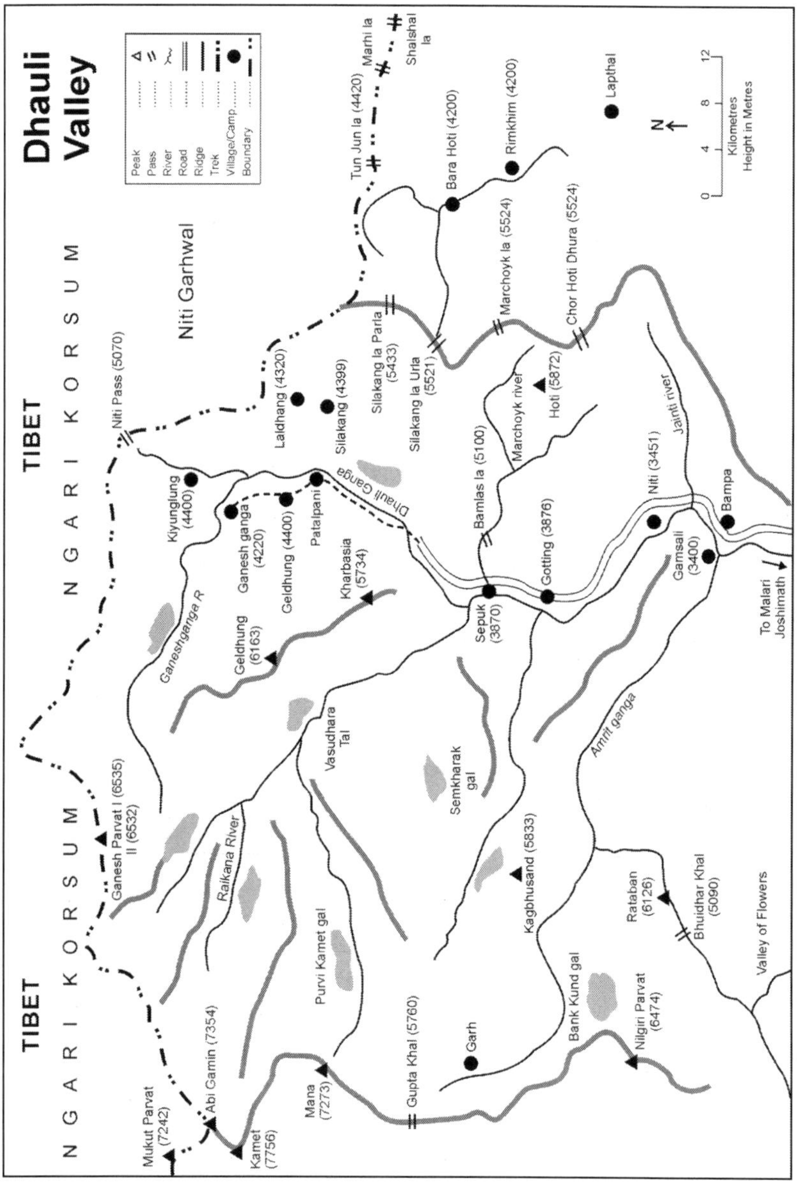

Dhauli Valley – Niti Pass.

Ahead of Gamsali, the Dhauli creates a terrific gorge, on one side of which has been built a precarious road. After crossing the gorge lies Niti, the last village in the valley.

FRANK SMYTHE ON KAMET, 1931

The route to Kamet peak leads along the Dhauli Ganga. All expeditions to Kamet in the first half of the twentieth century rested in Niti to organise porters and supplies. In 1931, a strong party led by Frank Smythe reached the Dhauli valley and later made the first ascent of the high peak of Kamet. Smythe was enchanted by the lower valley of the Dhauli, and recalled his conversation with General Charles Bruce, comparing it to the Alps.[10]

Smythe, a pucca British Sahib, was happy to be in hills, away from conflicts of India's freedom struggle in the plains. He mentioned:

> We were no longer within range of Gandhi's activities, and, after the insolent stares of "Congress Wallahs" of the lower hills and plains, it was pleasant to be greeted with a respectful and friendly "Salaam Sahib" or "Salaam Huzoor" from the villagers we met on the path.[11]

Smythe also observed about the people of Niti:

> At first appearance they seemed a wild, almost ruffian-looking crowd. Their faces had never seen, or their bodies experienced, soap and water. They exuded strong odours of yaks and other things. Their tattered garments consisted for the most part of coarse sackcloth. They walked barefoot or with feet encased in clumsy cloth, Tibetan boots or layers of sackcloth. But their gait was the gait of the hilman – slouching and slow on the level, rhythmical and deceptively fast uphill.[12]

---

10. 'I can bear him [*Bruce*] witness, for the Dhaoli Valley above Malari bears a striking resemblance to the Gastern Thal [*in the Alps*] only the Dhaoli Valley is on a more lavish and magnificent scale. The splintered rock peaks of reddish granite, of Alpine size in themselves, are mere outposts of greater peaks behind. Half a mile above Gamsali, the Dhaoli Valley narrows to one of the grandest defiles in the Garhwal Himalaya. From either bank of the Dhaoli River the precipices rise smooth and sheer, as though sliced by a titan's knife.' Smythe, F S, *Kamet Conquered,* Victor Gollancz, London, 1932, p. 239.
11. Ibid., p. 96.
12. Ibid., p. 105.

Frank Smythe and his party trekked at a leisurely pace, interacting with the villagers.

> Before leaving Surai Thota we were told of a belief which we were to hear repeatedly in the Kamet and Badrinath districts. When Doctor Longstaff climbed Trisul in 1907, one of his Gurkhas, Karbir by name, who accompanied him to the summit, was questioned by villagers on his return as to the view he had seen from the top. Being somewhat inventive and a mischievous turn of mind, Karbir replied with a grave face that they had seen far over the foothills to the great plain where they could see the cities of Delhi and Bareilly. And then, of course, it was easily possible to see Bombay, and beyond Bombay was the Black Ocean, and beyond that England, and he knew it was England because he'd been there! Thus does folk-lore originate, and we were questioned more than once as to whether we were climbing Kamet in order to see England from the summit.[13]

During our stay at Niti we asked around about this legend, but the present generation, fed on television, looked at us as though we had lost it! They knew where Bombay (now Mumbai) was and what lay beyond the ocean. We also aroused amusement when we spoke of another belief mentioned by Smythe. He had heard that a notion existed in the area 'that on the summit of Kamet there is a palace of pure gold tenanted by a powerful god'.[14]

A few kilometres ahead towards the Niti pass is the Gotting valley. It was compared by Smythe to the remote and serene valleys near Everest, as depicted in the paintings of T Howard Somervell. Today, a wide road passes through Gotting, which has turned into a ghetto of road workers and has a large presence of the defence forces. We stayed here for a few nights to acclimatise and undertook some walks in the side valleys. Several trails descend from Bara Hoti (4500 m) around Gotting. The trails from several passes, Chor Hoti Dhura (5429 m), Marchoyk la (5524 m) and Bamlas la (5100 m) descend to Gotting. The Raykana river from Vasudhara tal and Kamet merges with the Dhauli at Gotting.

The existing road ends at Kharbasia (4200 m), a little ahead of Gotting. A steep walk of six kilometres leads to Geldung (4400 m). This was our base camp. In front of us was the famous Niti pass (5070 m). It was a major depression in the long, running ridge, and by taking a detour we could avoid

13. Ibid., p. 87.
14. Ibid., p. 87.

all the steep sections of the ascent to the pass. Trading caravans to Tibet in the past have stayed in Kyunglung (sometimes the name is also used for the Niti pass) and crossed the pass to camp at Hoti in Tibet. Rising from the plateau was the shapely monolith of Geldung (6163 m).

Swami Pranavananda, a Hindu sage, used this pass in the 1930s to visit Kailash and Manasarovar – as this was the shortest approach to those holy spots. He stayed many months at Manasarovar and has described most of the routes leading there.[15] Niti villagers crossed the pass regularly for trade with the Tibetans. Gyanima Mandi was the nearest market in Tibet for them. Carrying wood and grains to Gyanima Mandi they brought back rock salt. The rich Tibetans were happy to offer diamonds in exchange for large quantities of grains. The trade continued until China took over Tibet in 1959.

To the west of Geldung is the Ganesh Ganga valley, winding its way to the Ganesh Parvat (6535 m) group of peaks. Two of these peaks were climbed by the Indo-Tibet Border Police teams in the early sixties, soon after the Chinese aggression. They used the approach from the Raykana glacier near Vasudhara tal, possibly to avoid proximity to the troubled border.

SMALLER PARTIES AT BARA HOTI

To our south and east was the valley of Silakang la, (5433 m) which led to the Bara Hoti plains. In the 1920s, several trekking parties visited the Bara Hoti area. They crossed and re-crossed several passes. In August 1929, Major G W P Money travelled from Almora to Malari and then up the Dhauli. He crossed Chor Hoti Dhura to Rimkhim (4200 m) and Bara Hoti and returned via the Damjan pass. (c. 4000 m). Eight Bhotias were killed by falling rocks in September 1927. Major Money and his party too faced severe blizzards, but luckily, they suffered no casualties.[16]

In 1931, Lt Hugh Rose crossed several passes: Balcha Dhura to Lapthal and Rimkhim to Shalshal pass (4908 m). He reached Tun Jun la (4420 m); attempted to cross Silakang la to Geldung, failing that he tried Marchoyk la (5524 m). Unable to cross back to the lower valleys owing to heavy snow on these passes, he crossed into Tibet to Sarkia and from there into upper

15. Refer to the book Pranavanand, Swami, *Kailash – Manasarovar*, S P League, New Delhi, 1949.
16. Mason, Kenneth, editor, 'Minor Himalayan Travels', *Himalayan Journal*, Vol. 1 1929, p. 98.

Garhwal via the Niti pass. He enjoyed excellent views from the passes, particularly of Kailash. Those were happy days when no boundaries stopped explorers and they roamed the valleys as they desired.

In 1954, Indian explorer Gurdial Singh and his friends roamed the Upper Garhwal and adjacent Tibet in an epic journey that lasted three months. He had climbed Trisul with Roy Greenwood in 1951 and now returned to the area of the Dhauli valley, crossing Chor Hoti Dhura to Bara Hoti. They climbed a peak near Silakang la (Parla), going up by the south ridge to the 5431-m summit. They crossed to Tibet via the Tuan Jun la (4420). When they reached Kailash, he observed: 'the mountain is beautifully proportioned. A mighty cathedral; it seems to be the creation of some divine architect. No wonder it is considered so sacred by millions of Hindus and Buddhists'.[17]

They made their way back from Tibet via the Marhi la (c. 5100 m) to India. The slopes to Bara Hoti were covered with the familiar flowers, rippling streams so refreshing to the eyes, the first view of the Hoti amphitheatre in the mellow afternoon light after three weeks in harsh Tibet was most welcoming. They returned via Marchyok la (5524 m) and Bamlas la (5100 m). 'We had returned, intact, to the zone of rose finches, snow cocks, ruby throats, meadow-buntings and, to quote Longstaff, "to soft airs, warmth, trees and flowers"'.

In 1959, Gurdial Singh returned to Bara Hoti from the south. His only companion, Aspi Moddie, wrote: 'A time comes when a man wishes to have his mountains and enjoy them painlessly. Then there are no summit ambitions, and one is content to see "heaven in a wildflower"'. This was the aim of this party of two stalwarts. They started from Kumaun in the south and went across Unta Dhura and Khingur La to Lapthal. Entering the Bara Hoti plains, they stood on Bancha Dhura pass (5364 m) on the border, enjoying stupendous view of Garhwal peaks. As they turned their faces to the east, they saw the peak of Kailash. "There Kailash was, fifty miles away, the only white mountain in a brown land. It had the quality of Shangri-La, a remote and heavenly place."[18]

17. Singh, Gurdial, 'Three Months in Upper Garhwal and Adjacent Tibet', *Himalayan Journal*, Vol. 19 1955-56, p. 3.
18. Moddie Aspi, 'A High Walk in the Central Himalaya', *Himalayan Journal*, Vol. 22, 1959–60, p. 146.

Theirs was the last civilian party to roam around freely in these areas. In two years' time, both the Indian as well as the Chinese armies started to occupy the area and no visitors were allowed in the upper Dhauli valley.

1962: FACE TO FACE WITH THE CHINESE ARMY

For the Niti pass and its surroundings, 1962 was a game-changing year. The India–China war saw the introduction of the Indian army at high altitudes. One of the first defence posts was created at Bara Hoti Grazing Ground (BGG) across the Silakang pass from the Dhauli valley. Then, in early 1962, the Indian Army received information that the Chinese were planning to occupy BGG no sooner than the snow melted. The BGG is a gigantic amphitheatre at about 4200 m. On its northwest and southwest rims are ridges three hundred to a thousand metres higher than the BGG plateau-floor. But its northeast rim, which forms the international boundary with Tibet (China) is barely 150 m higher than the surroundings, and therefore, provided an easy gateway for the Chinese to BGG over the Tun Jun la (4420 m).

On 27 April, an Indian defence party led by Lt Gen Baljit Singh managed to reach Rimkhim with great difficulty and established a post on the plateau with the Indian flag flying. They disguised themselves as a Revenue Collection Party (RCP), set up to collect taxes for cattle grazing at Bara Hoti – so that their presence might not be called a military occupation of Bara Hoti.

The Chinese army detachment of ten soldiers and 30 laden ponies arrived at Bara Hoti from Tibet on 12 May and attempted to bypass the Indian camp. The Indian soldiers obstructed their paths, physically blocking their manoeuvring, all the while drawing their attention to the fluttering tricolour Indian flag. After a few minutes of heated gesticulations, the Chinese pitched their tents about 20 m away from the RCP, inside a disused graziers' stone-walled enclosure. Sadly for the RCP, the 30 ponies of the People's Liberation Army were the only livestock pastured in the BGG – and they refused to pay the revenue!

Though there was no fighting, in a short while the Chinese took possession of the un-held Tun Jun la, named it Hu Ji and set up a post at the site where they had stopped. Since then both sides have consolidated their positions, thus making it difficult for mountaineers and trekkers to visit.[19]

19. Singh, Baljit, *India Defence Review*, Internet Edition 18 September 2012.

OUR RETURN

As we returned to Niti, local elections were being held. Democracy has its roots here too, with posters everywhere, loudspeakers blazing and polling parties travelling up and down. Rich Niti villagers who migrate to the plains every winter had returned for a day to vote and a festive atmosphere prevailed. Thanks to the road, today they arrive here in cars and vans instead of on mules; there are solar lights, telephones and televisions. The road had been a boon for the villagers and the defence forces.

As with many other Himalayan valleys, this one, so remote in the first days of exploration in 1811, has become well connected to the world outside. There are those who might be tempted to call this the end of the age of exploration in the area. But they underestimate the breadth and scope of the mighty ranges this valley is gateway to. New climbs, further valleys and greater exploration await here the mountaineers of the future

We have not journeyed across the centuries, across the oceans, across the mountains, across the prairies, because we were made of sugar candy.

Sir Winston Churchill

Temple bells, Kumaun (Geeta Kapadia).

21

A Hundred Years after Younghusband

Travels in Tibet

Travel becomes most meaningful in retrospect, after we have had a chance to paint it up a little in our minds. With time, all scenes of travel become part of remembered landscape, effected by the chemistry of time and distance.

At the western end of the road below Potala Palace in Lhasa stands a huge chorten with a gate in the centre and wide roads on either side. On 3 August 1904, the British army marched through this gate, symbolising the fall of Lhasa. Younghusband reached and 'unveiled Lhasa' a week later. We stood opposite this historic chorten exactly a 100 years to the date after the event.

The Younghusband expedition 1903–04 was organised to thwart Russian interest in Tibet, so it was thought. Lord Curzon, the then Viceroy of India, felt that the Russians were supplying weapons to Tibet. He persuaded the British government to authorise a major military expedition to Lhasa, which had been closed to visitors for a long time. Thus, the Younghusband mission was born. Soldiers gathered in Darjeeling; Sikh, Dogra and other Indian sepoys under British officers, including L A Waddell and F M Bailey, and marched across Nathu la at the height of winter in December 1903. Supply lines were built up with usual British military efficiency and they penetrated deep inside the Chumbi valley. Finally, Lhasa was reached but, as in present-day Iraq, no WMD (Weapons of Mass Destruction) or Russians were found. After signing a one-sided treaty which established a permanent British presence in Tibet, Younghusband returned.[1]

---

1. Charles Allen, *A Mountain in Tibet*, Sterling Publishing Co Inc, 1982.

LHASA AND SURROUNDINGS

Much water has flowed in the Tsangpo since, as the adage goes. Tibet has undergone change, political upheaval, ethnic rivalries, development of its infrastructures and is now a part of the international tourism circuit. Many border roads have been built and entry points opened. A modern international airport and a super-fast railway line with modern carriages to Lhasa will be ready in time for the Olympics to be organised in Beijing in 2008 . After the symbolic opening of Tibet by Younghusband, the world has changed for the Tibetans.

A modern jet operated by the Chinese airlines connects Lhasa to Kathmandu. They serve some of the worst food, but the view compensates for everything! The panorama opens with Gaurishankar, Everest and Makalu, a grand view almost beyond imagination. As the aircraft takes a sharp northerly turn, the focus shifts to the right as the Kangchenjunga massif and peaks of Janu and Jongsong come into view. Soon 'the Plateau' of the north, Sikkim, is seen and then we fly over Tibet. It was now time to fasten seat belts for the landing at Gonggar airport, which was under renovation and expansion. Younghusband had taken more than nine months to reach here, with guns drawn on *ekkas*[2] and long supply lines. We reached in two hours and the only formalities required were a passport and visa. We drove the 96 km to Lhasa on a four-lane highway crossing the Tsangpo at the Gonggar bridge, imagining the crossing by the early teams on inflated yak skins – romantic but dangerous.

This was my third visit to the Tibetan plateau, each time by a different route.[3] I have witnessed many changes in Tibet under the Chinese rule. Over decades the only thing that has not changed is the Chinese ruler's hatred of the Dalai Lama, whose photographs and literature are banned, and anyone found with it is deported. However, faith survives, and most Tibetans wear a locket with Dalai Lama's photo. Prayer houses in remote villages have his

---

2. Guns were mounted on an open bullock-cart pulled by Yaks. This was the first time that any kind of wheels were introduced in Tibet.
3. 1999: trekking from Simikot to Purang, Manasarovar area.
   2000: Lhasa to Raga, northern route to Shinquen, Manasarovar, Everest base.
   2004: Lhasa, Shigatse, Gyantse, Kailash, Tirthapuri, Guge and Tsaprang.

photo – well hidden from view but very much in the hearts of people, and that's what the Guru wanted in the first place!

Lhasa and its surroundings, a major showpiece of Tibet, has changed beyond recognition. Old pictures show a big shantytown opposite the Potala. This area has been cleared by 'cajoling' its occupants to move to the outskirts. The square has been beautified and is now a major tourist attraction called Potala Square. It wears a festive look with several Chinese statutes and a four-lane highway passing at the foot of the Potala. Lhasa and the surroundings have excellent roads and well-planned townships. Fancy streetlights, taxis, museums, huge billboard signs, posh hotels and brightly-coloured restaurants gives it a feel of Hong Kong. Progress yes, but then ideologically no one, least of all the Tibetans, has any say, as to whether they want this progress or what it means to them. Schools teach Tibetan as a language, locals can travel to mainland China and many are employed in the tourism industry. No political dissent is tolerated and no one is willing to voice any views, specially as many Han Chinese have settled in Tibet and are in position of power.

The Potala was painted in white, symbolising religious power, and the centre was painted maroon stating political authority. Nowadays, as there are so many visitors here, *only* 5000 are allowed in everyday and that too for a very short period. Many of the visitors are Chinese who are here to see the cultural heritage of 'their' country. For preservation of the monument, photography is prohibited, and continuous maintenance work is carried on. Lhasa is beyond recognition since Younghusband's time of course, but it had grown even since last I visited, four years ago.

At the centre of the Potala square flutters the Chinese flag, near the site of a pillar that was erected in 821 signifying the Sino-Tibetan treaty. This treaty gave China its first foothold in Tibet, the roots of their claim date thus far back. It was at this place during the 1959 'Lhasa uprising' that hundreds of Tibetans gathered to protest. They were dispersed and the Dalai Lama fled to India. The rest, as they say, is history.[4]

The spiritual centre of Lhasa is the Jokhang temple with the Barkhor circuit around it. At any time of the year, you will find devout pilgrims from far away villages, performing *chham*, the Tibetan way of bowing to the deity.

4. Tsepon, W D Shakabpa, *Tibet: A Political History*, Yale University Press, 1967.

The temple wore a colourful look, and in small stalls on the mall, statues of Mao were being sold along with those of Buddha! Near the temple and in Potala square, boards were pasted with Chinese circulars, and statues of liberated peasantry were erected in Beijing style. Tibetans read them with curiosity. They live without much fear and not much poverty was evident – less than you would see in India.

The three monasteries around Lhasa are as ancient as they are holy. Sera is the nearest one with Ganden and Drepung a little away. Each of these represent a way of life with hundreds of lamas being trained here. When we visited, they were flourishing, well maintained and with several lamas performing rituals. Norbulinka, the summer palace of the Dalai Lama was another attraction. With its Japanese-style garden and long walls, it was peaceful haven for his holiness when he stayed here. A large radio, presented by the Prime Minster of India in 1952 is displayed and one wonders how it must have been ferried across passes by humans and mules.

YOUNGHUSBAND MISSION

Soon it was time for us to start on our journey across the Tibetan plateau. In 2004, the road to Gyantse was being repaired and widened into a four-lane highway. Soon a wide road from Gyantse to Yatung would join the road from Nathu la in Sikkim and on to Kolkata. As per the agreement reached between India and China, large container traffic from the warm water port of Kolkata would drive across this road to supply Lhasa, giving fillip to trade and bringing supplies to Lhasa directly rather than driving across the entire Chinese mainland.

We passed the beautiful Yamdrok tso (lake), Karo la (pass) and the foot of Nojin Kang peak. From your car you are within a touching distance of its icefall. Nakartse was as dirty at can be. In fact, throughout our travels in Tibet, we always wished for better hygiene, the one thing that has been missing in the development of tourism beyond Lhasa. As a rule, toilets were dirty; rooms and streets left much to be desired. Gyantse township was being improved with wider roads, and celebrations to mark the 100th anniversary of Younghusband's expedition were under way – called 'The Younghusband invasion and the defeat of British'. Gyantse fort, in the centre of town, witnessed fights between Younghusband's troop led by General

McDonald and Tibetan forces. Today, as one climbs up to Gyantse fort, at the entrance there is 'The British Hate Museum'. It contains stories of how brave Tibetans defeated the British. Of course, history records that the Tibetans were soundly beaten, though not without a fight. From the early part of the last century deceptions by Chinese and twisting of history has remained their hallmark.

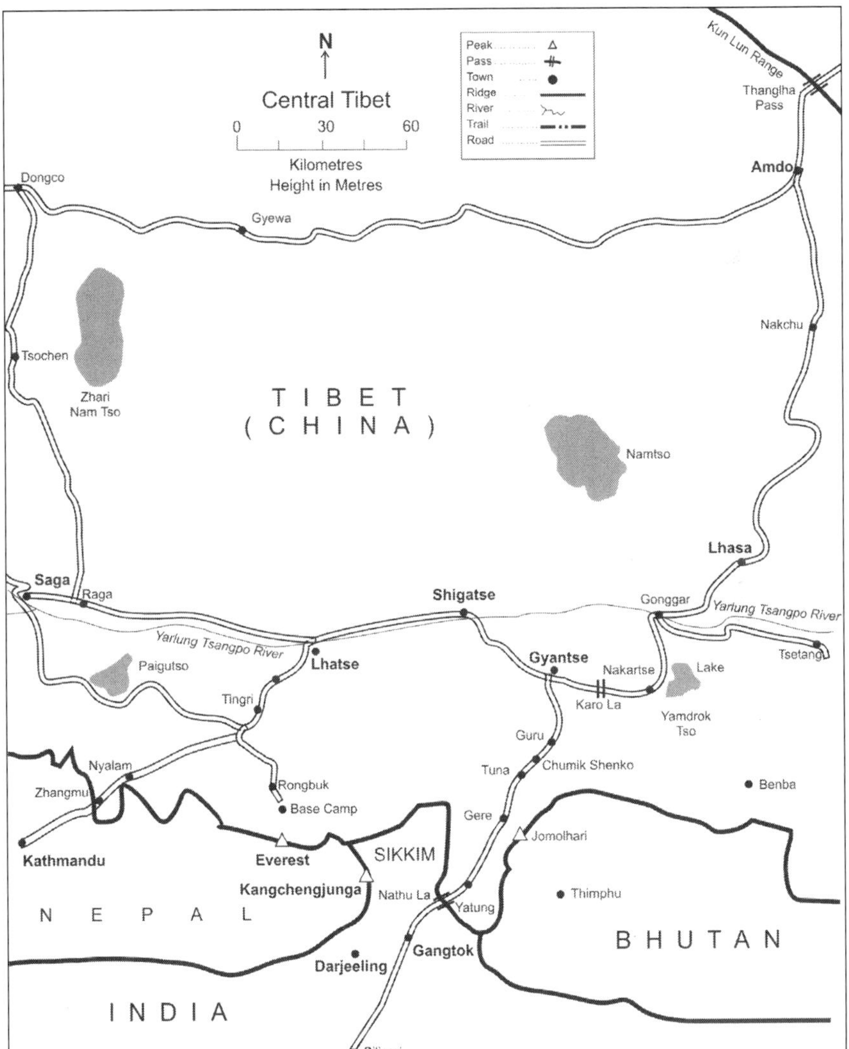

Central Tibet.

As the Younghusband expedition entered Tibet the first major battle was at Chumik Shenko where the Tibetan general from Lhasa had gathered a large army with primitive weapons. As both the armies met, there were friendly exchanges, and the Tibetans admired the machine guns and modern weaponry that the British had brought. Someone from the Tibetan side fired one of these and threw stones. This led to Indian soldiers opening fire and killing over 3000 Tibetans, a truly gory example of any battle (also see p. 67).

Going through several gorges the Younghusband expedition soon reached Gyantse. The Tibetans fled from the fort, which was quietly taken by the British. Presuming that the battle for Gyantse was over, a large contingent of soldiers marched towards Lhasa across Karo la. The Tibetans, realising their opportunity, returned in strength and re-conquered Gyantse. The British then found it difficult to dislodge them. Finally, fresh reinforcements from the famed Gorkha regiment were called for. As the main column returned, on 30 June 1904, the Gorkhas mounted a major assault to re-capture Gyantse fort. After establishing defences, they fired mortars and artillery to make a gaping hole in the walls and its defences.

The final storming of the fort began at 3.30 am, on 6 July 1904. Lt J D Grant and Havildar Karbir Pun led the assault. They climbed a cliff as the Tibetans threw stones and mud down on them. They got nearer to the wall along a route the stones could not reach, but many climbers slipped. Finally, at 6 pm, these two reached the top, followed by others. As the Gorkhas made a charge with their khukris, the Tibetans ran to the top and jumped off the cliff to their deaths. Over 500 Tibetans died in the assault. The 8th Gorkha Regiment received a special citation for bravery. Lt J D Grant was awarded the Victoria Cross and Havildar Karbir Pun was awarded a First-Class Order of Merit. The Gorkhas marched ahead across Karo la, Yamdrok tso and entered Lhasa through the chorten without any resistance.

GYANTSE AND SHIGATSE

The other important aspect of Gyantse is the Kumbum *stupa*. Built in the ninth century and rising seven storeys high, this unique structure is an architectural wonder. On every floor there are small temples with exquisite paintings that have lasted centuries. The top offers views of Gyantse fort and the wall that was climbed by Lt Grant.

The wide road connecting Gyantse and Shigatse, the second most important town in Tibet, covered the distance quickly. Shigatse was a mini-Lhasa with modern facilities and its centrepiece was the Tashilumpho monastery, the headquarters of Panchan lama. The Swedish explorer Sven Hedin had drawn excellent black and white sketches of the monastery and comparing them a century later, one could see that little had changed, the streets and buildings are the same. One can only hope that faith has remained the same, for there are disputes about who is the 'real' Panchan lama. While we were in Shigatse, the Panchan lama drove through the streets in a cavalcade strictly guarded by Chinese soldiers. People bowed to him quietly, and some celebrations were held. We interacted with lamas, locals and guides and, as Indians, were given respect by the locals ('you come from the country where the Dalai Lama lives'). They were comfortable talking to us, but their eyes were always alert for eavesdroppers, even within their own group.[5] Grains are collected as tax from rural areas and at vantage points there were clusters of road builders' huts. Many Tibetans felt that what China took from Tibet (gold, precious metal, gems, food) was far greater than what was given back to them (roads, houses, infrastructure).

From Shigatse starts the second part of Tibet. The road is rough and as you drive across the Tibetan plateau, population is sparse and towns become smaller. Lhatse stands at the junction where a bridge across the Tsangpo leads south to Kathmandu, while the road west goes along the river. There is a pass to be crossed and that is where we met Mr Po, a Chinese cyclist who was going across from Peking to Central Asia, 'to see *my* country'. He was staying with Tibetans and had no qualms about travelling alone among them. On the road, we frequently saw double-decker buses carrying Chinese tourists visiting Lhasa and proceeding to the extreme west of Tibet. These tourists looked interested in the country, but it was difficult to judge whether they were sponsored by their government or were travelling on their own.

THE NORTHERN ROAD

Little before Saga, which is a major military station, a bifurcation leads north going across very inhospitable terrain. It was this route that I had

5. During my third visit to Tibet, no Chinese liaison officer accompanied us as was required five years ago. There was more openness and Tibetan guides were running the show.

followed during my second trip to Tibet. Immediately after the bifurcation lies one of the wonders of this plateau – 'the Geysers'. Huge springs of hot water that burst out high into the sky and splash over a vast area. There are also many small bubbles of sulphur water. There is a small rest house and geological study station here, maintained by the Chinese government. The road ahead becomes rougher and rougher, and no human settlement can be seen. We passed Zari Namtso and the small township of the Tsochen (Coquen) that stands almost on its shore. Further north we were on the Shinquen – Amdo 'highway' and turned west, passing Gertse and Gakyi to reach Shinquen, which borders Ladakh. This was a barren stretch to drive through but, amid the cold winds we would suddenly find a large flock of sheep grazing on the stony plateau. We always wondered, 'grazing what?' When we stopped, curious shepherds would gather around and look at us without making any trouble. All nomads have standardised quarters on the outskirts of towns. Much of the population consists of Han Chinese who have been given incentives to come and settle here. Many herds of Tibetan antelope ran along the road, unafraid of our cars. We heard stories of Chinese soldiers using guns to hunt wildlife while travelling on this route.

At regular intervals, after driving about 200 km with no human beings in sight, a modern township would suddenly spring up from nowhere: Tsochen, for example. It had bank (China Bank) that would change dollars, hotels, modern amenities, water supply, school (Chinese teachers), telephones (China telecom, mobile phones, internet), postal facilities (China Post which operates daily services), good restaurants (Chinese) and of course, the Chinese army garrison quarters. One wonders what these people eat, where they work and why they are settled in these smaller towns.

Shinquen (old Ali) is the largest town in western Tibet – with nightclubs and a disco! A special tourist guesthouse is built here and permits are checked at a local Tibetan office lined with posters of Indian film actors and playing Indian film music! It is a huge military headquarters with a small airstrip and it was from here that Chinese troops attacked India in 1962. The Aksai Chin road, linking it to Central Asia; Khotan, Yarkand and Kashgar, starts from here. The war was fought by the Chinese to protect this illegal road running through Indian territories. Today, regular bus services operate on this route for locals and tourists.

Rutok (Rudok) is on the banks of the Pangong Lake, two-thirds of which is in China and a third in Ladakh. Having visited this lake in Ladakh, I compared with amazement the features and water of the lake. Like territories, even water was caught between the two political giants.

On return, one of the Tibetan guides cajoled us to climb a small hill, called 'Lovers Hill'. It offered a magnificent view of the great Himalayan range dividing this part of China and Himachal Pradesh of India. Leo Pargial (Rio Purgial) rising above the Satluj gorge, Shipki la pass, Gya and all the peaks were clearly visible. But amazingly, we also saw a large cantonment of the Chinese army with a huge star of People's Liberation Army painted on the hill and an airstrip behind it. It seemed that the Chinese did not mind tourists overlooking their military establishments, which I would have found it difficult to believe anywhere else. We were photographing the peaks with a telephoto lens, when suddenly we noticed a group of Chinese soldiers approaching us. 'It looks like now we will return via Beijing', I murmured. But the soldiers were also tourists like us, they came, looked at us, peered through our lenses at the peaks and murmuring, *verly good, verly good,* ran down again, smiling!

From Shinquen we drove to Demchok, which is about couple of kilometres from the Indian border and the Indus, for a brief visit. Across the political line stood the Indian Demchok. A small monastery was all that it had to offer. What really surprised us was that our Indian passports did not deter the Chinese from allowing us travel to any of the border areas as long as we had paid our fees and our visas were stamped with these places marked on them. In fact, during my three visits no officials, army or administrative, ever raised any objections to my Indian passport or ever looked up with a suspicious glance.

We were now to enter the third part of Tibet, where the holy places of Kailash, Manasarovar, Tirthapuri and Tholing math are situated. Some of these areas have strong associations with India as many Hindu pilgrims throng here.

TREK FROM NEPAL TO WESTERN TIBET

During my first visit to Tibet, I had trekked across the border from Nepal, a most favoured route for trekkers. We flew from Kathmandu to Nepalgunj and Simikot. Trekking along the Karnali we slowly gained ground to reach the border across Nara la. On some stones we saw slogans – *Maowadi Zindabad* (*Hail Mao Communists*). Little did we realise that this was the start of the trouble that has since engulfed western Nepal and stopped any approach through this route. Soon, we approached the border where a stone marked 'The entry point into Tibet'. Ironically, it was erected in early 1962 when China resolved its border problems with Nepal, but, later the same year, it attacked India for the same problem. We passed Khojarnath, our first huge monastery; its situation next to the border was what saved this monastery from destruction during the infamous Cultural Revolution when hardened bands of Red Guards destroyed much of the cultural heritage of Tibet. The lamas ran away across the border with almost everything and returned only after the fury was over. It has a huge Hindu influence, and many parts have paintings of Hindu gods and goddesses.

Purang, the district headquarters for this part of Tibet was nearby. We completed entry formalities and found special quarters for Indian tourists and pilgrims as well as with many hotels. The streets have a variety of goods being sold (Indian currency was accepted!) and barbeque meat it seemed, was the preferred delicacy. Walking the streets, we suddenly came across a group of fancily dressed ladies. Obviously they were not locals, but 'comfort girls'. They had travelled the long distance from mainland China to practise the 'oldest profession of the world' for the benefit of the large garrison of the Chinese soldiers. They are apparently a regular feature near all army stations in Tibet. On a hill at the outskirts of Purang, stood the ruins of the Purang (Taklakot) fort. This was the fort that had housed several prisoners who were tortured. In his book *Spy on the Roof of the World,* Welsh mountaineer Sydney Wignall, mentions his internment in this fort and the sufferings he had to endure there.

The road from Purang passes Toyo village, which houses a memorial to the great Dogra General, Zorawar Singh who died here in battle. Starting from Kishtwar, the Dogras had conquered Ladakh and then marched eastwards into Tibet. The Chinese and Tibetans withdrew and allowed them deep inside. When the winter approached, the Dogra army was trapped in these inhospitable surroundings and was attacked by the defenders.[6] On December 12, 1841, gallant Zorawar Singh fell to a bullet in the war – his army was massacred with the usual Mongol ruthlessness. Taklakot (Purang) was abandoned. The flag of Lahore Durbar, however, continued to flutter in Leh. The Tibetans believed Zorawar to be a powerful person and in their primitive superstition began chopping his body and collecting different parts for strength. Some body parts were buried at Toyo where a monument was erected, and the place of worship is locally known as 'Singhba chorten'.

MANASAROVAR AND KAILASH AREA

A long winding two-lane road now takes visitors, quickly and in comfort, to Raksas Tal and Manasarovar with a grand view of the holy Kailash. We gave a lift to a Chinese army officer in our car. After some initial hesitation, I got chatting with him as he spoke fluent English and seemed rather friendly. He was a stamp collector and we agreed to exchange Indian and Chinese stamps, which we did later by post. At the first view of Manasarovar and Kailash, I watched him curiously. As we alighted, he did a proper namaste to Kailash and Manasarovar and kneeling on ground like any other Tibetan performed a *chham*. We Indians were brought up with suspicion towards the Chinese, but such gestures and our experiences clearly illustrated that all are not cruel and non-believers as western writers would like us to believe. We met many friendly Chinese soldiers and, other than once at Saga, we were never stopped from photographing anything that we wanted to.

A lot has been written about Manasarovar and Kailash, which has a central place in Hindu philosophy and the Indian mind. The real reason could be geographical as four major rivers, which supply water to India, originate in the vicinity of this lake and mountain. The Indus flows towards the west and, after entering Ladakh, takes a huge turn to flow south across Pakistan into the Arabian Sea. The Yarlung Tsangpo (or only the Tsangpo) originates at the foot of Mayum la near Manasarovar and flows across the Tibetan plateau to the east where its passage is blocked by the great massif of

6. This also happened five decades ago when the German army attacked Russia in World War II in a similar fashion. See the book on Zorawar Singh, *Footprints in the Snow* by Brig G D Bakshi. The Jammu and Kashmir Light Infantry of the Indian army originates from Dogras of Zorawar's army.

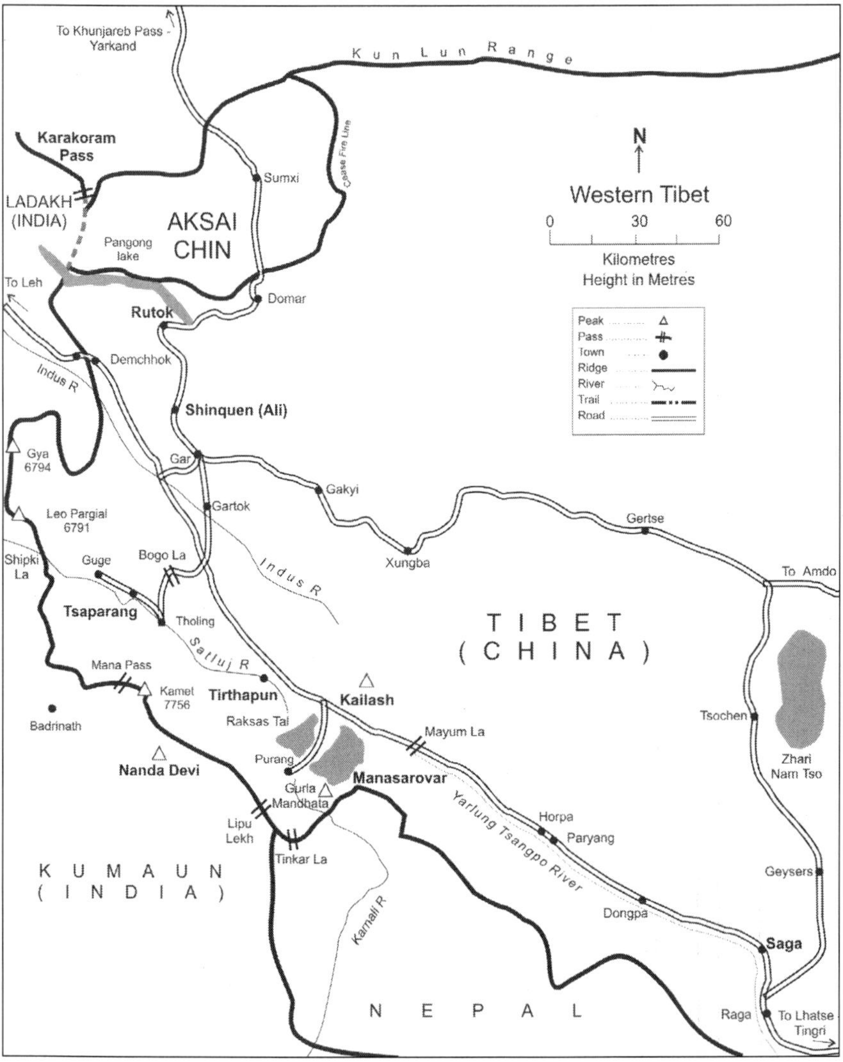

Western Tibet.

Namcha Barwa and Gyala Peri. Making a stupendous gorge between these two peaks, it finally turns south and enters the plains of Assam, where it is called the Brahmaputra. Finally, it merges with the Bay of Bengal.

From the southwest of Manasarovar near Tirthapuri originates the Satluj, flowing past the old kingdom of Guge. It passes through a gorge at foot of Shipki la to enter Kinnaur and flow into the Punjab plains to finally merge with the Indus. Towards the south from the foot of Gurla Mandhata originates the Karnali river, which flows through Nepal to join the Ganga. Thus, the major water sources of the Indian subcontinent, apart from the Ganges, originate north of the Himalaya, and particularly from vicinity of the Manasarovar and Raksas Tal lakes. The channel between these two lakes, called Ganga chu, is situated almost on the same longitude as the holy confluence of Ganga, Jamuna and the mythical Saraswati at Allahabad in India! These factors may have given a religious halo to the peak and the area. Perhaps, someday, a researcher would discover that early saints and Indian *shastras* (holy books) actually knew about the geographical significance and hence declared the area holy. There are gold mines at Thok Jalung, on the channel between the two lakes.[7]

The greatest view from Manasarovar area is of the Indian Himalayan peaks rising in the south and seen at about at same height due to curvature of earth. No wonder Tibet is called the 'Roof of the World'. Extending from Nanda Devi, Kamet, Abi Gamin, Mukut Parvat, the range extends towards the peaks of the western Himalaya. This is a stupendous panorama, and it is worth travelling here just for this view.

Amongst the several travellers and pilgrims to have visited these areas, the Indian sage Swami Pranavanand, stands out. He stayed here for several years and thoroughly explored all its aspects. His books, *Kailash and Mansarovar* and *Explorations in Tibet* are the most authoritative references on the area.[8] E Kawaguchi, a Japanese monk who travelled here in disguise, has also narrated experiences in the area in his book *Three Years in Tibet.*

TIRTHAPURI, TSAPRANG AND GUGE

We travelled southwest from Manasarovar to Tirthapuri and as tradition has it, a Tibetan pilgrim has to pay obeisance here before visiting Kailash. This was the extent of Hindu influence into this area as Indian gurus from the south had reached here centuries ago. The Satluj originates from the plains below Tirthapuri where the watershed divides the Indus and the Satluj river

7. The early exploration interest in Tibet was to locate these gold mines. Pandit Nain Singh passed from here in 1877.
8. These books were so accurate that initially the Chinese had banned them, and one could not travel into Tibet with copies.

systems. There are several shapes of mountains, which curiously resemble Nanda Devi. There is a hole through which you put your hand and pick up three stones: three white stones signify your karma to be very pure leading you to heaven, three black stones send you towards hell. Luckily everybody falls in between, picking some white and some black stones!

From Tirthapuri we drove across Bogo la to enter the southernmost district of Tsaprang. No words can describe the landscape, which must be seen to be believed. Surreal colours of mountains, deep gorges, backdrop of range after range of unbelievable shapes of peaks, was captivating. The high peaks of the Himalaya and Mana pass were on the horizon. The Satluj flowed in the centre of the range, forming a wide gorge. No wonder so many travellers and pilgrims were attracted here. We camped little before the Satluj gorge and on the next day crossed a bridge to reach the small township of Tholing (Thuling). The Tholing *math* (a typical Indian expression for a Hindu ashram), was established by Adi Guru Shankaracharya who was among the earliest people to have crossed the Himalaya through Mana pass from the Hindu shrine of Badrinath. He performed initiation rites on the king of Guge, under whose kingdom this area fell. The statue he carried back, a mix of Buddha and Vishnu, was consecrated at the Badrinath temple. Later an earthquake destroyed it and a new statue has now been consecrated.

The Tholing *math* was in ruins and had a very eerie feeling. In the centre was a typical square where a *havan* (puja with fire) would have been performed and the wall must have had huge statues of Hindu gods and goddesses. All this was ripped apart during the Cultural Revolution in 1967–1974. Today, the *math* lies in ruins. As a sign of changing times, and a kind of an expression of regret, the Chinese had put up boards that these temples were destroyed during the Cultural Revolution. We could see Chinese archaeologists measuring and photographing the area and were told that a major restoration drive based on old pictures was likely to be conducted.

A few kilometres from Tholing stand the ruins of Guge, a place of mystical quality. A huge fort stood here and today, though only the ruins can be seen, you are still awestruck by its magnificence. From the Satluj valley at its foot you see a high hill in a brilliant setting, with many holes, which soon turn out to be caves, mud walls and monuments. Inside are paintings, which have luckily remained intact, showing the variety of visitors to the court of the King of Guge and Hindu gods and goddesses. Jesuit Father Andrade had crossed Mana pass after Shankaracharya had stayed here and converted the king to Christianity! After a few years, the local lama clergy took objection and rose in revolt. The king had to run away for a few years, and when he returned to restore the kingdom, it was as a Buddhist.

The centrepiece of attraction at the Guge ruins is the Winter Palace. It is a huge cave through which one has to descend and its dark rooms with small windows are uniquely placed to keep the king and his entourage warm during the very cold winters of the Tibetan plateau. It offers a good view and gives you the feeling of how the king must have spent long months of winter, warm but without many of the modern-day comforts.

This is what Lama Govinda, a spiritual traveller from England, had to say about Tsaprang and Guge.

> It may be that the others might have felt oppressed by the loneliness and strangeness of the place, but to us it was just paradise – an enchanted world of rock formations which had crystallised into huge towers, shooting up thousands of feet into the deep blue sky, like a magic fence around an oasis, kept green by the waters of springs and mountain brooks. A great number of these nature-created towers had been transformed into dwellings – into veritable "skyscrapers" – by the people who had lived here many hundreds of years ago. They had ingeniously hollowed out these rock-towers from within, honey combing them with caves, one above the other, connected by inner staircases and passages, and lit up by small window-like openings.[9]
>
> Lama Angarika Govinda, *Way of the White Clouds,* p. 232

RONGBUK AND EVEREST BASE CAMP

With this the third part of Tibet was over and all that remained was the visit to the Rongbuk monastery at the foot of Everest. We crossed the Tsangpo by ferry at Saga (where a bridge is now being built) and drove to the banks of the beautiful Paigu Tso, admiring the northern face of Shisha Pangma. A rough road, now a major shortcut, took us to the Rongbuk monastery, looked after by several nuns.[10] Many Everest expeditions have camped here and today, vehicles reach the base camp, which has built-in toilets, quarters for liaison officers and in season you can imagine over 300 tents spread around.

9. Govinda, Lama Angarika, *Way of the White Clouds,* Rider, London, 1966, p. 232.
10. The original road drove over Pang la and offered a wide panorama of Everest peaks. It is still worth the extra drive.

The stories of ascents of Everest from the north are many. As a vignette from the Younghusband days, small colourful *ekkas* drawn by mules would have taken tourists from the monastery to the base camp. The Everest was within touching distance and the play of light at different times of the day has to be seen to be believed. The last rays of sun made the mountain golden, soon followed by reflections of radiant moonlight. One from our group had tears in her eyes looking at this magnificence.

RETURN

We drove back to Tingri for the descent from the Tibetan plateau, cutting across the Himalaya at Thorong la. It was a natural route passing between wide gorges, the Milarepa Cave en route was a holy place, but the townships of Naylam and Zhangbo, were as crowded and dirty as can be, and filled with moneychangers and trucks. Custom formalities were completed here and soon we passed the Chinese flag to cross the 'Friendship Bridge' to Nepal. Hundreds of Nepali porters scrambled to carry luggage across the bridge for a small payment.

As we had our first coffee, the Indian influence was all around us. Several pictures of Hindu gods, film stars and cricketers adorned the walls of every restaurant, barber's shop and shopping area. But the major statement was made by the Dalai Lama's picture displayed at every place -- a picture the Chinese have banned from being taken into Tibet. Having experienced Tibet's material development under China, which perhaps Tibetans would have never achieved by themselves for a long time, triggered many discussions on what was better – the material progress we had seen or the Dalai Lama's photograph, which symbolised freedom and spiritual realism? It was a hard choice.[11]

In a shop we saw stickers being sold – the Indian flag with a message written on it, 'India – Love it or Leave it' – a message from the Dalai Lama for the Tibetan population now sheltering in India. Our choice of course, was obvious. We loved India and were soon back home having experienced Tibet from Younghusband's days to modernity.

---

11. The Dalai Lama has appealed to followers to accept Chinese rule in Tibet and has plans to dissolve the Tibetan government-in-exile at Dharamsala, India.

22

Across Bhutan in Eighteen Days

A Journey across the Dragon Kingdom

The invasion and subjugation of Tibet by the Chinese Communist Army was one of the most tragic events of modern times; not only because it resulted in the annihilation and torment of countless innocent victims, but also because mankind is in eminent danger of losing one of its ancient and most successful cultures. For, whatever its imperfections in terms of modern democracy and in spite of its material poverty, the Tibetan theocratic system seems to have produced a people as content, as tolerant, as courageously independent and as free from cramping taboos as can be found anywhere. Today, Bhutan is almost the only place where this remarkable culture still thrives on its native soil. Like Tibet itself, this small mountain kingdom has remained beyond the reach of all, but a very few western travellers. Like Tibet, true, it has in the past owed its immunity to foreign influence, largely to the policy of the Government of India to define the political integrity of neighbouring states. Unlike Tibet, it is still independent, though how long it will retain this happy position if you would dare to guess.

Foreword by Eric Shipton.
From the book *Two and Two Halves to Bhutan*
by Peter Steele.

The flight from Kolkata to Paro was short. We could see the Himalayan range from Kangchenjunga to Masagang almost on border with Arunachal Pradesh. The aircraft made a delicate manoeuvre and we landed at the small airstrip at Paro. We were in Bhutan, called by many names: The

Dragon Kingdom, the Hidden Kingdom or Shangrila.[1] Till recently, Bhutan had kept its doors closed to onslaught of tourism and only a restricted number of visitors were allowed. Television, internet and films were not freely permitted till 1998. The benevolent King had intentions of protecting the traditions, culture and environment of the Kingdom – almost like what was envisaged by Shipton in the quote above.

At the airport 'foreigners' had to pay steep visa fees and a hefty charge per day of visit.[2] For Indians entry was free, no per day charges and we could use Indian currency – we are not foreigners in Bhutan other than our passports. Paro (2100 m) was a beautiful town, surrounded by forest. On the first evening we visited the small bazaar which was almost time-wrapped, with carved-wood windows, small houses and dominated by a huge *dzong* (fort). This was to be the usual pattern for our travels in Bhutan and we visited several huge *dzongs*. We planned to drive across the country – from west to east and partake of its culture, history and beauty.

EARLY HISTORY

The eighth century AD king Sindhu Raja, who was converted to Buddhism by Padma Sambhava (Lotus Born), was one of the earliest rulers of Bhutan. For several centuries after him many Tibetan kings crossed the passes to ravage the green valleys of Bhutan. In 1527, the lama Dujom Dorjee was the first Bhutanese who repulsed Tibetan invasions and took control of the entire country with the name 'Dharma Raja' (a king rules as per religious truths). It was he who built most of the *dzongs* as defence. Preferring to devote all his time to religion, he set up the institution of 'Deb Raja' (a king who dispenses bounty) to run the country.

The first Europeans to enter Bhutan were Fathers Estevao Cacella and Joao Cabrel in 1627. They met the second king, who was visiting Bhutan

---

1. Bhutan originated from the word *Bhotente:* Tibet was known as *bhot* and *ente* means a border land, thus, *A land on borders of Tibet.* However, the Bhutanese know their country as *Druk-Yul*: Druk- Thunder Dragon, Yul- Land – The Land of Thunder Dragon. (Rustomji, Nari, *Bhutan the Dragon Kingdom in Crisis,* Oxford University Press, Delhi, 1978, p. 4).
2. In 2004 all foreign visitors (except Indians) had to pay US $ 200 per day all-inclusive.

from his home at Ralung monastery near Gyantse in Tibet. They trekked with the king and wanted to preach Christianity, but were politely denied permission. They left for Shigatse in Tibet, from where Cacella, and later Cabrel crossed back to India from Nepal.

The areas south of hilly borders of Bhutan were called 'duars', fertile, flat lands that are today home to many tea gardens. This narrow strip of land is only about 40 km wide and 400 km long with 18 passes (doors or *duars*). In 1772, Deb Judhur swept down to Cooch-Behar from Bhutan and challenged the British who were in control of the area. Warren Hastings responded by sending an army under Captain Jones. Deb Judhur compromised and requested Hastings for peace and in 1774, George Bogle was commissioned to represent the British in Bhutan, the main intention being to open routes into Tibet.[3]

Dr Hamilton (1775), Captain Samuel Turner (1783), Captain Pemberton (1838) and Ashley Eden (1864) followed to further open up Bhutan and establish relations with British India. Ashley Eden's mission was badly treated by the Bhutanese and was forced to sign a treaty for restitution of the Assam duars. To punish the Bhutanese, in 1865 the British declared what came to be called the 'Duar War'.

There were three major Duars: Char Duar, Alipur Duar and Buxa Duar. By the early 19th century, the British knew the importance of these tea-growing areas and occupied them. Bhutan attacked the British but was repulsed. Finally, the 'Sinchula Treaty ' was signed, which gave these areas, including Darjeeling and Kalimpong, to the British and later to India. The compensation to be paid was Rs 10,000 per year, later raised by the Punakha Treaty to Rs 50,000. Today, it amounts to a large sum, which the Indian government pays by adjusting it against grants given to Bhutan!

Twenty years later the last civil war was fought in Bhutan. The Paro and Tongsa Penelop joined hands to defeat Thimphu and Punakha Dzong chieftains. Later Bhutan closed its doors to all outsiders.

The 1904 Younghusband expedition to Lhasa was a turning point in the history for Bhutan too. The Tongsa Penlop accompanied the expedition as

3. Dr Hamilton, who was with Bogle, carried large supplies of potatoes, which he planted at many places. This was the first introduction of the plant in Bhutan – today it is a staple food.

a mediator and in return for his services was awarded the 'Order of Knight Commander of Indian Empire'. John Claude White went to Bhutan laden with gifts, to award this honour in person on behalf of the British government. He attended the installation of the Tongsa Penlop as Gyalpo or king, which happened the following day.[4] The Dharma Raja had died, and no incarnation was found so the Deb Raja held both offices. But he was a recluse following a spiritual life, thus power fell into the hands of strong men of the country. At this gathering, lamas, officials and laymen unanimously voted to abolish 400-year-old offices of Deb and Dharma Raja and proclaimed Sir Ugyen Wangchuk, as the first Gyalpo (king) and declared the title hereditary. Britain signed a treaty in 1910 agreeing not to interfere in the internal administration of Bhutan, which in turn, agreed to be guided by an advisor from Britain in matters of defence and external relations. The Gyalpo visited Delhi for the Durbar of King George V. Sir Ugyen Wangchuk died in 1926 and was succeeded by Jigme Wangchuk. Bhutan's doors during this time remained tightly shut for the outside world and only a few foreigners entered the country.

PARO AND THIMPHU

We climbed to Tiger's Nest monastery (Takstang gompa) near Paro. This is a beautifully located monastery perched on a huge rock. Legend has it that a lama rode a tiger to reach here. We also visited the stupendous Paro Dzong, built in 1647, and Drukyal Dzong . The drive to Gele la (3988 m) gave us a glimpse of Ha district and Chomolahri peak. Everything seemed little familiar for these natural monuments are featured in many books and magazines. Modern goods were available everywhere and the contrast was worth experiencing – centuries old buildings juxtaposed with hordes of tourists sipping cold drinks, beer and eating chocolates at exorbitant prices. Not to overlook the hundreds of photos being clicked every hour.

We drove to Thimphu (2200 m), 55 km of winding narrow road in a dusty and barren valley. Thimphu is like any other Indian hill town, with shops full of 99 per cent Indian goods, crowded streets and pollution. We could have been back home!

4. Claude White, *Sikkim and Bhutan.*

The *dzong* here is the seat of the Bhutanese government. This was also the seat of the religious head, Je Khenpo. The Potala in Tibet represents religious as well as political power and common head is the Dalai Lama. This unison created a conflict, as the same person may not be suited to rule both. Bhutan has, in the last 100 years, bifurcated the institutions. The king is a hereditary monarch, whereas the head lama is a religious head called Je Khenpo. There have been many assassinations attempting overthrow each other but in last 50 years, especially with support from India, the king has become all powerful. All for the better, as Bhutan has had some excellent kings.

MODERN TIMES, CHANGING TIMES

Following the Gurkha invasions in Nepal, many fleeing Nepalese had settled first in the duars and later in the foothills of Bhutan for almost four generations now. Some of them served as slaves of Bhutanese nobles till 1963 when slavery was abolished. The father of the present King set them free. It is strange that until the early sixties they were slaves! There are many Nepalese in Bhutan, many speak Nepali but the stigma of being a slave still remains, and there are no intermarriages.

We watched an archery contest – archery is the national sport. Two colourfully dressed teams competed against each other, shooting arrows to hit the bull's eye at a good distance. The contest was accompanied by songs and dancing after each shot. We also saw the advent of modernity, such as the internet, telephones and television in Bhutan. While most visible in Thimphu, these facilities could be seen in remote parts too. With them, life is changing; scantily dressed ladies dance at parties to western tunes, couples live together without marriage, dress codes are turning western and attitudes are changing to the extent of causing an HIV scare. The youth are turning to India for work. Things are better, as compared to Nepal, but the winds of change are blowing from all directions. Bhutan's forests need to be protected so 2 June, the king's birthday, has been declared 'Tree Planting day'. At present, there is reportedly no corruption except at lower levels, but if this catches on and more roads are built, the forests may be in danger. Bhutan also has the highest birth rate 1: 3.5 in the world. Today's population of 900,000 thousand may triple soon and that may cause major environment pressure. Although it looks difficult, one prays that this small kingdom will survive as it is today.

EXPLORATION AND MOUNTAINEERING

Bhutan received few western visitors who wrote about it with knowledge and affection. Claude White, who was appointed Political Officer here in 1910s, travelled and studied a lot, cared for the people and bullied the officials! His book *Sikkim and Bhutan* is still a classic as he was a painter and sketched many features of Bhutan. Dr Peter Steele who was a doctor on Everest, trekked to remote areas with his two young kids sitting on a horse! His account *Two and Two Halves to Bhutan* is fun to read. These are just two names from a long list of visitors. A classic book is by Nari Rustomji, who followed the developments in Bhutan keenly, visiting on several occasions as a Political Agent of Sikkim. His book *Dragon Kingdom in Crisis* was the first book after Indian independence in 1947.[5]

The earliest climber to visit Bhutan was Spencer-Chapman. He had seen Chomolahri (7500 m) on the border of Bhutan and Chumbi valley of Tibet and climbed the peak via the south ridge in 1937. For decades after that the peak was left alone. Then, in 1970, an Indo-Bhutan armies' team, led by Col N Kumar attempted the peak. Two Bhutanese and two Indian officers including Col Prem Chand and Dorjee Lhatoo reached the summit. A second attempt was mounted two days later and though three climbers attempting the peak were spotted near the summit, they were never seen again. While at first it was thought that Chinese may have shot them, the Chinese co-operated in trying to locate their bodies on the Chumbi side but there was no trace of them.

After a few years, Junko Tabie, the Japanese woman mountaineer who had climbed Everest, came to climb Masagang, the highest peak of Bhutan on the border of Tibet. She failed narrowly but based on her experience, a strong Japanese team reached the summit the following year. Doug Scott, Victor Saunders and Sharavathi Prabhu climbed Jitchudrake.

Soon the government of Bhutan closed peaks for climbing, so in the last two decades there have not been any major expeditions. A large section of the Himalaya thus remains unexplored for climbers to attempt when these areas are opened.

---

5. Rustomji was a personal friend of the ruling family of Bhutan (as he was with Chogyals of Sikkim) and was advisor to the Gyalpo (the king) during the most troubled times, again as in Sikkim. What a man!

PUNAKHA

We drove 60 km from Thimphu on a winding road with good forest cover. En route we crossed Dochu la (3150 m) and descended to the Wangdi Phodang valley with a large river flowing in centre. Punakha Dzong (1500 m) was 17 km away standing between two rivers.

This is a huge and intricate fort and one of the best in Bhutan. There are several rooms, each beautifully decorated and preserved. As there were Tibetan attacks in later years and there was no cultural revolution as in China and Tibet, the artefacts here are well preserved and well maintained. However, a major earthquake had destroyed this *dzong* and with it, a lot of the written history of Bhutan.

The *dzong* has a very interesting story associated with it. Guru Zhabdrung Ngwang Namgyal was in the Ralung monastery south of Lhasa. The king did not like him and ordered his execution. Namgyal ran away to Bhutan with a rare golden statue of Buddha. After few year, the Tibetan discovered the loss and attacked Bhutan several times to recover it. The *dzong* was built by Namgyal to hide the statue. When a large Tibetan force attacked, he reasoned that the statue was cause of all troubles, so he made a duplicate. When the Tibetans came to the *dzong,* he threw the replica into the river. The Tibetans were shocked, called all Bhutanese mad for throwing away such a precious statue, but they went back, never to attack again. The original statue is still at Punakha Dzong but can be seen only by the Gyalpo (King) or Je Khenpo (chief lama) once a year.

CENTRAL BHUTAN; BUMTHANG

We travelled 200 km east to Central Bhutan crossing Pele la (3390 m) and Yotong la (3425 m). En route we passed Tongsa Dzong and stayed at Jakar in a well-built wooden farmhouse with a villager. Though we missed views of the high mountains we were amply compensated by forest – what a forest! Only in Arunachal Pradesh, which is not destroyed by development, was the forest as unbelievably virgin! It must be seen to be believed and enjoyed.

Now we were in the ancient and historically important part of Bhutan, replete with legends. The father of the first king saw a white bird flying towards central Bhutan. So he followed it here and a prophecy told him that he would be a king. He found employment with the local chieftain of the huge Tongsa Dzong. When the chieftain retired he was given charge for five years, as the successor was a young child. However, after five years, he refused to hand over power and a civil war ensued. As a solution, the chieftain's child was made Penlop at Jakar-Bumthang.

The elder was made Tongsa Penlop (crown prince to succeed the king) and when he died his son became the first king of Bhutan. Thus the crown prince is given title of Tongsa Penlop and he then becomes a king naturally. The present crown prince was declared Tongsa Penlop a day before we arrived at Tongsa. But as Tongsa Penlops were always fighting in civil war, the name was changed to Chokhor Penlop for future kings.

There was much to enjoy around Bumthang. Mo Bar, the burning lake, had a legend: Once, a lama in search of treasure stepped into this lake with a lighted lamp. Not only did he come out with treasure, the lamp was still burning brightly! Then there was the legend of a lama, who acted as a mad man to popularise religion. While travelling he lost a load of berries at three places. He established huge chortens at each place, Ruku *ji*, Chiende *ji* and Tamsu *ji* – all ending with *ji*, meaning berries, as a clever ploy to establish religion.

We walked to the monastery of Shedung. Again, we were in the midst of ancient history and modern western tourists. A camera bag was forgotten by one of our companions in one of the three monasteries we visited and was later not traceable. We made a big fuss and took a policeman to the monastery. The bag was returned quietly. It is sad that winds of civilisation are blowing here too and, in few years, as in Nepal or in India things like this will happen more frequently. But we hope that this process is delayed as much as possible

The next day Bumthang was buzzing with tourists and locals as the Jambey Lhakhang dance festival was to be held. This monastery is one of the 1008 monasteries built by a high lama in one night, as it was destroyed by demons who would not allow it to be rebuilt. So, on a full moon midnight, the villagers dance naked to cheat the demons – make them think something is wrong and flee in fear. During the day a mela is held where goods are sold and archery contests held, along with gambling, drinking and eating.

EASTERN BHUTAN

We were now driving to Mongar (1500 m) and Trashigang (1700 m) in eastern Bhutan. This was a thickly forested area, much less travelled. Usually tourists do not proceed east of Bumthang, as there are fewer facilities. We travelled across two passes, Shertang la (3000 m) and Thrumsing la (3780 m), the latter being the highest motorable road in Bhutan. We missed the views but the forests again were great. Trashigang[6] is the eastern most town in Bhutan.

This was botanist country, well-surveyed first by F M Bailey in 1924, when he travelled around west and central Bhutan and found some rare Himalayan poppies. Two other botanists, G Sheriff and Frank Ludlow made extensive journeys to every corner of Bhutan. In 1933, they crossed from west to east and in 1934 and 1936 they collected plants from the east and crossed into Tibet. They made more two plant-collecting expeditions soon after the war, mainly in eastern Bhutan. Sheriff and Ludlow knew Bhutan as no foreigner had ever before.

These areas have seen much modern history too. After India gained Independence, an Indo-Bhutanese Treaty of Friendship and Co-operation was signed in 1949. This allowed Indians and Bhutanese full access to each other's countries.

The 1962 Indo-China war changed everything for Bhutan. It is believed that while fleeing from the Chinese in 1959, the Dalai Lama wanted to enter Bhutan from Tibet. The king refused, as he was naturally scared of the Chinese army following him into the kingdom. (The Dalai Lama has not visited Bhutan since, nor has the king, who keeps the Chinese happy, invited him.) It was a wise decision as the Chinese, using that as a ruse, may have taken over Bhutan for good. The Dalai Lama then entered India from the far eastern corner of the Bhutan–Arunachal Border at Khinzemane, an area held by India but within few kilometres of the Bhutanese borders. During the war, Indian troops were on the Thagla ridge, which Bhutan claimed as theirs and they protested, but mildly. In fact, many injured, retreating Indian soldiers came down to safety through Bhutan. The fearful (of the Chinese) king signed a comprehensive treaty with India and almost everything in Bhutan since then is linked to India. India pours in lots of money and goods, undertakes road construction and both armies jointly patrol the borders

6. The lady owner of our small hotel was named Jambey Eden. Eden is quite a non-Bhutanese second name. The only reference could be that of Ashley Eden mission to Bhutan in 1864 !

with China. Bhutan's conducts its defence and foreign affairs in consultation with India.[7] The king is wise and does not irritate Delhi. In 1971 when Bangladesh was created, at India's calling Bhutan, a member of the UN, was first to recognise it as a new country.

THE FAR EAST

From Trashigang we drove to Rangjung monastery, 16 km away. This wonderful monastery was renovated by lamas from Mysore (south India) and had old connections with Ralung gompa near Shigatse. We were allowed to photograph inside and young lamas studying the scriptures were least bothered by our presence.

Goma Chorten, was en route to Trashiyangtse. As the story goes, there was a huge rock, signifying the evil in one's mind, that Guru Padmasambhava cut with a sword to purify himself – you can see the mark. Then he meditated here; the mark of his head on the rock can also be seen. He conquered the evil mind with meditation, but evil spirits still cropped up in his head as a serpent. He cleverly buried it under the evil mind itself – under the rock. That was his simple message: conquer evil in the mind by burying it under the mind itself.

The last place we visited was Kora Chorten at Trashiyangtse, a holy circle also visited by Arunachalis. It was just about 10 km away from Arunachal Pradesh – the point where I had stood a year ago! It was a touching moment for me. Many passes lead across from here to India and for locals and Indians, borders are open.

With this our travel in Bhutan, west to east was complete. Ideally, we would have liked to drive out to India from Samdrup Jonkhar in the south, a much shorter route. But this road is closed due to terrorism, and this was one of the last chapters in the history of Bhutan in 2000–2003. Many Bodo and ULFA[8] militants of Assam, who were fighting India for separation, had entered lower eastern Bhutan in 1990s, established camps in the thick forest and operated from there. As the Indian army could not enter Bhutanese territories to flush them out, this provided them a safe haven.

---

7. Bhutan has an army of only 15,000 soldiers.
8. Bodos are fighting for a separate Bodoland while ULFA is the 'United Liberation Front of Assam'. Both are militant, terrorist organisations.

Much pressure was put on Bhutan by India to fight these terrorists. The king pleaded against bloodshed, fearing the threat to himself and his people if he fought the militants. Finally, he agreed to act and appeals were made by him to militants to give up arms. When they did not respond, the king personally led a Bhutanese army brigade to attack the camps. The militants fled and as they entered Assam, the Indian army took over. The queen mother has built a series of chortens on Dochu la (3150 m) (near Thimphu) as thanksgiving to gods for this brave action by the king.

All that remained was to drive back the way we had come to complete our eighteen-day journey across the Dragon Kingdom. What we had witnessed and enjoyed was unparalleled natural beauty, friendly and honest people, rich culture and history with controlled tourism development. With the world changing fast, Bhutan cannot be in isolation for long and we wondered what the next decade will bring for the country. The king cannot keep Bhutan closed forever. Afterall, an open-air museum for future generations as well as the welfare of people is at stake. On the other hand, the country cannot allow all carpetbaggers who wish to visit. Bhutan will have to find the golden mean to develop the state and preserve its culture and environment. As a Buddhist tenet states: 'Peace is not absence of chaos, it is peace within chaos'.

While returning we saw a figure in red sitting on a rock on the banks of the river. He was the rimpoche (Precious Teacher) of a nearby monastery and was meditating. Not disturbed with our presence, he did not even look at us, but continued chanting and meditating, as he must have done for decades. His disposition was very pleasant, calm and serene. As I went near him, he opened his eyes. I had never seen a calmer face and quieter eyes. He continued prayers silently as we photographed him at close quarters and was not upset. As we left, he waved us goodbye with a faint smile but continued with his prayers. To me this was the true spirit of Bhutan. As long as such devotion continues, Bhutan will remain the major bastion of Buddhism, peace and serenity.

23

Himalayan Disaster – Nature's Fury or Man-made Calamity?

A Look at Himalayan Floods in Recent Memory

On the night of 15–16 June 2013, scientists at Wadia Institute's weather station recorded 315 mm of rain in Kedarnath valley, which is extremely rare for this time of the year. The rain soon brought down huge avalanches from the glacier slopes of Kedarnath peak and the nearby 'Rock Tower' peak. These peaks form the backdrop to the Kedarnath temple on a long ridge, behind which lies the Gangotri glacier. The avalanches crashed down into Chorabari lake at its foot. This wide lake had never held much water and did not have the capacity to contain such vast amounts of water and debris. As its banks burst, water cascaded down from the lake towards the Kedarnath temple with great fury, bringing with it huge rocks and debris. In its normal course, the Mandakini river flows on both sides of the temple plateau. But this time, the flow was so furious that it breached the plateau on which the temple is built and rushed towards the temple complex. A huge rock rolled towards the temple, smashing into the memorial to Adi Shankracharyya behind the temple and came to a stop. It is possible that this event saved the temple from destruction as other rocks, stones and floodwater that followed were diverted and forced around it. However, they smashed the shops in the bazaar, burying many pilgrims there.

The devastation caused in downstream was staggering, making the Uttarakhand catastrophe 'one of the most extreme events of the century'. In the lower valleys more than 70,000 pilgrims were trapped, and many died. Unplanned roads, makeshift construction on riverbanks and an overwhelming number of pilgrims multiplied the scale of the disaster.

Nature's fury certainly started the destruction but it turned into a man-made catastrophe. It will take years before we are able to enjoy the Himalayan mountains in the Kedarnath area.

Traditionally, villagers built homes far above reach of the river, safe from floodwaters. Although the destruction of roads cut off these traditional habitations and they suffered from a lack of supplies, they remained relatively safe. Those villagers who had not followed traditional wisdom and built homes near the river and road for commercial reasons were wiped out.

This devastation was caused by just two glaciers and one lake. The Indian Himalayan region is home to over 7,000 glaciers, covering an area of 8,500 km. They play a crucial role in shaping and influencing the environmental conditions in India. Siachen, Gangotri, Zemu, Milam, Bhagirath Kharak and Satopanth are only some of the important glaciers located in the Indian Himalayan region. Approximately 968 glaciers drain into the Ganga basin in Uttarakhand and over 4,660 glaciers feed the Indus, Shyok, Jhelum and Chenab river systems. The Ravi, Beas, Chenab and Satluj river systems are fed by 1,375 glaciers; 611 glaciers drain into the Teesta and Brahmaputra basins, contributing between 50–70 per cent of the annual discharge. If the higher Himalayan region is not treated with due respect, any of these glaciers can cause havoc anytime.

Himalayan glaciers and natural dams have caused havoc in the past. It may be interesting to recall just a few of these events.

GONA TAL

Gona tal was a largish lake created by natural landslide in the early part of the last century. A serene lake with clear green water, it was situated in the Birehi valley, about 24 km from Pipalkoti, on the banks of the river Alaknanda and used to be a popular halting place for pilgrims to Badrinath.

As young students, two of us had trekked to this lake in 1966. This is what I wrote in my diary:

JUNE 5, 1966: We left at 7 a.m. for Gona tal (13 km; 1710 m) where we intended to spend a few days. The path we followed went through thick forest and kept going downwards. After covering nearly 12 km we were in the hot valley near the Gona village from where the lake was three km ahead. It had been a horrid, hot, sweltering journey, at the end of which we found a beautifully located Forest Rest House facing the green, clear water of Gona tal. Two days passed quickly; mostly boating and swimming in the lake.

Three days in paradise were not enough but we had to leave mainly because our food stock was over, and we had to eat the local food which we did not relish. On the 8th, we left Gona tal for Birehi, 16 km away. We could see the forests burning in the distance in the darkness of the night. After our 170 km trek over 16 days, we were psychologically drained. There was no question of walking even a kilometre more, and Pipalkoti was 8 km away. It sounded like eternity. Providence was on our side, for the engineer whom we had met at Gona tal was going to Pipalkoti in his jeep and he was kind enough to give us a lift. We spent a day at Pipalkoti, on the banks of Alaknanda.

Five years later we heard tragic news. In 1971, at the peak of summer, the natural dam that had created the Gona tal suddenly burst, causing floods and havoc. Fortunately, only half the retaining wall had broken, or else the tragedy would have been far greater. Water rushed down the valley where we had walked and in a flash, it reached the Alaknanda, though luckily below Pipalkoti. The impact was the same as in the 2013 Kedarnath disater – roads were wiped out, many pilgrims who were on the road were killed and their bodies carried down to Rishikesh by the floodwaters. But then there were not the hordes of tourists and pilgrims as in 2013. Thus, the devastation in terms of human deaths was far less. After about a decade, engineers allowed the controlled bursting of the remaining wall and the lake was drained without causing more damage.

Now only an empty bowl exists at the 'paradise' where we had enjoyed three wonderful days!

SIKKIM

In 1976, Zerksis Boga and I were camping at the foot of Kangchenjunga, at the head of the Zemu glacier. This was the spot where many explorers had camped in the 1930s. Douglas Freshfield (see his book *Round Kangchenjunga*), Paul Bauer and his German team, G O Dyhrenfurth, John Hunt, H W Tilman amongst others. Everything was the same, except that the 'Green Lake' they all had camped at had disappeared and we were staying next to an empty crater.

In addition to all its other natural beauty, Sikkim is a land of glaciers. The main ones are Zemu, Rathong and Lhonak . These glaciers are surrounded by potentially dangerous glacial lakes that can burst and cause floods at any time; scientists say that Sikkim is a ticking time bomb. Glacial lakes are formed by melting glaciers and a sudden discharge of large volumes of water and debris from them is termed 'glacial lake outburst flood' or 'GLOF'. The famous Green Lake in west Sikkim was a moraine dammed lake that had formed due to the retreat of long Zemu and its subsidiary glaciers. Another glacial lake is being formed behind the terminal moraines due to blockage of the melt.

In north Sikkim, the area of one of the lakes in the Gurudongmar complex increased nearly four times between 1965 and 1989. The Khanchung Chho, origin of the river Teesta, is another moraine dammed lake that has grown noticeably over the past few years. The Chho Lhamo, a glacial lake situated on 'The Plateau', near the border of Sikkim and Tibet, had also grown significantly in size. Dr Alexander Kellas, T H Braham and John Claude White have written about the Chho Lhamo as one of the most beautiful places on earth. Now only a small portion remains – we photographed it in 2012.

'Teesta floods' are a regular phenomenon in the area. The Green Lake and glacial lakes of the Zemu glacier breach natural dams and cause misery downstream. The devastation of lower Zemu glacier is to be seen to be believed, the stone-bed goes on for several kilometres. The glaciers in the northern areas contribute to the floods with the level of water increasing to wipe out roads and habitations. The effects have been felt right down in the Bengal plains and Bangladesh. A severe earthquake hit the region in September 2011. The epicentre near Talung gompa was about 10 km below the surface. Hence it caused destruction of ridges faraway but the Talung gompa, near the epicentre was not totally destroyed! Thus, a major catastrophe was avoided.

LEH FLOODS

Ladakh, situated at around 3500 m above sea level, is described as a 'high altitude cold desert'. The area receives sparse rainfall (around 100 mm/yr), and a heavy downpour is a rare occurrence. The average rainfall in Leh for the month of August is 15.4 mm, with highest rainfall ever recorded during a single 24-hour period being 51.3 mm, on 22 August 1933.

But then, on the night of 6 August 2010, the unbelievable happened. In space of 30 minutes Leh received 75 mm of rain due to a cloud burst. This implies that it received around a year's worth of rainfall in half an hour! Moreover, the intensity was concentrated within a six km band. Suddenly debris was falling and Leh, not being used to so much rain was in disarray. Homes were destroyed; hospitals, schools and many buildings were damaged. The death toll was about 250. Much of the destruction was caused by debris flowing from the rocky sidewalls of the valleys, not by the flooding itself.

The village of Choglamsar at the outskirts of the city was particularly badly hit. This settlement had sprung up in the last few decades, in the direct line of walls of mud. Thus, the traditional wisdom of Ladakhi village building was violated and the villagers paid a heavy price for it. Traditional villages, on the plateau, did not suffer much damage. Though the cloud burst was a natural calamity, by not respecting Nature's laws, people paid the price.

CHONG KUMDAN GLACIER DAM

One of the earliest bursting of the glacier dams recorded was in the east Karakoram area. There are several huge glaciers in this area, which records extreme temperatures.

Over a century ago and repeatedly later, large natural dams have been created at the junction where the Chong Kumdan glacier meets the Chip Chap river. The word itself in Yarkandi language, means 'big dam' (chong: big, kumdan: dam)

The Chong Kumdan glacier has, over the years, often advanced rapidly. As it takes a sharp turn at this junction, it presses against the eastern walls opposite. The forceful movement of mass puts tremendous pressure on the walls. This blocks the flow of the Chip Chap river. However, the glacier is also liable to retreat and weakened by the retreat, the dams break and outbursts of water occur.

Such dam-bursts have taken place in 1780, 1826, 1835 and 1839, and have been a regular feature for many years from then on. The water marks from when the dam-waters rose for about 125 m at the peak can still be seen. The dam was studied by Ney Elias and Godwin-Austen in 1877.

All the dammed water rushed out causing death and destruction right up to Attock Fort, about 1200 km downstream. A battalion of Sikh soldiers stationed there suffered many casualties. Hence, the river acquired the name Shyok – 'the river of death'.

In 1926, floods released caused by the Chong Kumdan dam destroyed Abudan village and the surrounding land at a distance of 400 km from the outburst.

Another major dam-burst occurred in 1929. Mr T Durgi of the Public Works Department was then posted at the dam-site to warn against a future burst. In 1932 he sent two runners to Khalsar over the Saser Pass to warn people about the oncoming floods. Flood waters had already reached Khalsar, but by this phenomenal, fast trek (130 km in 28 hours) they did manage to pass on a warning.

Kenneth Mason, the first editor of *The Himalayan Journal,* took keen interest in this dam. He collected large amounts of material, and recorded observations and diagrams. He also calculated the frequency of the advance and retreat of Kichik ('small dam') and Chong Kumdan glaciers and predicted:

> As I shall not be here to be proved wrong, I will be precise. The Chong Kumdan will advance rapidly during the winter of 1968–69; the Shyok valley be blocked; a lake will form above it, some 10 miles long; and there will be floods caused by the collapse of the dam in autumns (July to September) of 1971, 1974 and 1977, the first one occurring probably in the autumn 2½ years after the glacier has advanced.

However, as per all the available records, the last major burst that caused destruction occurred on 16 August 1929. Since then, minor bursts have taken place in 1932–33 and 1937–39. The dam waters escaped slowly in these cases and no major damage was caused. But no bursts of dams have occurred after that. The Karakoram glaciers in this region are in a state of retreat. Indian forces have been stationed in the area since long and their records of the Shyok water-level do not speak of any floods.

Is it likely Mason may still prove correct about the future? Curiously, he gave the year 2013, for the last advance of the glacier and its dam. But perhaps the 'global warming' phenomenon has nullified his prediction.

We camped at this lake in 1991, exactly 62 years to the date of the last major burst. The line created by highest point of lake could be seen clearly on the retaining wall. The huge vacant area was sometimes filled with ice-penitents. A little lower down the Kichik Kumdan dam ('smaller dam') was still active but not enough to cause damage. We could compare our photos with those published in *The Himalayan Journal* in 1930.

As these examples indicate, the Himalayan and Karakoram glaciers are prone to floods. This has probably been accentuated by the phenomena of global warming causing cloud bursts.

But what about roads that are built on a wrong axis, dams that change the course of rivers, uncontrolled and unplanned building of hotels and habitation on riverbanks, the load of pilgrims and tourists on fragile valleys? This is far more than Nature can bear – therefore disasters like the recent one in Uttarakhand (2013) are bound to happen. It is best to understand the Himalaya and its glaciers and respect them.

She has a rainbow in her heart.
And quiet beyond the moon.
She is earth, hill, water, cloud
All faith-kept things.
Treat, oh treat her well, for we
Soon leave the secret room.

– Annon

Select Bibliography

GENERAL

Aitken, Bill. *Touching Upon the Himalaya*. New Delhi: Indus Publishing Co., 2004.

Aitkinson, E.T. *The Himalayan Gazetteer*. Allahabad: Government of India, 1882.

Bauer, Paul. *Kangchenjunga Challenge*. Translated by E. G. Hall. London: William Kimber, 1955.

Braham, Trevor. *Himalayan Odyssey*. London: George, Allen & Unwin Ltd, 1974.

Bruce, C.G. *Twenty Years in the Himalaya*. London: Arnold, 1910.

Jackson, J. A. *Adventure Travels in the Himalaya*. New Delhi: Indus Publishing Company, 2005.

Kapadia, Harish. *High Himalaya Unknown Valleys*. New Delhi: Indus Publishing Company, 1993.

——. *Meeting the Mountains*. New Delhi: Indus Publishing Company, 1998.

——. *Trekking and Climbing in the Indian Himalaya*. London: New Holland Publishers, 2001.

——. (ed). *A Passage to Himalaya*. Mumbai: Oxford University Press, 2001.

——. *Into Untravelled Himalaya*, New Delhi: Indus Publishing Company, 2004.

——. *Trekking in the Himalayas*, Outlook Traveller, 2016.

Kohli, Captain M.S. *Mountaineering in India*. New Delhi: Vikas Publishing House Pvt Ltd, 1989.

Longstaff, T.G. *This is My Voyage*. London: John Murray, 1949.

Mason, Kenneth. *Abode of Snow*. London: Rupert Hart Davis, 1955.

Mehta, Soli & Harish Kapadia. *Exploring the Hidden Himalaya*. London: Hodder and Stoughton, 1990.

Mumm, A.L. *Five Months in the Himalaya*. London: Arnold, 1909.

Nakamura, Tom. *East of the Himalayas*. Japan, 2018.

Neate, Jill. *High Asia*. London: Unwin Hayman, 1989.

Waddell, Major L.A. *Among the Himalayas*. Westminster: Archibald Constable & Co, 1899.

Wilson, Andrew. *The Abode of Snow*. Kathmandu: Ratna Pustak Bhandar, 1979.

SIKKIM AND NORTH-EAST

Allen, Charles. *A Mountain in Tibet*. London : Andre Deutsch, 1982.

Bauer, Paul. *Himalayan Campaign: The German Attack on Kangchenjunga*. Translated by Summer Austin. Oxford: Basil Blackwell Oxford, 1937.

Bauer, Paul. *Himalayan Quest*. Translated by E. G. Hall, London: Nicholson and Watson, 1938.

Bhattacharji, Romesh. *Lands of Early Dawn*. New Delhi: Rupa & Co, 2002.

Bailey, F.M. *No Passport to Tibet*. London : Rupert Hart-Davis, 1957.

Cooke, C.R. *Dust and Snow*. London: Private, 1988.

Cox, Kenneth (Ed.). *Frank Kingdon Ward's Riddle of the Tsangpo Gorges*. Suffolk, The Antique Collector's Club, 2001.

Elwin, Verrier. *The Tribal World of Verrier Elwin*. New Delhi: Oxford University Press, 1988.

Freshfield, D.W. *Round Kangchenjunga*. London: Arnold, 1903.

Hunt, John. *Life is Meeting*. London: Hodder and Stoughton, 1978.

Kapadia, Harish. *Across Peaks and Passes in Darjeeling & Sikkim*. New Delhi: Indus Publishing Company, 2001.

——. (Ed). *Legendary Maps from the Himalayan Club*. Roli books, 2018.

Maxwell, Neville. *India's China War*. Dehra Dun: Natraj Publishers, 1997.

Risley, H.H. (ed). *Gazetteer of Sikkim*. Calcutta: Government of Bengal, 1894.

Rustomji, Nari. *Enchanted Frontiers*. Bombay: Oxford University Press, 1971.

White, J Claude. *Sikkim and Bhutan: Twenty-one Years on the North-east Frontier, 1887-1908*. London: Edward and Arnold, 1909.

UTTARANCHAL

Aitken, Bill. *The Nanda Devi Affair*. New Delhi: Penguin, 1994.

Boardman, Peter. *The Shining Mountain*. London: Hodder and Stoughton, 1978.

Bonington, Chris. *Changabang*. London: Heinemann, 1975.

Gansser, A & H Arnold. *The Throne of the Gods*. London: Macmillan, 1939.

Kapadia, Harish. *Across Peaks and Passes in Garhwal*. New Delhi: Indus Publishing Company, 1999.

——. *Across Peaks and Passes in Kumaun*. New Delhi: Indus Publishing Company, 1999.

Kohli, Capt. M. S. (with Kenneth Conboy). *Spies in the Himalayas.* New Delhi: Harper Collins, 2002.

Murray, W.H. *The Scottish Himalayan Expedition.* London: JM Dent & Son, 1951.

Murray, W.H. *Evidence of Things Not Seen. A Mountaineer's Tale.* London, Baton Wicks, 2002.

Roskelley, J. *Nanda Devi: The Tragic Expedition.* Harrisburg: Stackpole Books, 1987.

Saunders, Victor. *No Place to Fall.* London: Hodder and Stoughton, 1994.

Smythe, Frank S. *Valley of Flowers.* London: Hodder and Stoughton, 1938.

——. *Kamet Conquered.* London: Victor Gollancz Ltd, 1932.

Shipton, Eric. *Nanda Devi.* London: Hodder and Stoughton, 1936.

——. *That Untravelled World.* London: Hodder and Stoughton, 1969.

Tilman, HW. The *Ascent of Nanda Devi.* Cambridge: University Press, 1937.

Venables, Stephen, *A Slender Thread,* London: Hutchinson, 2000.

KULLU AND LAHAUL

Gill, M.S. *Himalayan Wonderland.* New Delhi: Vikas Publishing House Pvt Ltd, 1972.

Harcourt, A.F.P. *The Himalayan Districts of Kooloo, Lahoul and Spiti.* New Delhi: Vikas Publishing House Pvt Ltd, 1972.

Kapadia, Harish: *Across Peaks and Passes in Himachal Pradesh.* New Delhi: Indus Publishing Company, 1999.

Khosla, G.D. *Himalayan Circuit.* London: Macmillan, 1956.

Noble, Christina. *At Home in the Himalayas.* London: Collins, 1991.

KINNAUR

Bajpai, S.C. *Kinnaur.* New Delhi: Indus Publishing Company, 1992.

Conway, Captain CWWS. *Sunlit Waters.* Bombay: Thacker, 1942.

Gerard, Captain Alexander. *Account of Koonawur in the Himalaya.* New Delhi: Indus Publishing Co, 1996.

Mamgin, M.D. *Kinnaur District Gazetteer.* Shimla: Government of Himachal Pradesh, 1971.

Mukherjee, Hirendra Nath. *The Great Tibetologist Alexander Csoma de Koros.* New Delhi: Sterling Publishers, 1981.

Pallis, Marco. *Peaks and Lamas.* London: Cassell, 1939.

Sanan Deepak & Dhanu Swadi. *Exploring Kinnaur & Spiti in the Trans-Himalaya.* New Delhi: Indus Publishing Company, 1998.

SPITI

Holmes, Peter. *Mountains and a Monastery*. London: G Bles., 1958.

Kapadia, Harish. *Spiti: Adventures in the Trans-Himalaya*. New Delhi: Indus Publishing Company, 1996.

Thomson, Thomas. *Western Himalaya and Tibet*. New Delhi: Cosmos Publications, 1978.

Handa, O.C. *Buddhist Monasteries in Himachal Pradesh*. New Delhi: Indus Publishing Company, 1987.

——. *Tabo Monastery and Buddhism in the Trans-Himalaya*. New Delhi: Indus Publishing Company, 1993.

KASHMIR

Jackson, John A. *Sonamarg Climbing and Trekking Guide*. Srinagar: Government of Jammu & Kashmir, 1976.

Neve, Dr E.F. *Beyond Pir Panjal*. London: Church Missionary Society, 1914.

Younghusband, Francis. *Kashmir*. London: John Murray, 1909.

Neve, Dr Arthur. *Thirty Years in Kashmir*, Lucknow: Asian Publications, 1984.

Tyndale Biscoe, C.E., *Kashmir in Sunlight and Shade*, New Delhi: Dilpreet Publishing, 2002.

ZANSKAR

Deacock, Antonia. *No Purdah in Padam*. London: Harrap, 1960.

Workman, W.H. and F.B. Workman. *Peaks and Glaciers of Nun Kun*. London: Constable, 1909.

Peissel, Michel. *Zanskar, the Hidden Kingdom*. London: Collins and Harvill, 1979.

Pierre, Bernard. *A Mountain Called Nun Kun*. London: Hodder and Stoughton, 1955.

LADAKH

Drew, Frederic. *The Jummoo and Kashmir Territories*. New Delhi: Capital Publishing House, 1997.

Francke, A.H. *Ladakh the Mysterious*. New Delhi: Cosmos, 1978.

Harvey, Andrew. *A Journey in Ladakh*. London: Jonathan Cape, 1983.

Keay, John. *When Men and Mountains Meet*. London: John Murray, 1977.

Rizvi, Janet. *Trans-Himalayan Caravans: Merchant Princes and Peasant Traders in Ladakh*. New Delhi: Oxford University Press, 1999.

——. *Ladakh: Crossroads of High Asia*. New Delhi: Oxford University Press, 1983.

Vigne, G.T. *Travel in Kashmir, Ladakh, Iskardoo*. New Delhi: Sagar Publication, 1981.

EAST KARAKORAM

Galwan, G.R. *Servant of Sahibs*. Cambridge: W Heffer & Sons, 1923.

Kapadia, Harish. *Across Peaks and Passes in Ladakh, Zanskar & East Karakoram*. New Delhi: Indus Publishing Company, 1999.

——. *Siachen Glacier – the Battle of Roses*, Rupa Publications, 2010.

Kulkarni, Lt Gen Ramesh (with Karpe, Anjali) *Siachen 1987*, Harper Collins, 2022.

Lall, John. *Aksai Chin and Sino-Indian Conflict*. New Delhi: Allied Publishers, 1989.

Maxwell, Neville. *India's China War*. Dehra Dun: Natraj Publishers, 1997.

Palit, Major General D.K. *War in High Himalaya*. London: Lancer International, 1991.

Poncar, Jaroslav. *Siachen Expedition 1978*, Germany, 2021.

Saunders, Victor. *Elusive Summits*. London: Hodder and Stoughton, 1990.

Shipton, Eric. *That Untravelled World*. London: Hodder and Stoughton, 1969.

Singh, Major General Jagjit. *The Saga of Ladakh*. New Delhi: Vanity Books, 1983.

Venables, Stephen. *Painted Mountains*. London: Hodder and Stoughton, 1986.

Workman, F.B. and W.H. Workman. *Two Summers in the Ice-Wilds of Eastern Karakoram*. London: T Fisher Unwin, 1917.

Young, Peter. *Himalayan Holiday*. London: Herbert Jenkins, 1943.

Index

Across Bhutan 201
Alipur Duar 203
Amrit Ganga valley 177
Anchri tal 161

Bara Bangahal 93-95, 97
Bara Hoti 172, 174, 176, 180-83
Bhaderwah 48-49
Bhiundhar 125-27, 129-30
Bhut nala 48, 53-54, 56, 58
Bhutan 12, 16, 20, 26, 69, 201-11
Borum la 28-29
Braham, Trevor 28-29, 31, 114, 120-21, 123-24, 215
Brocken Spectre 12, 14, 98
Buxa Duar 203
Byans 155, 157, 163

Char Duar 203
Chauhan, Nanda Singh 127, 130
Chhongtash 77
Chhota Bangahal 93, 95-97
Cho Lhamo 34-35
Chomolahri 204, 206
Chong Kumdan glacier 216
Chor Hoti Dhura 174, 180-82
Col Italia 72, 78-79

Da Namgyal 3-4
Dainasar lake 93, 97
Dalai Lama 67, 69, 186-88, 191, 200, 205, 209
Danpur 137, 155
Darma (valley) 134, 155-62
Daulat Beg Oldi 77
Deoria tal 151
Dhaula Dhar 84, 86-88, 93, 95, 97
Dhauli valley 172, 178
Dhodu 144, 170
Dodsar lake 44-45
Donkhya la 28-29, 34
Dorjee Lhatoo 4, 9, 206
Duars 203
Dzongu Valley 22

Early explorers 27, 42, 77, 108, 114, 122
Eastern Kumaun 155
Everest 2-3, 5, 8-10, 12-13, 16, 27, 30-31, 34, 70, 101, 153, 174-75, 180, 186, 199-200, 206
Explorers in Kashmir 42

Galwan 74-76
Galwan, Rasool 74-75
Garhwal 104, 125, 128, 137, 143-44, 146-47, 151-53, 167, 172, 176, 179, 182
Giagong valley 30-31
Girthi Ganga 175-76
Gona tal 213-14
Great Game 60, 62, 64, 70-71
Green Lake 215
Gromchevsky, Colonel 64-65
Guge 106-07, 109, 157-58, 186, 196-99
Gulabgarh 53-54, 58
Gupt Khal 177
Guru 24, 67, 111, 126, 187, 198, 207, 210
Gurudongmar lake 33
Gyalzen Mikchen 3
Gyantse 67-69, 186, 188-91, 203
Gyundi 105, 112-13, 115

Hango 109-11
Hangrang 105, 108-11
Hanle 105-07, 109-10, 112, 158
Himalayan Disaster 212
Himalayan Mountaineering Institute 1, 7, 13, 26

Johar 155-56
Jolingkong lake 164

Kablas Lakes 48
Kailash 111, 117, 157-58, 163, 165, 181-82, 186, 193, 195, 197
Kalindi Khal 158
Kamet 35-36, 125-26, 172, 174-75, 179-80, 197
Karakoram Pass 62, 77-78
Karcha valley 113-15
Kashmir 36-43, 46-49, 56, 58, 63, 65, 70, 78-79, 87, 90, 106, 173, 195
Kedar Kantha 142-46
Kedarnath 142-43, 147-50, 212-14
Killar 58-59
Kim 62, 108, 116-18, 124
Kishong lake 24
Kishtwar 48-51, 53-57, 194
Kolahoi 39-40, 42-45, 47
Kullu valley 93
Kuthi valley 156

Lassar Yankti 160-61
Leh floods 215
Lhasa 66-70, 185-88, 190-91, 203, 207
Lidderwat 37-39, 43-45

Machail 54, 58
Madhyamaheshwar 149-51
Manasarovar 157-58, 164-65, 173, 181, 186, 193, 195-97
Mangalsinh, Harsinh 134
Marsar lake 45
Memories 1
Mistry, Kaivan 77, 79, 113, 137
Mobile in the Himalaya 99

Narayan Ashram 157-58, 165
Narayan, Bansi 152-54
Neve, Arthur 38, 42, 49
Neve, Ernest 42-43
Niti pass 172, 178
Nubra valleys 72, 79

Obra gad 167-69

Padmanabh 72, 79-81
Pahelgam 37-38, 46
Pallis, Marco 92, 111, 119, 124
Paro 201-04
Pauhunri 27, 34
Prem Chand of Gorkhas 3
Purang 186, 194-95

Ranglana 144, 168, 170
Rongbuk monastery 199
Rudranath 151, 153-54

Sach pass 59
Sandakphu 12-13, 16, 18-21
Saryu valley 132-34, 139-40
Satluj 108-11, 117-18, 144-45, 193, 196-98, 213
Scottish Himalayan Expedition 157, 176
Shaksgam valley 63-64, 78-79
Sherpa Guide School 7
Sherpas 1-5, 7-11, 31, 132, 150
Shigatse 186, 190-91, 203, 210
Shin la 163
Shyok 72-74, 76-77, 79, 213, 217
Siachen glacier 63, 68, 80-81
Sikkim 5-6, 8-9, 12, 16-18, 22-24, 26-28, 32, 34-35, 66, 82, 119, 186, 188, 206, 215
Singalila ridge 12
Sirdar Wangdi 6-7
Smythe, Frank 125, 128-29, 130-31, 172, 177, 179-80
Sonamarg 38, 45-46

Tarsar lake 39, 45
Temples 143, 147-50, 154, 190, 198
Tensing Norgay 1, 3-4, 6-9, 23, 30
Teram Shehr plateau 72, 79-80
The Plateau 26-35, 186, 215
Thimphu 203-05, 207, 211
Tholing 106, 157, 193, 198
Tholung (monastery) 22-24, 29
Thula 115
Tibet mission 66
Tirasang 111
Tirthapuri 186, 193, 196-98
Toyo 194-95
Travel to Darjeeling 1, 13
Travels in Tibet 185
Treks in Kashmir 36
Treks on ancient trails 116
Tsaprang 157, 186, 197-99
Tungnath 151

Urgen 111

Valley of Flowers 125-31, 177
Vasuki tal 149
Vishnu Ghar range 153

YOL 82-84, 86, 88-91
Younghusband, Sir Frances 60
  Younghusband Mission 27, 66, 69-70, 188
Yurgolak fort 73

Zajimarg valley 45